10⁷⁵

THE

COMPLETE POEMS OF ROBERT SOUTHWELL,

S.J.

MEMORIAL-INTRODUCTION.

ST. PETER'S COMPLAINT. MYRTÆ, OR MYRTLE-WREATHS.

MÆONIÆ. MELOFOLIA, OR APPLES IN LEAVES.

POEMATA LATINA.

THE COMPLETE POEMS

OF

ROBERT SOUTHWELL

S.J.

FOR THE FIRST TIME FULLY COLLECTED AND
COLLATED WITH THE ORIGINAL AND EARLY EDITIONS AND MSS.
AND ENLARGED WITH
HITHERTO UNPRINTED AND INEDITED POEMS FROM MSS. AT
STONYHURST COLLEGE, LANCASHIRE,
AND ORIGINAL ILLUSTRATIONS AND FACSIMILES IN THE
QUARTO FORM.

EDITED, WITH MEMORIAL-INTRODUCTION AND NOTES,

BY THE

REV. ALEXANDER B. GROSART,

ST. GEORGE'S, BLACKBURN, LANCASHIRE.

GREENWOOD PRESS, PUBLISHERS
WESTPORT, CONNECTICUT

Originally printed in London in
1872 for private circulation

Reprinted from an original copy in the collections
of the Yale University Library

First Greenwood Reprinting 1970

Library of Congress Catalogue Card Number 69-14086

SBN 8371-4102-8

Printed in the United States of America

TO

THE REV. JAMES MARTINEAU, M.A.

AS AUTHOR OF

'ENDEAVOURS AFTER THE CHRISTIAN LIFE,'

TO WHICH, IN COMMON WITH MULTITUDES, I OWE MUCH,

AND TO WHOM

NOT ADMIRATION ONLY BUT LOVE IS FELT BY ALL OF US,

I DEDICATE

THIS EDITION OF A 'SWEET SINGER ;'

REMAINING VERY GRATEFULLY

ALEXANDER B. GROSART.

CONTENTS.

I place on the left figures 1, 2, 3, &c. in these Contents, in order to show the sequence of the Poems in the Author's Stonyhurst MS. volume. There is no title-page to it, and never has been. On the seventh page (three leaves blank) begins the Letter to his Father (pp. 29). Next three pages blank; then the Triumphs ouer Death (pp. 33)—the last page and half containing the Latin and English poems as printed by us (pp. 182-3). After the Latin and English verse on the Lady of the Howard family, there are other three pages blank, then comes the Preface, commencing 'Poets, by abusing,' &c. (2 pp.) Then, to the Reader, and the poems in succession as numbered. The Poems occupy 36 leaves and part of a page = 72 or 73 pages, with five blank leaves. The Prose occupies 31½ pp. G.

III. MÆONIÆ, 113-168.

ILLUSTRATIONS *in the illustrated Quarto only.*

PREFACE.

VEXED by the travesties on editing and mere carelessness of WALTER earlier (1817) and TURNBULL later (1856) in their so-called editions of the Poems of FATHER SOUTHWELL—of both of which more, with specific proofs, in the sequel—I had long wished worthily to reproduce this 'sweet Singer;' and having fortunately come into possession of the original and early editions —each rarer and costlier than another—and a still more fortunate '*find*' of his own MSS. in STONYHURST COLLEGE—all of which were cordially and unreservedly placed at my service by the Rector, the very Reverend FATHER PURBRICK, S.J.,—I am at last enabled to do so, not without a 'good hope' of grateful acceptance by competent students and lovers of our poetic Literature.

I would now give account of previous editions, and thereafter show what we have tried to accomplish in advance of them.

As distinguished from some of his Prose Writings, which were furtively printed in his own house in London (1593-4),[1] the Poems of SOUTHWELL were wholly

---

[1] *Father John Gerard*, the Poet's friend, is our authority. His words are : ' P. Southwellus, qui in modo juvandi et lucrandi animos excelluit, totus prudens et pius, mansuetus etiam et amabilis .... *in domo suâ Londini prelum habuit ad imprimendos*

POSTHUMOUS, although, from the Epistles to his 'louing cosen' and to the Reader prefixed to ST. PETER'S COMPLAINT and related pieces (1595 and in after-editions), it is clear that he had himself intended their publication. Our collation of the Poems in the STONYHURST MSS. reveals that originally and continuously they have suffered from the want of the Author's own supervision: for over and over, as our Notes show, there are most annoying misreadings and misprints, whereby epithets bright as dew are changed (so-to-say) into blotches of ink, and the meaning reversed, and delicacies not only missed but absolutely spoiled, as in rough handling of a moth's wing. Certainly his small and difficult handwriting offers an excuse for the original Editors.

The following is the title-page of the first edition (1595), from the CAPELL copy preserved in TRINITY COLLEGE, CAMBRIDGE:

Saint

Peters

Complaint,

With other Poemes.

Printer's ornament.

London

Imprinted by Iohn Wolfe.

1595.

---

libros suos, quos quidem edidit egregios.' (MS. Autobiography of Father Gerard, quoted by the very Reverend Dr. Oliver in the Catholic Magazine for September 1832.)

The collation is 38 leaves in forms—signatures A to K²
—ending with ' From Fortune's Reach ;' and it may be
noted that the two leaves C and C² (pp. 11-14) of the
undated [1596] edition, beginning ' Euill president' &c.
and closing ' Darts of disdaine' &c. are omitted in that
place and inserted after ' Come in, say they' &c. (p. 30
of 1596 edit.), so as to form sigs. E and E². This thin
quarto, which is identical with another of the same date,
' At London, Printed by I. R. for G. C. 1595' [= James
Roberts for Gabriel Cawood], contained St. Peter's Com-
plaint and these shorter poems: Mary Magdalen's Blushe;
Mary Magdalen's Complaint at Christ's Death; Tymes
goe by Turns; Looke Home; Fortune's Falsehoode;
Scorne not the Leaste; A Childe my Choice; Content
and Ritche; Losse in Delaye; Love's servile Lott; Life
is but Losse; I dye Alive; What Joy to live; Life's
Death, Love's Life; At Home in Heaven; Lewd Love is
Losse; Love's Gardyne Greife; From Fortune's Reach;
The Nativity of Christe; Christe's Childhoode,—the last
two coming in between Scorne not the Leaste and a Chylde
my Choyse. With the exceptions above noted, the 1595
and 1596 editions correspond page for page as far as p. 46.

Following this volume speedily was the ' Mæoniæ'
of the same year, 1595. Its title-page will be found at
page 115, with relative Epistle by the Publisher (JOHN
BUSBIE)—not, be it noted, named as, but in all probability
really, the Publisher of 'St. Peter's Complaint and other
Poems.' This volume, of which a beautiful copy is in
Jesus College, Oxford, contained those additional Poems
ever since printed under the title of ' Mæoniæ.' It was
a precious gift JOHN BUSBIE gave in ' Mæoniæ :' for
there can be no question that in these relatively minor

poems we have SOUTHWELL at his deepest, tenderest,
and best. Issued in 1595, these two volumes must have
been read by those whose eyes were yet wet from weep-
ing over their Author's tragic end.

The next edition of the Poems is without date, but
I assign it, after careful thought, to 1596 (early). Its
title-page is given in fac-simile in our illustrated quarto
edition: the ' wording' of it at page 3. It will be
noticed that this edition bears to be ' Newly augmented
with other Poems.' These augmentations were not 'Mæ-
oniæ'—which is not included in it even to the extent of
a single poem—but the following: A Phancy turned to
a Sinner's Complainte; David's Peccavi; Synne's heavy
Loade; Josephe's Amazement; New Prince, new Pompe;
The Burning Babe; New Heaven, new Warre. The col-
lation is 42 leaves: and throughout, this edition agrees
in its contents with that of 1615 (4to). My accomplished
friend Deputy-Inspector-General DR. BRINSLEY NICHOL-
SON has favoured me with full notes on WILLIAM LEAKE
the Publisher of this undated edition, whereby it appears
that he was a somewhat humble and often-changing
Bookseller from about 1594-5 (at latest) onward for a
decade (at least). He has also called my attention to
the head-pieces and tail-pieces ornamenting the volume,
specially that ' bluff King Hal,' and early incidents of
the Reformation, are (seemingly) introduced into them.
But inasmuch as these were common to other contem-
porary books, it is scarcely worth while recording the
details, save that I invite ˋcritical readers to solve the
meaning of the monogram in the title-page, as shown
in our fac-simile. It has the look of a combination of
R. S. as = ROBERT SOUTHWELL with L. = LEAKE; but

the numerals below, which at first I thought might indicate the Poet's age at death (32-3) scarcely yield this, unless the final X. be = II.[1] as a cross. I assign Leake's edition to 1596, because it is so marked in a contemporary hand in my copy and in another reported to me, and because there are certain misprints in it that are partially corrected in the edition of 1597 as also in those of 1599 and 1602, which editions I merely name, as they are identical in their contents and of no special worth or authority, although as books they fetch extravagant prices in their 'few and far between' occurrence in Library-sales and Book-catalogues. DR. HANNAH favoured me with the use of his copy (formerly Park's) of 1599 edit. In the centre of its woodcut title-page is an Æsculapian device, with the mottoes 'Nosce teipsum, Ne qvid nimis' and 'Love and lyve.'

As a bibliographic curiosity I give on the next page the title-page (which is within a border) of an early Scottish edition. DAVID LAING, ESQ. LL.D., has kindly forwarded me this, and he conjectures that its date was probably 1597 or 1598. From its incompleteness CALDECOTT supposed it to be the '*first*' edition, that is, previous to the edition of 1595: but this is most improbable.

---

[1] As I pass this through the press, my excellent friend the Rev. S. Sole thus writes me : ' I was thinking whether IESWS MARYE could not be made out of the monogram. You will remember Southwell has prefixed these names to one of the Elegies. F. Haigh of Erdington Catholic Church, well known in the circle of Archæologists, showed me that it could be done, and suggests it as the explanation. Notice the lengthening of the upright line of the E in the monogram on the left of the page ; this may be the I of Iesus ; which otherwise can be formed without much stretch. The monogram would thus read R. S. Jesus Marye.'

Moreover, incompleteness is no evidence, inasmuch as
the St. Peter's Complaint, with only 'Content and Ritche'
of Edinburgh, bears the much later date 1634, while
1616 and 1620 editions of London are exceedingly imper-
fect. The exemplar now described is that of the Anglo-
Poetica, where it was priced 21*l*. The memorandum
date of 1595 in Chalmers' copy I suspect was simply a
note that it was a reprint of the 1595 edition. It would
seem that Professor JOHN JOHNSTON of St. Andrews—
a notable man, as shown in M'Crie's Life of ANDREW
MELVILLE and Dr. Irving's 'Lives of Scottish Writers'
—had some oversight of this edition.

Saint

Peters Com-

Plaint

With other Poëms.

```
Printer's
ornament.
```

Edinbvrgh

Printed by Robert Walde-graue

Printer to the Kings Majestie
cum Privilegio Regis.

A Sonnet bearing Johnston's initials is oddly inserted at
page 30, at close of Saint Peter's Complaint. It may
find place here, the more so that it has never since been
reprinted :

SONNET: A SINFULL SOULE TO CHRIST.

I lurk, I lowre in dungeon deepe of mynd,
In mourning moode, I run a restles race;
With wounding pangs my soulè is sorelie pyn'd,
My griefe it growes, and death drawes on a pace:
    What life can last except there come releace?
Feare threats, dispaire; my sinne infernall wage.
I faint, I fall: most wofull is my cace;
Who can me helpe, who may this storme assuage?
    O Lord of life, our peace, our only pleaye,   *plea?*
O blesful light, who life of death hast wrought,
Of heau'nlie loue the brightsome beame, and bage,   *bay?*
Who by Thy death˙ from death and hell vs brought,
    Reviue my soule; my sinnes, my sores redresse,
    That liue I may with Thee in lasting blesse.   I. I.

The collation is in all 28 leaves: sigs. A to G: and the contents (except the addition of JOHNSTON's sonnet) correspond with those of 1595, and follow the same order. The Epistles only are awanting. Another Scottish edition of Saint Peter's Complaint, with Content and Ritche— already named—bears the imprint ' Edinbvrgh, Printed by Iohn Wreittoun, Anno Dom. 1634' (4to, 19 leaves). That assigned to Robert Waldegrave, Edinburgh, 1660 (4to), by TURNBULL, I suspect to be an imagination: at least I have failed to trace a copy anywhere.

These are all the quarto editions known. Others are in duodecimo, and are combined with more or less full collections of the Prose Writings. On the next page is the title-page of the earliest smaller edition, of which the collation is: Title-page; Epistle-Dedicatory ' To my worthy good cosen, Maister W. S.' 2 pp.; The Avthovr to the Reader (*bis*), 2 pp.; St. Peter's Complaint, pp. 1-34; St. Peter's Peccaui [*sic*, = David's Peccavi and Sin's Heavy Load], St. Peter's Returne Home [= Look

Home], Saint Peter's Comfort [= Scorn not the Least
and Times go by turns], Saint Peter's Wish [= Life is
but Loss], pp. 35-42; 'Finis' being placed on the last.
Then follows Sainte Mary Magdalen's Fvnerall Teares
[prose], pp. 43-157; 'Finis' again being placed on the
last. Then St. Mary Magdalen's Blvsh, No Ioy to Liue,
St. Mary Magdalen's Traunce [= Lewd Love is Losse],
Sainte Mary Magdalen's Farewell [= From Fortune's
Reach], At Home in Heauen, Christ's Natiuity, Christ's
Childhood, and the Christian's Manna (of which more
immediately), pp. 158-170, and 'Finis' once more on
the last. The edition of 1620 is identical throughout
with the preceding.

S. Peters

Complaint.

And

Saint Mary

Magdalens

Fvnerall Teares.

With sundry other selected,
and deuout Poems.

By R. S. of the Society of Iesvs.

*Is any among you sad? Let him pray. Is he of a
cheerfull hart? Let him sing.* Iac. 5.

[Doway] Permissu Superiorum. M. DC. XVI.

Of ' The Christian's Manna' TURNBULL thus speaks:
' This [edition 1620] has annexed to it "The Christian's
Manna," a poem not in any other edition [a mistake, as
it had previously appeared with the same heading in
1616 edition]. But MR. PARK considers it "has no le-
gitimate claim to be considered as his production." On
this point I am neither able myself to form an opinion,
nor give others an opportunity for doing so; since, in
spite of every effort, I have been unable to find a copy
of the edition' (Ritson, Bib. Poet. 341 n.)—(p. xxxvi.).
Later, MR. J. PAYNE COLLIER, in his ' Bibliographical
Account' (s. n.), in recording the 1620 edition of London,
which also contains the ' Short Rules of Good Life,' ob-
serves: 'To the present copy is added a poem called "The
Christian's Manna" not found elsewhere [a mistake, as
with TURNBULL], but which, though not reprinted by Mr.
Turnbull, there is no sufficient reason for doubting to be
by Southwell;' and then with high praise follows a quo-
tation. Still later, MR. W. CAREW HAZLITT, in his ' Hand-
book of Early English Literature' (1867), has this note
under the 1616 edition: 'This edition and the next
contain the very doubtful piece entitled The Christian's
Manna, which was not included in the English and Scot-
tish editions.' All have been misled by the Anglo-Poetica.
After all this, our Readers will be amused to learn that
' The Christian's Manna' is only ' Of the blessed Sacra-
ment of the Aulter' under a new title, as pointed out in
our Notes and Illustrations in the place. Of course this
establishes its genuineness, seeing that the poem is not
only in Addl. MS. 10.422, but in our STONYHURST MS.
It was printed unknowingly by TURNBULL (pp. 157-160).
None of the other changes of headings in 1616 and 1620

have before been observed. There were enlarged editions
—the additions being Prose—in 1630 and 1634. That
of 1630, ' London, printed by I. Haviland, and sould by
ROBERT ALLOTT' (the same engraved title-page with the
London edition of 1620), has all the Poems of 1596 and
of ' Mæoniæ' 1595, and Marie Magdalen's Fvnerall Teares,
Triumphs over Death and Short Rules of Good Life.
BARRETT the Publisher dedicates this edition ' To the
right Honorable Richard, Earle of Dorset,' who was the
third earl and second son of Robert Sackville, second earl,
by his first wife MARGARET, only daughter of Thomas
Howard, fourth duke of Norfolk, on which ' fair lady's'
death our Worthy wrote his 'Triumphs of Death.' He
was also the patron-friend of DONNE and BISHOP HENRY
KING. The Epistle follows :

' My Lord,—The entertainment which this worke in
the seueral parts therof hath formerly found with men
of exact iudgment, may be a sufficient testimony, that
it is not (now) offered vnto your Lordship for that it stands
in need of protection (the vsuall apologie of euery tri-
uiall Pamphletter), much lesse to emendicate any others
suffrages, beyond the knowne worth thereof : the onely
reason of this present boldnesse, and my excuse for thus
presuming to recommend it to your honorable hands,
being, that as the Author thereof had long since dedi-
cated some peeces of the whole to sundrie particular
branches of that noble stocke and familie whereof your
Lordship is (and long may you be a strong and flourish-
ing arme !), so now my selfe hauing first collected these
dismembred parcels into one body, and published them
in an entire edition, I held it a kinde of sacrilege to de-

fraud your noble name of the right which you may so justly challenge thereunto, which by the sunshine of your fauour shall bee as it were reanimated; and he encouraged to further endeuours, who in the meane time is at your Lordship's seruice.   'W. BARRET.'

The allusions in this Epistle-dedicatory are explained by the Verse-dedication of the ' Triumphs over Death' to ' the Worshipfull M. Richard Sackuile, Edward Sackuile, Cicily Sackuile and Anne Sackuile, the hopefull issues of the honorable gentleman, Master Robert Sackuile Esquire.' This verse-dedication follows :

Most lines do not the best conceit containe ;
Few words, well coucht, may comprehend much matter
Then as to use the first is counted vaine,
So is't praise-worthy to conceit the latter.
The grauest wits that most graue works expect,
The qualitie, not quantitie respect.

The smallest sparke will cast a burning heat,
Base cottages may harbour things of worth :
Then though this volume be, nor gay nor great,
Which under your protection I set forth :
Do not with coy disdainefull ouersight
Deny to read this well meant orphan's mite.

And since his father in his infancy
Prouided patrons to protect his heire :
But now by Death's none-sparing crueltie,
Is turnd an orphan to the open ayre :
I, his unworthy foster-sire haue dar'd
To make you Patronizer of this ward.

You glorying issues of that glorious dame,
Whose life is made the subiect of Death's will :
To you, succeeding hopes of mother's fame,
I dedicate this first of Southwel's quill :
He for your unkle's comfort first it writ,
I for your consolation print and send you it.

Then daine in kindnesse to accept the worke,
Which he in kindnesse writ I send to you :
The which till now clouded, obscure did lurke :
But now opposèd to each Reader's view,
May yeeld commodious fruit to every wight,
That feeles his conscience prickt by Parcæs spight.

But if in ought I haue presumptuous beene,
My pardon-crauing pen implores your fauour :
If any fault in print be past unseene,
To let it passo, tho Printer is the crauer :
So shall he thanke you and I by duty bound,
Pray that in you may all good gifts abound.   S. W.

F. G. WALDRON, who in 1783, in an appendix to
an edition of Ben Jonson's 'Sad Shepherd,' gave a few
pieces from SOUTHWELL, and which were reprinted by
HEADLEY in his 'Beauties,' supposed the above verse-
dedication to have been composed by SOUTHWELL him-
self, and the initials (S. W.) to denote S[outh] W[ell].
TURNBULL repeats this without correction. The suppo-
sition is of the wildest. It is neither suggested nor sup-
ported, but contradicted by the sense and style of the
verses, and in the third and fourth stanzas his death is
distinctly named. If I might hazard a more likely con-
jecture, the S. W. is = W. S. the 'loving cosen' of the
Epistle-dedicatory of the Poems of 1595, that is, in such
case, his 'loving cosen' had something to do with the
edition, and added his initials reversed. But of course
the full signature of JOHN TRUSSEL in 1596 edition gives
the Verses to him.

Such were the original and early editions of the
Poems of SOUTHWELL : and I have now to show that
they all prove faulty in their text when collated with the
Author's own MSS. at Stonyhurst College. Taking LEAKE'S

edition (1596, though undated) as a basis, I submit these dozen examples of errors ; others are pointed out in our Notes and Illustrations :

1. 'Yet higher poures [= powers] *must* think though they repine,' in 'Scorne not the Leaste' (st. i. line 5), misreads 'most' for 'must.'

2. '*Untowched* of man, yet mother of a sonne,' in 'Our Ladye's Spousalls' (st. i. line 2), misreads 'Vntaught' for 'Untowched.'

3. 'Unwonted workes with wonted *veyles* to hide,' in the same poem (st. i. line 6), misreads 'wiles' for 'veyles.'

4. 'O blessèd man, betroth'd *to such* a spouse,' in the same (st. ii. line 5), misreads 'betrothd too much' for 'to such.'

5. 'Thus had *she* virgins', wives' and widowes' crowns,' in the same (st. iii. line 5), misreads 'the' for 'she.'

6. ' In thee *their* joy and soveraigne they agnize,' in 'Our Ladie's Salutation' (st. ii. line 2), misreads ' they' for ' their.'

7. ' With weeping eyes His mother reu'd His smart,
     If blood from Him, teares rann from *her* as fast,'

in ' The Circumcision' (st. iii. lines 1-2), misreads ' his' for ' her;' and again in line 4, ' The payne that Jesus *felt* did Mary tast,' misreads ' set' for ' felt.'

8. 'And from a *thorne* nowe to a floure He fledd,' in ' Christe's Return out of Egipt' (st. ii. line 6), misreads ' throne' for ' thorne.'

9. ' His *worthes* all prayses farr exceed,' in ' Lauda Syon Sal.' (st. i. line 5), misreads 'workes' for 'worthes.'

10. 'The *prime* use of this mystery,' in the same poem (st. iii. line 6), misreads ' prince' for ' prime.'

11. 'No heed of their *deceivinge* shiftes,' in 'The Pro-

digall Chylde's Soule Wracke' (st. xii. line 2), misreads
'receiuing' for 'deceivinge.'

12. 'The world with *jesses* of delight,' in 'Man's Civill
Warre' (st. iii. line 3), misreads 'lesses' for 'jesses:' and
in the same (st. v. line 3), 'Foes senses *are* to vertue's
lore,' misreads ' and' for ' are:' and again (st. vi. line 4),
'Or *truce* of halves the whole betraye,' misreads ' trust'
for ' truce.'

I have selected these out of (literally) scores similar,
because, with the exception of the egregious one of 'throne'
for 'thorne' (No. 8), the first edition (1595) has the same
blunders, and so the other early editions enumerated by
us. Our Notes and Illustrations will supply abundantly
more. TURNBULL corrects NONE of these misreadings,
save the very few corrected for him in his text of 1634,
and, as we shall see, superadds as many of his own.

It will be evident that none of the printed texts from
1595 to 1856 is to be regarded as accurate or authori-
tative. This being so, I turned to the British Museum
Manuscripts (Addl. MSS. 10.422 and Harleian MSS. 6921):
but after a laborious collation, these, while yielding by a
happy chance better occasional readings—and which are
confirmed by the Stonyhurst MSS.—proved flagrantly
blundering. The Addl. MSS. 10.422 is unquestionably
the superior : but taking St. Peter's Complaint, here are
specimens of its misreadings :

1. St. i. line 2, 'Full fraught with *teares*' for 'full
fraught with grief,' the ' teares' being caught from the
preceding line.

2. St. ii. line 4, ' *in* penance wed' for ' *to* penance.'

3. St. xii. line 2, 'now *least*' for ' now *left*.'

4. St. xiii. line 3, 'What trust *to* one' for '*in* one.'

5. St. xviii. line 1, 'a sea of *showres*' for 'a sea of sours.'

6. St. xxii. line 4, 'With hellish dunge to fertill *heavenly* desires' for '*heaven's* desires.'

7. St. xxiv. line 5, 'My *other* were stones . . .' for 'My *oaths.*'

8. St. xxxviii. line 4, 'Soule's wilfull *fame*, synne's *lost* stealing face' for 'wilfull *famine*' and '*soft*-stealing.'

9. St. xliii. line 5, '*unquanted* hunger' for '*unacquainted* hunger.'

10. St. xlvi. line 1, 'ah! that *ever I* saw it' for 'ah! that I ever saw it.'

11. St. lxii. l. 3, 'You nectar'd *ambrose*' for '*ambries.*'

12. St. lxviii. line 6, 'all the *skrikes*' for '*scribes.*'

13. St. lxxii. line 2, 'God *soone*' for 'God, sun.'

14. St. xcvii. line 3, 'To *blame* your babes' for '*embalm.*'

15. St. cxvii. l. 6, 'shop of *share*' for 'shop of *shame.*'

It were endless to enumerate the dropping and misplacing of words and the uncouth orthography. The same result is obtained in collating the shorter poems. I adduce only half-a-dozen examples:

1. '*Flye* fortune's subtleties' for '*Sly*,' in 'Fortune's Falsehood' (st. i. line 2).

2. '*Some*-dying mirth' for '*soone*-dying mirth,' in 'Marie Magdalen's Blush' (st. i. line 6).

3. 'Lett thy *farewell* guide thy thought' for '*forewit*,' in 'Losse in Delay' (st. ii. line 6).

4. 'Where pleasure's upshott is to *denye* accurst' for '*die* accurst,' in 'What Joy to liue' (st. v. line 6).

5. '*Such* hyde the light' for '*Sunne*, hyde thy light'
('Death of our Ladie,' st. iii. line 5).

6. 'For sith no price can thy worth amount' for '*to*
thy worth,' in 'The Presentation' (st. i. line 5).

Similar errors might be exhibited to almost any extent,
but it cannot be required. It was this MS. WALTER and
TURNBULL consulted and used. It had formerly been in
the HEBER collection. From its contents and arrange-
ment I was inclined to think it must have been the same
Manuscript that is stated by DR. OLIVER (as before)
to have been in the Catholic Church of Bury St. Ed-
munds, and which has long been missing there : but the
presence of St. Peter's Complaint in full in it seems to
make this doubtful. Seeing that 6921 (Harleian MSS.) is
of like and even faultier character, I do not deem it ne-
cessary to record the result of our collation of it. Both
swarm with mistakes of every conceivable sort, in addi-
tion to a punctuation that is chaos. Yet, as our Notes
and Illustrations show, both yield some admirable correc-
tions of the printed edition.

It is pleasant to turn from the printed texts and these
MSS. to the STONYHURST MSS. The principal MS. of the
Poems is a handsome volume, one plainly upon which the
Jesuits set much store. It is daintily bound in vellum,
with gilt edges, and written very beautifully throughout
in one hand, with the exception of one poem, viz. The
Prodigall Chylde's Soule Racke, which, though occur-
ring in the body of the volume, is wholly in Southwell's
autograph. The badge of the Society of Jesus is upon
the cover. This MS. must have been prepared for the
Author himself, inasmuch as while now and again self-

correcting mistakes are left inadvertently, there are re-
peated corrections IN HIS OWN AUTOGRAPH, revealing care-
ful reading and interest. Our fac-similes (in the illus-
trated quarto) show both the MS. and a correction, and
also from another autograph MS. the Poet's handwriting
and signature. Besides this Volume, there are various
separate MSS. in SOUTHWELL's own autograph, notably the
LATINA POEMATA, which it is my privilege to print for
the first time. But as these, with the exception of the
remarkable Latin poems, are in Prose, I reserve farther
notice of them for our Memorial-Introduction.

It may be well to give proof of the value and autho-
rity of the STONYHURST MS. Our waning space forbids
enlargement : but in Notes and Illustrations other ex-
amples will be found in plenty. I shall select instances
that will at the same time serve to show TURNBULL's er-
roneous readings.

Turning to the 'Visitation' (st. i. l. 5), we read in the
early editions and British Museum MSS. ' Her youth to
age, *herselfe* to sicke she lends.' So it stood in the ori-
ginal text of the Stonyhurst MS.; but SOUTHWELL has
made it ' Her youth to age, her *helth* to sicke she lends,'
giving meaning to what was nonsense. TURNBULL per-
petuates the nonsense.

Again, in ' David's Peccavi' (st. ii. line 4), the Stony-
hurst MS. reads ' My garments *gyves*' [=fetters]. TURN-
BULL has ' My garments *give*.'

Once more, in ' Seeke Flowers of Heaven' (st. v.
lines 3-4) reads in TURNBULL, ' Most glittering gold
in lieu of glebe, These fragrant flowers *do* yield.' So
also the Stonyhurst MS. originally, but corrected by the
Author as the sense requires, ' *doth* yield.'

Yet again, in ' Mary Magdalen's Complaint' (st. v. line 2), TURNBULL reads, ' In the *sunne* of happiness :' the Stonyhurst MS. corrects ' In the *summe.*'

Farther, in ' What Joy to live' (st. iii. l. 1), TURNBULL misreads, ' Here *loan* is lent :' the Stonyhurst MS. corrects ' loue' for ' loan ;' and so in st. iv. line 5, for TURNBULL'S ' luring *gain*,' SOUTHWELL corrects by ' ayme.'

Again, in ' Love's servile Lot' (st. vi. line 2), TURN- BULL reads haltingly, ' Yet doth draw it from thee :' the Poet fills-in in the Stonyhurst MS. ' she' before ' draw.'

Once more, in ' Love's servile Lot' (st. xii. line 1), TURNBULL reads, ' With soothèd words enthrallèd souls :' the Stonyhurst MS. corrects ' soothèd' into ' soothing.'

Farther, in ' Content and Ritche' (st. vi. line 3), TURN- BULL reads, ' Effects *attend*, or not *desire* :' the Stony- hurst MS. ' Effects *atteyn'd* or not *desired.*'

Again, in Dyer's Phancy' (st. i. line 3), TURNBULL reads, ' Whose hope is *salve* :' the Stonyhurst MS. ' Whose hope is *falne.*'

Finally, in ' I die Alive' (st. iii. line 1), TURNBULL reads, ' Thus still I dye, yet still I do *remayne.*' So ori- ginally in the Stonyhurst MS. as in the Harleian MS. But in the former there has been study to make the line of which it is the final word accord in rhyme with the line which is balanced with it, and which ends in ' alive.' First of all the word ' *relyve*' was substituted ; and that not satisfying, ' revive' was finally adopted. The radical changes and the study evinced reveal the Poet's own au- thority and care. Moreover, when we consider that the Harleian MS. has the word ' remayne' and the consequent defect of rhyme ; and that the same care which has ren- dered the Stonyhurst MS. superior here and in many similar cases, down to minute corrections of orthography (and so in the Prose MSS.), has been bestowed upon the whole work—not to speak of the fact that this Volume is and always has been in the hands of the Society of which SOUTHWELL was a member, and that the beauty of the MS. confirms one's expectation that to his own brethren he would have presented a copy of his own poems worthy of him and of them—the Stonyhurst MS. must (*meo judicio*) be assigned the highest, if not absolute authority. Accordingly I have taken it for my text, albeit in Notes and Illustrations I have pointed out the ' various readings' of the early printed editions, and adopted an occasional correction of the Stonyhurst MS. oversights. The STONYHURST MS. is arranged as shown in our Contents, and includes all those in the BRITISH MUSEUM MSS. published by WALTER and TURNBULL. Curiously enough, St. Peter's Complaint is given only in an abbreviated form, as recorded in the preliminary Note to our reprint, and I have reports of various MS. copies of a similar kind.[1] I know not that the extension of the Poem has added to its value. Its absence from the Stonyhurst MS. in full would seem to argue that it was a later poem than the others. For the text of St. Peter's Complaint I have selected LEAKE's edition of 1596, with relative Notes and Illustrations at the close.

Our Notes and Illustrations throughout will furnish sorrowful examples of the utter carelessness of TURNBULL (in addition to the foregoing). I may farther refer to pp. 46, 47, 48, 50, 53, 54, 55, 65, 70, 71, 75, 81, 86, 90, and so onwards *ad nauseam*. Of WALTER's edit. (1817)

---

[1] See more on the formation of St. Peter's Complaint in our Memorial-Introduction.

suffice it to say generally, that in the complete Poems
(apart from our additions for the first time) there are in
all 57, while WALTER gives only 15, and 3 from Addl.
MSS. 10,422.   Specifically his manipulation of the ad-
dress of the ' Author to the Reader' will be enough.   In
1595 edition (his avowed text) st. ii. thus reads :

> If equities euen-hand the ballance held,
> Where *Peters* sinnes and ours were made the weightes:
> Ounce, for his Dramme : Pound, for his Ounce we yeeld :
> Ilis ship would groane to feele some sinners frightos.
> So ripe is vice, so greene is vertues bud :
> The world doth waxe in ill, but waine in good.

In WALTER we have this without a shred of authority :

> If Justice' even hand the balance held,
>   Where Peter's sins and ours were made the weights,
> *How small his share, compar'd to what we yield!*
>   His ship would groan, &c.

He gives only three out of the four stanzas of this poem,
and tacks on for the missing fourth stanza the closing one
of the first address to the Reader, omitting the others there-
in.   Then in ' A Fancy turned to a Sinner's Complaint,'
after stanza iv. no fewer than eight verses are omitted,
and another, and other five, and again other three, and
twice one ; and so throughout.   TURNBULL said con-
temptuously, ' I refrain from criticism on MR. WALTER'S
text :' severe but not undeserved, only his own is scarcely
one whit better, and in places worse.   I deplore the sad
necessity laid on me thus to pronounce on one so labori-
ous as TURNBULL.   Our finest Literature would get cor-
rupted, if such editing were not exposed and censured.

In basing my edition on the STONYHURST MSS., I can-
not sufficiently utter my sense of indebtedness to the
custodiers of them, seeing that they not only give us a

superior and authoritative text, but the hitherto unprinted
Latin Poems. Nor must I omit very cordially and grate-
fully to acknowledge the loving and careful helpfulness
of the REV. S. SOLE, of St. Mary's College, Oscott, Bir-
mingham, in collating and recollating the text, and in re-
reading our proofs with the MSS. 'To err is human,' so
that I cannot hope to have presented an immaculate edi-
tion ; but I can in all honesty say no pains, no toil, has
been spared to try to make it worthy of the Poet. It
may be as well to state, that I may have failed to repro-
duce literally an occasional 'u' for 'v' and 'v' for 'u,' and
perhaps 'hee' for 'he,' and the like. I have also thought
it expedient to introduce the apostrophe and the usual
capitals in divine names and personifications (nouns and
pronouns), and, as explained in relative Notes, have ad-
opted our 'Thou' instead of 'Thow,' 'too' for 'to,' and
'thee' for 'the,' as in present usage. The Notes and Il-
lustrations at close of each poem discuss various read-
ings, punctuation, obscurities, &c. &c.; and here I wish
most heartily to thank Deputy-Inspector-General DR.
BRINSLEY NICHOLSON for his varied and luminous com-
munications in elucidation and illustration of the text.
As in VAUGHAN and CRASHAW, and as in MARVELL,
DONNE and SIDNEY forthcoming, my editions owe much
and will owe more to his affluent reading, rare insight,
and most generous willinghood to aid us in our 'labour
of love.' The Shakesperean Reader will thank DR.
NICHOLSON for putting us in the track of the Shake-
speare allusions noted in our Memorial-Introduction, only
one of many like services.

    As before, I have to thank my helpers on the other
Worthies for continued and increasing interest in my

books. To the authorities of Jesus College, Oxford, I
am indebted for the use of the extremely rare 1595 edi-
tions of St. Peter's Complaint and other Poems and
Mæoniæ, and to the same at Stonyhurst College for use
of other early editions; and also to DR. HANNAH of
Brighton, for scarce editions and some annotations and
suggestions.

In our illustrated quarto edition I have the satisfac-
tion to present a photo-facsimile by Pouncey of Dor-
chester of the CHRIST of LEONARDO DA VINCI's renowned
fresco in the convent Maria delle Grazie, Milan, of ' The
Last Supper.' It may be permitted me to state, that
after days and days' study of the very best engravings (*e.g.*
Morghen's) of this mighty picture, while seated before
the original, I never have seen a faithful reproduction
of it, emphatically never have seen even an approach to
faithfulness in the face of The Lord. I must regard our
photograph—specially taken for me and under my own
eyes in MILAN—as an infinite advance on the engravings.
The sorrow-laden eyes, lids heavily, burningly, tearlessly
pressed down in fathomless sorrow and shame under the
coming Betrayal (how large-orbed if the lids were raised!);
the quivering lips as the awful words are spoken, ' Verily
I say unto YOU, that one of YOU shall betray ME;' the
wasted cheek, broad-shadowed; the ineffable sweetness of
the mouth and dimpled chin; the magnificent dome of
brow—no nimbus there, and not needed, any more than is
a crown needed to mark out the true king; the thin, pre-
maturely blanched, though abundant hair,—are brought
out, as I think, with incomparable superiority in our fac-
simile—all the more that the pathetic marks of ' Time's
effacing fingers' are inevitably given. I have seen many

CHRISTS by the great Masters, but Leonardo da Vinci's conception abides unapproached and unapproachable. As an illustration of SOUTHWELL's poems, all so radiant with the light of His Face, every one will agree it is most fitting. Besides the Christ, as already named, I furnish two Fac-similes, by WORT, of New Oscott, Birmingham, of SOUTHWELL's MSS. from Stonyhurst—(1), from the author's MS. of Poema de Assumptione B.V.M.; (2), from the Stonyhurst MS. volume. With reference to the former, an examination of the MS. satisfies that the poem and signature were written by the same hand and at the same time as the latter and larger portion. One is a careful measured hand, suited to the writing of a poem in a complete form ; the other is his own signature, written freely as he naturally would write in signing his name. It is in the same dark ink. III. The same of the title-page of the 1596 edition of St. Peter's Complaint and other Poems.

For other things I refer my Readers to our Memorial-Introduction and Notes and Illustrations. I feel it to be no common privilege to be really the first worthily and adequately and in integrity to present SOUTHWELL as a Poet.

ALEXANDER B. GROSART.

15 St. Alban's Place, Blackburn, Lancashire.
February 27th, 1872.

P.S. I add here the judgment of EDMUND BOLTON, whom WARTON calls ' a sensible [old] Critic,' on SOUTHWELL's works, from Hypercritica (Oxon. 1772, written before 1616): ' Never must be forgotten " St. Peter's

Complaint," and those other serious Poems, said to be Father SOUTHWELL's ; the English whereof, as it is most proper, so the sharpness and light of wit is very rare in them.' This quotation from Bolton was first used by WARTON (H.E.P. iii. 230: 1781), next by HEADLEY (1787, p. lxv.), and next by PARK in a note to *Cens. Lit.* (ii. 78), whence WALTER copied it (p. xviii.) almost in Park's own words, and WILLMOT (i. 15 note) has also secured it. SIR EGERTON BRYDGES has it in his new edition of PHILIPS (p. 219 note) and RITSON (Bibl. Poet. 342). BRYDGES also quotes it in his Adv. to the reprint of ' Triumphs of Death'—and so the hackneyed words go from critic to critic. I hope our edition will lead some to read for themselves.

DR. BLISS, in his edition of the *Athenæ Oxoniensis* (s.n.), has corrected WOOD's odd mis-assignation of SOUTH-WELL's Poems to JOHN DAVIES of Hereford. We owe too much to WOOD to deal hardly with him for occasional slips of this kind. G.

MEMORIAL-INTRODUCTION.

I. The Life.

The Life-story of Southwell beyond his Writings is a
brief one on the earthly-side, albeit on the thither hea-
venly-side, I do not doubt it fills many a page of the
Great Biographer's 'Book of *remembrance*'— as does
every beautiful and meek life. And so in Eternity, and
through Eternity's audience, there 'remaineth' compensa-
tion over-against the large and clamorous 'biographies' in
Time and for contemporaries, of multitudes '*great*' only
in an unconsecrate use of the word. Sibbes' 'resurrec-
tion' of saintly 'memories, as well as of bodies,' is of the
certainties, and the demonstration that to be good, simply
and quietly, is the most abiding greatness. We are far
off from the Facts, and the Facts are few, of our Worthy's
life ; but a fragrance sweeter than cere-cloth perfumes is
blown to us across the centuries from it. So that, with
all the dimness, we can discern that in him England
held one who was of her truest, purest, bravest, lovingest,
Christliest sons.

Collins records of the Southwells that the 'antient
and honourable family,' whence all came, derived its name
from the town of Southwell, in Nottinghamshire, where
he says, the 'chief branch continued to reside until the

reign of Henry VI.'   The first ancestor, however, of the
Norfolk house—our Worthy's—found in the Pedigrees;
and I have wearied myself over well-nigh 'endless gene-
alogies'—was JOHN SOUTHWELL, of Felix Hall in Essex,
who was M.P. for Lewes in Sussex in 28 and 29 Henry
VI.   He had two sons, ROBERT and JOHN.   JOHN was
ancestor to the SOUTHWELLS now represented by VIS-
COUNT SOUTHWELL in Ireland.   ROBERT SOUTHWELL, the
elder son, succeeded his father at Felix Hall.   In 1415,
according to COLLINS, he was made trustee to the DUKE
OF NORFOLK.   He married ISABELLA, daughter of JOHN
BOYS, Esq. of Norfolk, and had by her RICHARD, his son
and heir, who in the Act of Resumption (3 and 4 Ed-
ward IV.) had his grant from the King saved.   This
RICHARD's first wife was AMY, daughter and heiress of
SIR EDMUND WYCHINGHAM, of Wood-rising in Norfolk
(by ALICE, daughter and heiress of SIR JOHN FALSTOLFE,
'a name to conjure with').   With her, he obtained the
manor of Wood-rising, 'where—quitting Felix Hall—he
fixed his residence, and there his posterity had a noble
seat and fine park, which continued in the family for
many generations.'   There were two sons of this mar-
riage; but SIR ROBERT, the elder, died without issue in
1513.   FRANCIS SOUTHWELL, his brother, was Auditor
of the Exchequer to Henry VIII.; and by DOROTHY,
daughter and co-heir of WILLIAM TENDRING, Esq., had
four sons—1. SIR RICHARD SOUTHWELL, his heir. 2.
SIR ROBERT, Master of the Rolls. 3. FRANCIS. 4. AN-
THONY.   For the descendants of the latter three I must
refer those curious in such matters to BLOMEFIELD's well-
known county History.   I limit myself, except in one
memorable thing to be after-noted, to SIR RICHARD

SOUTHWELL and his line. He was our Poet's grand-
father. Of him BLOMEFIELD, under Wood Rysing, thus
recounts his 'honours :' ' He was a great favourite of
King HENRY VIII.; one of the visitors appointed by
him of the monasteries in Norfolk on their suppression;
of the Privy-council to that King, Edward VI., and
Queen Mary; master of the ordnance and armory; one
of the executors to Henry VIII.; and high-steward of
the Duchy of Lancaster.'[1] Farther : ' In the reign of
Queen Mary he made a remarkable speech (1554) in the
House of Lords (sic) on that Queen's being with child,
and an act of Parliament thereon passed; about the
government of the realm, and the person of the child, in
case of that Queen's decease.'[2] The county History also
enumerates about thirty manors in Norfolk of which this
SIR RICHARD SOUTHWELL was lord in 37 HENRY VIII.
It also states, ' Great part of his inheritance, with this
lordship (Wood-rising), came to his nephew, THOMAS
SOUTHWELL, son of SIR ROBERT SOUTHWELL by Mar-
garet his wife, daughter and sole heir of THOMAS NEVILL,
fourth son of GEORGE, LORD ABERGAVENNY.'[3] Unhap-
pily this SIR RICHARD SOUTHWELL introduced not a few
bars sinister (if I may venture to use heraldic phraseo-
logy) into the House.[4] During the lifetime of his first

---

[1] Blomefield, vol. x. pp. 276-7, ed. 1809.
[2] Hollingshed, p. 1124.   [3] Blomefield, as before.
[4] Blomefield refers, in his account of the illegitimate family
of SIR RICHARD, to Sir Henry Spelman's History of Sacrilege,
p. 270. I may remark in passing (with all reverence) that it
was part of the 'humiliation' of The Lord to have in His human
descent not great and holy ones merely, but this record also :
' Salmon begat Booz of Rachab; and Booz begat Obed of Ruth'
(St. Matthew i. 5).

wife, by MARY, daughter of THOMAS DARCY, of Danbury
—who eventually became his second wife—he had a num-
ber of children. The first, RICHARD, was eldest son, of
Horsham St. Faith's, Norfolk, who was living there 27
ELIZABETH [1585-6]. He died a prisoner in the Fleet.
He was Father of our SOUTHWELL by Bridget, daughter
of SIR ROGER COPLEY of Roughway, county Sussex (by
Elizabeth, daughter of Sir William Shelley), his first
wife—his second wife having been MARGARET, daughter
of John Styles, Parson of Ellingham. Of the first mar-
riage—with which alone we are concerned—there were
issue as follows : 1. RICHARD, eldest son, of Spixworth,
county Norfolk, who married Alice, daughter of SIR
THOMAS CORNWALLIS of Brome, county Suffolk, whence
descend the Southwells of Kinsale in Ireland, Barons de
Clifford. 2. THOMAS, second son.

3. ROBERT, OUR POET.

4. MARY, who married Edward Banister of Idsworth,
county Hants, Esq. (MS. 2 D. 14.186 Coll. Armor.) 5.
Other four daughters. I do not think it necessary to
record other issue after the second marriage.

ROBERT SOUTHWELL was thus the third son of RICHARD
SOUTHWELL, Esq. of Horsham St. Faith's, which ' estate,'
and its acquisition, is thus described by BLOMEFIELD (as
before) : ' The site of this priory, with the lordship, lands,
appropriated rectory, and the rectory and advowson of
Horsford, were granted about the 36th of Henry VIII.
to SIR RICHARD SOUTHWELL, of Wood-rising in Norfolk,
and Edward Elrington (*not* Ebrington, as inadvertently
misprinted by TURNBULL). RICHARD SOUTHWELL, Esq.

held it in 1588, who sold it to SIR HENRY HOBART, the judge, and his son SIR JOHN inherited it.'

Turning back a moment, our Readers will have observed the occurrence of the name of SHELLEY in these genealogical details. It is to be remembered; for ELIZABETH, daughter of Sir William Shelley, and mother of BRIDGET COPLEY, in turn mother of our Worthy, links the Poet of ' Mæoniæ' and ' Myrtæ' with the mightier PERCY BYSSHE SHELLEY. A short table shows this :

John Shelley, Esq. = Elizabeth, d. and h. of John Michelgrove, of Michelgrove, co. Sussex.

| Sir William Shelley, Knt., eldest son ; one of the Justices of the Court of Common Pleas. | Edward Shelley, second son of the chief of the House, settled at Worminghurst Park, co. Kent, and from whom, says W. M. ROSSETTI, Esq., in his Memoir of J. P. SHELLEY, ' descends that branch of the family which has achieved some fleeting distinction in the way of a peerage and a second baronetcy (the first baronetcy, in the older line, dates from 1611), and an eternal distinction in giving birth to the " poet of poets." ' (*Works*, vol. i. pp. xxx.-i. 1870.) |

In other lines there is like association with other historic names — Sidney, Newton, Howard, Paston, and WILLIAM LENTHALL, Speaker of the Long Parliament. But the family branches and twigs, marriages and intermarriages, noble and base, renowned and commonplace, of the SOUTHWELL Family I must leave to be followed up by those wishful to do so. I place below helps and authorities.[1]

[1] Besides Blomefield, Collins, Burke and the usual authorities, I am indebted to my never-failing friend, the Rev. J. H. Clark, M.A., of West Dereham, Norfolk, for full notes from, among others, the 'Visitation of Norfolk' (1563), published by the Norfolk Archæological Society, continued and enlarged by the late Rev. G. H. Dashwood, M.A. F.S.A., and other Norfolk genealogists (1865). Harleian MS. 1178 is the basis.

Resident, as undoubtedly RICHARD SOUTHWELL was, at Horsham St. Faith's at the period, there seems no reasonable doubt that ROBERT was born there, and not in Suffolk, as PITS earlier, and FULLER copying him, stated. After-dates, that will come out in the sequel, enable us to fix his birth in 1560-1, or just about the time that Mary Queen of Scots—of whom he was destined to sing pathetically—'landed' from France in her native Scotland. A singular anecdote has been transmitted of him while an infant—curiously repeated in other Lives, as is familiar to all—viz. that he was stolen from his cradle by a vagabond woman or ' gipsy.' Being, however, speedily missed by his nurse, he was almost immediately recovered.[1] This ' deliverance' was tenderly and gratefully remembered in after years. ' What,' exclaims he, ' if I had remained with the vagrant ? how abject ! how destitute of the knowledge or reverence of God ! in what debasement of vice, in what great peril of crimes, in what indubitable risk of a miserable death and eternal punishment I should have been !'[2]

Where he began to ' learn letters' has not been told : but he was sent over ' very young' to DOUAI. Inquiries there have resulted in the information that *the* French Revolution made havoc of the Books and Papers there, so that no memorial exists of its early ' scholars.'[3] In his

---

[1] TURNBULL states that the vagrant ' substituted for him her own child,' and ' confessed to have been prompted to the crime for the sake of gain' (p. xiv.).

[2] TURNBULL, as before, quotes this p. xiv.

[3] From our correspondence with the Librarian of Douai we had hoped to find in the possession of H.E. the Archbishop of Westminster (Dr. Manning) an early MS. roll of *alumni* belonging to the College; but, in a courteous answer to my appli-

15th year he passed to PARIS, where he came under the
care, religiously and educationally, of a once famous
Englishman, Father THOMAS DARBYSHIRE, who, Arch-
deacon of Essex, for ' conscience' sake' made a sacrifice of
all his preferments on the accession of ELIZABETH.[1] This
' Master' was among the earliest from England to ' join'
the Society of Jesus; and we cannot doubt that his per-
fervid zeal and example quickened his pupil's desire to
give himself to the same Order.   In 1578 at Rome, be-
fore he was 17, he was enrolled ' amongst the children'
of St. Ignatius.   The date of this event—so central in
his short Life—is noticeable.   It was on the vigil of ST.
LUKE (17th October) : and it is pleasant to conclude
that as the vigil of St. Luke was also St. Faith's-day
(Old style), he chose that day in honour of his native
place, Horsham *St. Faith's*.   The thing has not hitherto
been pointed out; but it seems to verify itself as well as
confirm the birthplace.[2]

Young as he was, he had thought of it long before
he was ' received.'   Here is his plaint, rather than com-
plaint : ' Divulsum ab illo corpore, in quo posita sunt
mea vita, meus amor, totum cor meum, omnesque ef-
fectus.'[3] He still pursued his ' studies,' and spent a con-

cation, H.E. informed me that he had no such MS. Suggest-
ing that it might be preserved at Ushaw, I applied there also;
but Dr. Tate had to report that there was nothing of the kind
there.

[1] See Dr. Oliver's 'Collections towards illustrating the Bio-
graphy of the Scotch, English, and Irish members of the Society
of Jesus :' (1845) p. 80, and references to TANNER and to WOOD'S
Athenæ.

[2] I am indebted to the very Reverend Dr. Husenbeth, Cossey,
Norwich, for the interesting suggestion.

[3] Mori, Hist. Prov. Angl. Soc. Jesu, p. 173.

siderable portion of his 'noviciate' at Tournay in Bel-
gium, its climate being pronounced milder and more
suited to his constitution.[1]   The little Memoir in Bishop
Challoner's 'Memoirs of Missionary Priests, as well
Secular as Regular, and of other Catholics of both sexes
that have suffered death in England on Religious Ac-
counts, from the year of our Lord 1577 to 1684' (1741,
8vo), thus summarises these years : 'He was sent over
young to Doway, where he was, for some time, alumnus
of the English College or Seminary in that University.
From thence he went to Rome, and there was received
into the Society of Jesus when he was but sixteen [in
17th] years of age. Having finish'd his noviceship, and
gone thro' his course of Philosophy and Divinity with
very great satisfaction of his Superiors, he was made
Prefect of the Studies in the English College of Rome,
and took that opportunity of applying himself to the
study of his native language, in which he proved no small
proficient, as the elegant pieces, both in Prose and Verse,
which he has publish'd in print abundantly demonstrate.'[2]
    The name of Ignatius Loyola was still a recent 'me-

[1] We learn this from More : ' Ne videlicet ardentem sanctis
desideriis juvenem, immoderatis Italiæ æstibus nondum parem,
duo in uno corpore calores opprimerent, utque tam præclaris
dotibus ornato, et qui per ardorem quærendi spem excitaverat
eximia quædam adipiscendi, non sola Roma nobilitaretur.' (Mori
Hist. Prov. Angl. Soc. Jesu, p. 177.)

[2] P. 324. The same *data* are found in More (as before), as
follows : ' Romam Tornaco rursus vocatus ad philosophos, theo-
logosque audiendos, neque ingenio, neque industria, neque laude
studiorum, aut fructu, neque vita cum virtute acta cuiquam se
passus est esse inferiorem. Et ingenii quidem et industriæ laus
in universæ philosophiæ decretis propugnandis enituit; tum
etiam, cum post decursum theologiæ stadium, aliorum studiis est

mory' and power (he died on July 31st, 1556, or only at
most five years before SOUTHWELL's birth), and his mag-
nificent and truly apostolic example of burning love, com-
passion, faith, zeal, self-denial charged the very atmo-
sphere with sympathy as with electricity; so that it is no
marvel our Worthy gave himself with a fine self-forget-
fulness and consecration to that Work in which the great
Founder of the Order wore out his life. The Society
was then in its first fresh ' love' and force, unentangled
with political action (real or alleged); and I pity the
Protestant who does not recognise in LOYOLA and his
disciples noble men, who, in the fear of God and with a
passion sprung of compassion, went forth with the single
object to win allegiance to the Lord Jesus Christ. I
' *intermeddle*' not with later complications and actual or
imagined degeneracies into mere political interferences
and 'plottings.' I wish to hold up clear and high the
indubitable fact that LOYOLA himself and (I believe) the
great body of his followers at the period in which we are
concerned, were 'priests' seeking supremely to do spiri-
tual duty and not to engage in treasons, stratagems, and
spoils.

That SOUTHWELL and others contemporary had the
hearts of true Englishmen of ' gentle' descent, and that
what they sought was ' religious' good for their country
and countrymen, with not a shadow of thought or 'plot-
ting' against ELIZABETH, I cannot for a moment doubt

---

præfectus in Anglicano de urbe Seminario; in quo juventus id
temporis copiosissima, et ingeniorum varietate, et splendore
florentissima non facile nisi ab omnibus doctrinæ præsidiis ornato
atque instructo ducebatur.' (p. 179.)

in the face of their pathetic and (in the circumstances)
brave words as ' on oath ;' and none the less that as a
Protestant I must rejoice that The Reformation in Eng-
land was not undone. I have that faith in Truth that
makes me confident that it was no righteous way to pre-
serve The Reformation to 'persecute' and slay cruelly
and meanly those who held to the ' old Religion' in its
old forms. The contest might have been more prolonged
and the final issue different : but prolongation is not
always delay or loss, and difference does not necessarily
involve a less desirable result. Of this I am satisfied
that the ' Blood-shedding' tragically and sorrowfully re-
corded in Bishop Challoner's matter-full ' Memoirs' and
Dodd's great 'Church History of England,' and Dr. Oli-
ver's ' Collections,' wears as black a colour as any in
Foxe. There is no monopoly of martyrdoms.

Our Worthy repeatedly gives utterance to his love
for his Order, and Tanner furnishes many quotable bits:
e.g. ' Nescio an quis alius unquam post sanctissimum Pa-
rentem ejus Ignatium, majorem de Societate Jesu sen-
sum, majorem vocationis suæ foverit æstimationem, quam
Robertus Southwellus. . . . Scripsit aliquando in sua
ad socios Romam epistola S. Xaverius, æternum animæ
suæ exitium imprecans, si unquam ab amore dilectissimæ
suæ religionis descisceret : " si oblitus," inquit, " fuero
tui, O Societas Jesu, oblivioni detur dextera mea." Sed
an non sublimes ejus de hoc ordine conceptus adæquârit,
si non superâret Robertus, clarissimo in Anglia gentis
Southwelliæ natus sanguine, ex his quæ sua propria manu
consignavit, patebit.'[1]

---

[1] Tanner, Soc. Jesu Martyr. p. 30: quoted by Turnbull
(p. xv.).

Thus flaming with the very ' fire' of the dauntless
Founder, SOUTHWELL was ' ordained Priest' in the sum-
mer of 1584, and being appointed to the Mission to Eng-
land, proceeded to his native country. He left Rome on
8th May 1586.[1] He had earnestly sought the ' perilous'
commission, as appears from a letter to the General dated
20th February 1585, ' wherein his future martyrdom
seems rather to have been anticipated, than merely re-
ferred to as a simple possibility.'[2] Another letter from
Porto, written on 5th July 1586, while on his way to
England, breathes the yearning ' haste' of The Lord as
He went up for the last time to JERUSALEM. Even in
the quaint old Latin these ' Epistolæ' pulsate and throb
with emotion. I do not envy the Reader who can rise
with dry eyes from Father More's ' History' which con-
tains them.[3]

We get passing glimpses of our SOUTHWELL in the
Life of FATHER JOHN GERARD, published only recently
in the following very weighty and remarkable book : ' The
Condition of Catholics under James I. Father Gerard's
Narrative of the Gunpowder Plot. Edited, with his Life,
by John Morris, Priest of the Society of Jesus. 1871.
(8vo, Longmans).' I know not that I can do better than
at this point glean these notices. So far as I can make
out, the first belongs to 1588, and thus runs : ' On my
arrival in London, by the help of certain Catholics, I dis-
covered Father Henry Garnett, who was then Superior.

---

[1] Bp. Challoner (as before) inadvertently assigns the depar-
ture to 1584 (p. 324). It is plain by the Letters in More that
it was not until 1586, as Dr. Oliver states (p. 194).

[2] TURNBULL, p. xvi.

[3] See pp. 182-183, for these Letters.

Besides him, the only others of our Society then in England were Father Edmund Weston, confined at Wisbech (who, had he been at large, would have been Superior), *Father Robert Southwell*, and us two new-comers.'[1] Again: ' My companion, Father Ouldcorne, had already arrived, so the Superior was rather anxious on my account, as nothing had been heard of me; but yet for that very reason hopes were entertained of my safety. It was with exceeding joy on both sides that we met at last. I stayed some time with the Fathers, and we held frequent consultations as to our future proceedings. The good Superior gave us excellent instructions as to the method of helping and gaining souls, *as did also Father Southwell, who much excelled in that art, being at once prudent, pious, meek, and exceedingly winning.*'[2] Once more: ' Next morning [after account of a meeting in Worcestershire], about five o'clock, when *Father Southwell* was beginning Mass, and the others and myself were at meditation, I heard a bustle at the house-door. Directly after, I heard cries and oaths poured forth against the servant for refusing admittance. The fact was, that four Priesthunters, or pursuivants, as they are called, with drawn swords were trying to break down the door and force an entrance. The faithful servant withstood them, otherwise we should have been all made prisoners. But by this time *Father Southwell* had heard the uproar, and guessing what it meant, had at once taken off his vestments and stripped the altar; while we strove to seek out everything belonging to us, so that there might be nothing found to betray the presence of a Priest. . . . Hav-

---

[1] Pp. xxiv.-v.   [2] Ibid. p. xxv.

ing thus escaped the day's danger, *Father Southwell* and
I set off the next day together, as we had come.'[1] Far-
ther: In the 'journeying' of the Priests there was per-
petual danger of betrayal in their intercourse with the
'gentry.' One half-pathetic half-comic Incident is told
of a 'gentleman' who 'suspected' the Father. But he
observes, 'after a day or so he quite abandoned all mis-
trust, as I spoke of hunting and falconry with all the
details that none but a practised person could command.'[2]
He then adds: 'For many make sad blunders in at-
tempting this, as *Father Southwell*, who was afterwards
my companion in many journeys, was wont to complain.
He frequently got me to instruct him in the technical
terms of sport, and used to complain of his bad memory
for such things ; for on many occasions when he fell in
with Protestant gentlemen, he found it necessary to
speak of these matters, which are the sole topics of their
conversation, save when they talk obscenity or break out
into blasphemies and abuse of the Saints or the Catholic
faith.'[3]

These incidental Notices verify at once the hazard of
the time for Priests in England and the 'spiritual' cha-
racter of the work prosecuted by our Worthy. Every
other mention of him is in accord with this. It is re-
membered that he 'sought out' the woman—his nurse—
who had rescued him in his infancy from the 'gipsy' with
a view to her conversion ;[4] while the long, intense, wist-
ful, most eloquent and beautiful Letters to his Father

---

[1] Ibid. pp. xxxix.-xl.   [2] Ibid. p. xxiii.
[3] Ibid. pp. xxiii.-iv.
[4] Mori Hist. Prov. Angl. Soc. Jesu, p. 172.

and Brother remain as evidences of the ' one thing' cared
for by him.[1]

During his Mission in England he had always a ' re-
fuge' and home in London in the house of Anne, Countess
of Arundel, whose husband, Philip Howard, Earl of
Arundel, was imprisoned in the Tower and died there,
' the noblest victim to the jealous and suspicious tyranny
of Elizabeth, *non sine veneni suspicione,* as his epitaph
still testifies.'[2]   He and his companion had gone in the
outset to William third Lord Vaux of Harrowden, resi-
dent in then suburban Hackney.   But after a few months,
when the Confessor of the Countess of Arundel died,
SOUTHWELL was appointed her domestic chaplain and con-
fessor.   It was while in this noble Family that he com-
posed for the Earl's use his ' Consolation for Catholics'
—of which more hereafter.

If the phrase ' Reign of Terror' is historically used
of that in FRANCE called ' Red,' an examination of the
Facts—not merely as told by LINGARD, but as being in
our day revealed in the CALENDARS of the Period and in
such a book as MORRIS'S ' Condition of the Catholics'—

---

[1] See on this Letter in the second part of this Memorial-In-
troduction.

[2] Morris's ' Condition of Catholics,' as before, p. lvii. It is
impossible to over-rate the permanent historic worth of this
Work, nor the painstaking and thoroughness of the editing.
We may not agree in some of the verdicts, must see things dif-
ferently o' times: but none will deny the weight and value of
the book as a contribution to the ecclesiastico-historico litera-
ture of England. Might I suggest to FATHER MORRIS to explore
the MSS. at Rome for notices of English Catholics undoubtedly
lying there utterly neglected?   I and all who have to do with
our early Literature long for daylight being introduced into the
masses of correspondence buried in the great Libraries of Rome.

shows a ' White' ' Reign of Terror' in England for Ca-
tholics. It was a CRIME to be a Catholic: it was proof
of high-treason to be a Priest: it was to invite ' hunt-
ing' as of a wild-beast to be a Jesuit. Granted that in
our SOUTHWELL'S years 1588 is included, and that the
shadow of the coming of The Armada lay across Eng-
land from the very moment of his arrival. Granted that,
in the teeth of their instructions, there were Priests and
members of the Society of Jesus who deemed they did
God service by ' plotting' for Restoration of the ' old
Faith and Worship' after a worldly sort. Granted that
politically and civilly the Nation was in a sense in the
throes of since-achieved liberties. Granted that MARY all
too sadly, even tremendously, earned her irrevocable epi-
thet of ' Bloody.' Granted that the very mysticism, not
to say mystery, of the ' higher' sovereignty claimed for
him who wore the tiara, acted as darkness does with
sounds the most innocent. Granted nearly all that Pro-
testantism claims in its Apology as a Defence, it must
be regarded as a stigma on the statesmanship and a stain
on the Christianity of the ' Reformed' Church of England,
as well as a sorrow to all right-minded and right-hearted,
that the ' convictions' of those who could not in conscience
' change' at the bidding of HENRY VIII. or ELIZABETH or
JAMES were not respected ; that ' opinion,' or, if you will,
' error,' was put down (or attempted to be put down) by
force, and that the headsman's axe and hangman's rope
were the only instrumentalities thought of. The State
Trials remain to bring a blush to every lover of his coun-
try for the brutal and ' hard' mockery of justice in the
highest Courts of Law whenever a ' Papist' was con-
cerned—as later with the Puritans and Nonconformists.

Bp. CHALLONER has translated two Letters of our
SOUTHWELL from the 'History of the Persecutions in
England,' by DIDACUS YEPES, Bishop of Tarragona; and
I avail myself of them here, as follows:

THE FIRST LETTER.

1. 'As yet we are alive and well, being unworthy,
it seems, of prisons. We have oftener sent, than re-
ceived, letters from your parts, tho' they are not sent
without difficulty; and some, we know, have been lost.

2. 'The condition of Catholic recusants here is the
same as usual, deplorable and full of fears and dangers,
more especially since our adversaries have look'd for
wars. As many of ours as are in chains, rejoice, and
are comforted in their prisons; and they that are at
liberty set not their hearts upon it, nor expect it to be
of long continuance. All, by the great goodness and
mercy of God, arm themselves to suffer any thing that
can come, how hard soever it may be, as it shall please
our Lord; for Whose greater glory, and the salvation of
their souls, they are more concerned than for any tem-
poral losses.

3. 'A little while ago, they apprehended two priests,
who have suffered such cruel usages in the prison of
Bridewell, as can scarce be believ'd. What was given
them to eat, was so little in quantity, and, withal, so
filthy and nauseous, that the very sight of it was enough
to turn their stomachs. The labours to which they
obliged them were continual and immoderate; and no
less in sickness than in health; for, with hard blows and
stripes, they forced them to accomplish their task, how

weak soever they were. Their beds were dirty straw, and their prison most filthy.

4. ' Some are there hung up, for whole days, by the hands, in such manner that they can but just touch the ground with the tips of their toes. In fine, they that are kept in that prison, truly live *in lacu miseriæ et in luto fæcis* (Psalm xxxix.). This Purgatory we are looking for every hour, in which Topliffe and Young, the two executioners of the Catholics, exercise all kinds of torments. But come what pleaseth God, we hope we shall be able to bear all in Him that strengthens us. In the mean time, we pray that they may be put to confusion who work iniquity : and that the Lord may speak peace to His people (Psalm xxiv. and lxxxiv.), that, as the royal prophet says, His glory may dwell in our Land. I most humbly recommend myself to the holy sacrifices of your reverence and of all our friends. January 16, 1590.'

The Second Letter.

1. ' We have written many letters, but, it seems, few have come to your hands. We sail in the midst of these stormy waves, with no small danger ; from which, nevertheless, it has pleased our Lord hitherto to deliver us.

2. ' We have altogether, with much comfort, renew'd the vows of the Society, according to our custom spending some days in exhortations and spiritual conferences. *Aperuimus ora, et attraximus spiritum.* It seems to me that I see the beginnings of a religious life set on foot in England, of which we now sow the seeds with

tears, that others hereafter may, with joy, carry in the
sheaves to the heavenly granaries.

3. 'We have sung the canticles of the Lord in a
strange land, and, in this desert, we have suck'd honey
from the rock, and oil from the hard stone. But these
our joys ended in sorrow, and sudden fears dispers'd us
into different places : but, in fine, we were more afraid
than hurt, for we all escaped. I, with another of ours,
seeking to avoid Scylla, had like to have fallen into
Charybdis ; but, by the mercy of God, we passed be-
twixt them both, without being shipwreck'd, and are
now sailing in a safe harbour.

4. 'In another of mine I gave an account of the
late martyrdoms of Mr. Bayles and of Mr. Horner, and
of the edification which the people received from their
holy ends. With such dews as these the Church is
water'd, *ut in stillicidiis hujusmodi lætetur germinans*
(Ps. lxiv.). We also look for the time (if we are not un-
worthy of so great a glory) when our day (like that of
the hired servant) shall come. In the mean while I re-
commend myself very much to your reverence's prayers,
that the Father of Lights may enlighten us, and con-
firm us with His principal Spirit. Given March 8, 1590.'

These Letters are only two out of hundreds of the
like ; and I for one deplore that one so gentle and lov-
able as FATHER SOUTHWELL had his heart thus wrung.
But worse than 'fear' and haunting 'suspicion' inevit-
ably came. For about six years our Worthy laboured
with consuming devotedness and success, when his Mis-
sion was as in a moment ended by that old peril of St.
Paul, '*false brethren*,' in 1592. The circumstances are as

follows, from TURNBULL, verified by the authorities already cited. ' There was resident at Uxendon [Woxindon], near Harrow-on-the-Hill, in Middlesex, a Catholic family of the name of Bellamy, whom [which?] SOUTHWELL was in the habit of visiting and providing with religious instruction when he exchanged his ordinary [ordinarily?] close confinement for a purer atmosphere. One of the daughters, ANN, had in her early youth exhibited marks of the most vivid and unshakable piety; but having been committed to the Gatehouse of Westminster, her faith gradually departed, and along with it her virtue. For, having formed an intrigue with the keeper of the prison, she subsequently married him, and by this step forfeited all claim which she had by law or favour upon her father. In order, therefore, to obtain some fortune, she resolved to take advantage of the act of 27 Elizabeth, which made the harbouring of a priest treason, with confiscation of the offender's goods. Accordingly she sent a messenger to Southwell, urging him to meet her on a certain day and hour at her father's house, whither he, either in ignorance of what had happened, or under the impression that she sought his spiritual assistance through motives of penitence, went at the appointed time. In the mean while having apprised her husband of this, as also of the place of concealment in her father's house and the mode of access, he conveyed the information to TOPCLIFFE, an implacable persecutor and denouncer of the Catholics, who, with a band of his satellites, surrounded the premises, broke open the house, arrested his Reverence, and carried him off in open day, exposed to the gaze of the populace.'[1]

¹ Pp. xxii.-xxv.

Perhaps this account must be read *cum grano salis*
in so far as ANN BELLAMY is concerned, seeing that, in
a Letter of the justly-named ' bloodhound' TOPCLIFFE,
he boasts of the seizure of SOUTHWELL as his own act,
adding, with a penetration we at this later day must ac-
knowledge : ' It may please your Majesty to consider, I
never did take *so weighty a man*, if he be rightly consi-
dered.' The whole fawning, cruel, abominable Letter
appears in STRYPE.[1] JOHN DANYELL also claimed 'merit'
in the same ' arrest.'[2]

Carried by TOPCLIFFE to TOPCLIFFE's own dwelling,
he was there during a few weeks ' tortured' ten times
with such pitiless severity, that the unhappy prisoner
complaining of it to his judges, declared that death
should have been preferable. Nor did the ' tortures' end
when he was transferred to the Gatehouse and the Tower,
the former kept by the husband of the she-Judas who
had ' betrayed' him. How he was ' agonised' is simply
and affectingly told by TANNER and by MORE. Even
CECIL admitted the ' torture' of him to have reached
' *thirteen* times.'[3] There must have been pauses in the
cruelty, though not an hour's release in the imprison-
ment ; for his Poems bear hitherto unrecognised traces
of having been composed in (probably) the Tower, and
subsequent to the putting him ' *to the rack*' and kindred
atrocities that are not to be named. Let us turn to these
undoubted reminiscences of his prison-experiences of the

---

[1] Annals of the Church and State, vol. iv. p. 9 (edit. folio,
1731).

[2] TURNBULL, pp. xxvi.-vii., where a Letter from Danyell is
given from the State-Paper Office : Domestic, No. 200.

[3] Cf. More, as before, p. 193.

dolorous kind named. First of all, in 'Mary Magdalen's Complaint at Christ's Death,' we read,

> ' Sith my life from life is parted,
> Death, come take thy portion;
> *Who survives when life is murdred,*
> *Lives by mere extortion.*' (p. 62.)

The simile is somewhat forced, but 'extortion' is more than a rhyme-word with 'portion.' It is a synonym for 'racking' or 'tormenting;' and, alas, it was well, or rather, wretchedly known to him that one rendered senseless through violence became conscious again on renewal of torture. Thus it was natural to him to represent Mary as saying that in her surviving when Christ her life had been murdered, her sense of life was only due to the rackings and torments of her grief. Prisoner in the Tower, under the circumstances he did indeed 'couche his life in deathe's abode.'

But deeper and more painfully realistic still are his 'Life is but Losse' (pp. 81-3) and 'I die alive' (p. 184). Let the Reader at once turn to these unutterably tender and pathetic pieces, and slowly, and I doubt not with mist of tears, read them. Take meanwhile these lines in the former :

> ' *By force I live*, in will I wish to dye;'

and this complete stanza (iv.) :

> ' Come, cruell death, why lingrest thou so longe?
> What doth withould thy dynte from fatall stroke?
> *Nowe prest I am*, alas! thou dost me wronge,
> To lett me live, *more anger to provoke :*
> Thy right is had when thou hast stopt my breathe,
> Why shouldst thoue stay to worke my dooble deathe?'

Similar is the yearning, the 'panting,' the 'sighing of the

prisoner,' that God hears, the hunger for the benignant
release of Death, in ' I dye to live;' and there are like
touches in ' What joy to live' (pp. 85-6).   Surely, too,
the solace of Sleep's sweet forgetfulness takes new soft-
ness from the recollection of his own prison-sleep, in ' St.
Peter's Complaint,' thus :

> ' Sleepe, Death's allye, obliuion of teares,
> Silence of passion, balme of angry sore,
> Suspence of loues, securitie of feares,
> Wrath's lenitiue, heart's ease, storme's calmest shore,
> Sense's and soule's repriuall from all cumbers,
> Benumning sense of ill with quiet slumbers.' (St. cxxi.)

It gives a new and strange interest to these Poems thus to
find these erewhile overlooked autobiographic experiences
worked into them.   Their bearing on the inevitableness
of his poetic gift I shall speak of onwards.

Transferred to a dungeon in the Tower ' so noisome
and filthy, that when he was brought out at the end of
the month to be examin'd, his cloaths were quite cover'd
with vermin,' his Father—and one is grateful to know
that he was worthy of his son and of the Letter ad-
dressed to him —' presented a Petition to the Queen,
humbly begging " That if his son had committed any-
thing for which, by the laws, he had deserved death, he
might suffer death; if not, as he was a gentleman, he
hoped her Majesty would be pleased to order that he
should be treated as a gentleman, and not be confined
any longer to that filthy hole." [1]   It argued conscious
innocence politically, and absolute confidence in the ' *if
not*,' so to address Elizabeth.   It argued too recognition
in the highest quarters of the justice of the plea, that

---

[1] Challoner, as before, p. 325.

'the Queen was pleased to have regard to this Petition, and to order Mr. Southwell a better lodging; and to give leave to his father to supply him with cloaths and other necessaries; and amongst the rest, with the books which he ask'd for, which were only the Holy Bible, and the works of St. Bernard.'[1] The selection of books, *the* Book of Books and *the* Father of the Fathers for a Poet, is very noteworthy: and through all his weary imprisonment 'spiritual things,' not civil or earthly, were his theme when he 'discoursed' to his sister MARY (Mrs. Bannister), or others permitted occasionally to visit him.

BISHOP CHALLONER tells unexaggeratedly and simply the story of the 'beginning of the end,' and 'the Trial,' and the 'end,' deriving the 'Trial' from a MS. in Latin preserved in the Archives of the English College at St. Omer's. I have now to submit these successively: first, the 'beginning of the end,' as follows:

'He was kept in prison three years; and, at ten several times, was most cruelly rack'd, till, at length, a resolution was taken on a sudden in the Council to have him executed. Some days before his execution he was removed from the Tower to Newgate, and there put down into the hole call'd *Limbo*; from whence he was brought out to suffer, on account of his priesthood, the 21st of February 1594-5, having been condemn'd but the day before. Care was taken not to let the people know before-hand the day he was to die, to hinder their concourse on that occasion; and a famous highwayman was ordered to be executed at the same time, in another place, to divert the crowd from the sight of the last

[1] Challoner, p. 325.

conflict of the servant of Christ: but these precautions avail'd nothing, great numbers, and amongst them many persons of distinction, flock'd to Tyburn to be witnesses of his glorious martyrdom. Hither Mr. Southwell was drawn on a sled thro' the streets; and when he was come to the place, getting up into the cart, he made the sign of the Cross in the best manner that he could, his hands being pinion'd, and began to speak to the people those words of the Apostle (Rom. xiv.), Whether we live, we live to the Lord, or whether we die, we die to the Lord: therefore, whether we live or die, we belong to the Lord. Here the sheriff would have interrupted him ; but he begged leave that he might go on, assuring him, that he would utter nothing that should give offence. Then he spoke as follows : " I am come to this place to finish my course, and to pass out of this miserable life; and I beg of my Lord Jesus Christ, in whose most precious Passion and Blood I place my hope of salvation, that He would have mercy on my soul. I confess I am a Catholic priest of the holy Roman Church, and a religious man of the Society of Jesus; on which account I owe eternal thanks and praises to my God and Saviour." Here he was interrupted by a minister telling him, that if he understood what he had said in the sense of the Council of Trent, it was damnable doctrine. But the minister was silenc'd by the standers by, and Mr. Southwell went on saying, " Sir, I beg of you not to be troublesome to me for this short time that I have to live: I am a Catholic, and in whatever manner you may please to interpret my words, I hope for salvation by the merits of our Lord Jesus Christ. And as to the Queen, I never attempted, nor contrived, or imagined any evil against her; but have always prayed for her to our Lord; and for this short time of my life still pray, that, in His infinite mercy, He would be pleased to give her all such gifts and graces which He sees, in His divine wisdom, to be most expedient for the welfare, both of her soul and body, in this life and in the next. I recommend, in like manner, to the same mercy of God, my poor country, and I implore the divine bounty to favour it with His light, and the knowledge of His truth, to the greater advancement of the salvation of souls, and the eternal glory of His divine majesty. In fine, I beg of the almighty and everlasting God, that this my death may be for my own and for my country's good, and the comfort of the Catholics my brethren."

' Having finished these words, and looking for the cart to be immediately drove away, he again blessed himself, and, with his eyes rais'd up to heaven, repeated, with great calmness of mind and countenance, those words of the Psalmist, *in manus tuas*, &c., " into Thy hands, O Lord, I commend my spirit," with other short ejaculations, till the cart was drawn off. The unskilful hangman had not apply'd the noose of the rope to the proper place, so that he several times made the sign of the Cross whilst he was hanging, and was some time before he was strangled; which some perceiving, drew him by the legs to put an end to his pain; and when the executioner was for cutting the rope, before he was dead, the gentlemen and people that were present cried out three several times, " Hold, hold !" for the behaviour of the servant of God was so edifying in these his last moments, that even the Protestants who were present at the execution were much affected with the sight.

After he was dead he was cut down, bowelled, and quartered.'[1]

It is added by Turnbull: 'Lord Mountjoy (Charles Blount, eighth Baron Mountjoy), who happened to be present, was so struck by the martyr's constancy, that he exclaimed, "May my soul be with this man's!" and he assisted in restraining those who would have cut the rope while he was still in life' (pp. xxxi.-ii.).

Now comes the St. Omer's ms.:

'After Father Southwell had been kept close prisoner for three years in the Tower, he sent an epistle to Cecil, Lord Treasurer, humbly entreating his lordship, that he might either be brought upon his trial, to answer for himself, or at least, that his friends might have leave to come and see him. The Treasurer answered, that if he was in so much haste to be hanged, he should quickly have his desire. Shortly after this, orders were given, that he should be removed from the Tower to Newgate; where he was put down into the dungeon call'd *Limbo*, and there kept for three days.

'On the 22d of February, without any previous warning to prepare for his trial, he was taken out of his dark lodging and hurried to Westminster, to hold up his hand there at the bar. The first news of this step towards his martyrdom fill'd his heart with a joy which he could not conceal. The judges before whom he was to appear were Lord Chief Justice Popham, Justice Owen, Baron Evans, and Sergeant Daniel. As soon as Father Southwell was brought in, the Lord Chief Justice made a long and vehement speech against the Jesuits

[1] Challoner, pp. 325-27

and seminary priests, as the authors and contrivers of all the plots and treasons which he pretended had been hatched during that reign. Then was read the bill of indictment against Father Southwell, drawn up by Cook, the Queen's solicitor, to this effect:

" Middlesex.

" The jury present on the part of our sovereign lady the Queen, that Robert Southwell, late of London, clerk, born within this kingdom of England; to wit, since the Feast of St. John Baptist, in the first year of the reign of her Majesty; and before the 1st day of May, in the thirty-second year of the reign of our lady the Queen aforesaid, made and ordained priest by authority derived and pretended from the See of Rome; not having the fear of God before his eyes, and slighting the laws and statutes of this realm of England, without any regard to the penalty therein contained, on the 20th day of June, the thirty-fourth year of the reign of our lady the Queen, at Uxenden, in the county of Middlesex, traiterously, and as a false traitor to our said lady the Queen, was and remained, contrary to the form of the statute in such case set forth and provided, and contrary to the peace of our said lady the Queen, her crown and dignities."

' The grand jury having found the bill, Father Southwell was ordered to come up to the bar: he readily obeyed, and bowing down his head, made a low reverence to his judges; then modestly held up his hand according to custom; and being ask'd, whether he was guilty, or not guilty? he answered: I confess that I was born in England, a subject to the Queen's majesty; and that by authority derived from God, I have been promoted to the sacred order of priesthood in the Roman Church; for which I return most hearty thanks to His divine Majesty. I confess also, that I was at Uxenden in Middlesex at that time; when, being sent for thither by trick and deceit, I fell into your hands, as it is well known : but that I never entertained any designs or plots against the Queen or kingdom, I call God to witness, the revenger of perjury; neither had I any other design in returning home to my native country, than to administer the sacraments, according to the rite of the Catholic Church, to such as desired them.

‘ Here the judge interrupted him, and told him that he was to let all that alone, and plead directly guilty, or not guilty. Upon which he said, he was not guilty of any treason whatsoever. And being asked by whom he would be tried? he said, By God and by you. The judge told him he was to answer, By God and his country ; which, at first, he refused, alledging that the laws of his country were disagreeable to the law of God; and that he was unwilling those poor harmless men of the jury, whom they obliged to represent the country, should have any share in their guilt, or any hand in his death. But, said he, if thro’ your iniquity it must be so, and I cannot help it, be it as you will, I am ready to be judged by God and my country. When the twelve were to be sworn, he challenged none of them, saying, that they were all equally strangers to him, and therefore charity did not allow him to except against any one of them more than another.

‘ The jury being sworn, Mr. Cook began to prove the heads of the indictment, that Mr. Southwell was an

Englishman, and a priest, by his own confession; and
that his being so young was a demonstration that he
was made priest since the time mentioned in the statute,
&c. The judge ask'd him how old he was? He replied,
that he was about the same age as our Saviour, viz. 33.
Topliffe, who was present, took occasion from this ans-
wer to charge him with insupportable pride, in com-
paring himself to our Saviour. But Father Southwell
refuted the calumny, confessing himself to be a worm
of the earth, and the work and creature of Christ his
Maker. In fine, after Mr. Cook had declaim'd, as long
as he thought fit, against the servant of Christ, and
Topliffe and Lord Chief Justice Popham had loaded
him with reproaches and injuries, to which Father
Southwell opposed a Christian constancy and modesty,
the jury went aside to consult about the verdict, and, a
short time after, brought him in guilty. He was asked,
if he had any thing more to say for himself, why sent-
ence should not be pronounced against him? He said,
nothing; but from my heart I beg of Almighty God to
forgive all who have been any ways accessory to my
death. The judge (Popham) exhorted him to provide
for the welfare of his soul whilst he had time. He
thank'd him for this show of good-will; saying, that he
had long since provided for that, and was conscious to
himself of his own innocence. The judge having pro-
nounced sentence according to the usual form, Father
Southwell made a very low bow, returning him most
hearty thanks, as for an unspeakable favour. The judge
offered him the help of a minister to prepare him to die.
Father Southwell desired he would not trouble him upon
that head; that the grace of God would be more than

sufficient for him. And so, being sent back to Newgate,
thro' the streets, lined with people, he discovered, all the
way, the overflowing joy of his heart, in his eyes, in his
whole countenance, and in every gesture and motion of
his body. He was again put down into Limbo, at his
return to Newgate, where he spent the following night,
the last of his life, in prayer, full of the thoughts of the
journey he was to take the next day, thro' the gate of
martyrdom, into a happy eternity ; to enjoy for ever the
sovereign Object of his love. The next morning early,
he was called out to the combat, and, as we have seen
above, gained a glorious victory.

    ' Mr. Southwell's execution is mentioned by Mr.
Stow in his *Chronicle :* " February 20 (1594-5), says
the historian, Southwell, a Jesuit, that long time had
lain prisoner in the Tower of London, was arraigned at
the King's-Bench bar. He was condemned, and on the
next morning drawn from Newgate to Tyburn, and there
hanged, bowelled, and quartered.'[1]

    It is very pitiful to have the great name of COKE —
for the ' Cook' of the Manuscript was he—thus intro-
duced. Anything more relentless and ingeniously and
wickedly perverse than the ' meaning' put into SOUTH-
WELL's allusion to the age of THE LORD as (nearly)
equal to his own is inconceivable. To me it is an in-
finitely touching and unconscious revelation of how his
whole soul was filled with thoughts of the supreme Life,
so that, as perfume from a wind-shaken flower, the
Christ-linked remembrance of his age could not but be
uttered.

                [1] Challoner, pp. 330-34.

From Morris's ' Condition of the Catholics' (as be-
fore) we learn that there were ' conversations' on ' equi-
vocation' and kindred matters during the examinations,
and that one ' in authority' sought to break down the
' firmness' of another Catholic prisoner by a false as
malignant assertion that Southwell had ' conformed' and
sent for a Protestant ' minister.'[1] I care not to dwell
any longer on this judicial MURDER. I pronounce it to
be such; and it is the sorrow and shame of our com-
mon human nature and Christianity that ' both sides'
have like blood-wet pages. I must regard our Worthy
as a ' martyr' in the deepest and grandest sense—a
' good man and full of the Holy Ghost.'[2] I should

[1] As before, pp. ccxiv. ccxviii. and lxvii.

[2] I add the following as a foot-note, from the Transactions
of the London and Middlesex Archæological Society (vol. i. pp.
293-4): 'Robert Southwell, yᵉ Jesuit priest, was also discovered
and arrested at Uxenden, and it was admitted by him that he
had been often in Bellamy's house; and his friend John Gerard,
another Jesuit, defended yᵉ denial of yᵉ fact by one of yᵉ wit-
nesses, as being a denial authorised by yᵉ example of yᵉ Saviour.'
        In June 1592 it was ordered, ' That Mr. Justice Young, or
sume other lyke commissioner, do apprehend Richard Bellamy
of Oxenden, in yᵉ parryshe of Harrow on yᵉ Hyll, and his
wyffe, and the tow sonnes and ther tow daughters, in whose
house father Southwell, alias Mr. Cotton, was taken by Mr.
Toplay [Topcliffe?] a comyssyner, and wher a noumber of other
preests have bene recevyd and harberd, as well when Southwell
hathe been ther as when Mr. Barnes, alias Stranudge, al's Hynd,
al's Wingfeld, hathe beene ther a sojorner in Bellamy's house.
And they to bee comytted to severall prysons: Bellamy and his
wyfe to yᵉ Gaythouse, and ther tow doughters to yᵉ Clynck, and
ther tow soones to St. Katheryn's, and to be axamyned straytly
for yᵉ weighty service of yᵉ Qˢ Maᵗʸ.' The ' alias COTTON' is a new
fact in Southwell's biography. TURNBULL has given a genea-
logical table of the Bellamys, and related papers from the State-
Paper Office (pp. lxiv.-vi.): sufficient to have been once printed.

blush for my Protestantism, if I did not hold in honour,
yea reverence, his stainless and beautiful memory, all
the more that he was on the 'losing side,' none the less
that beliefs and forms and observances that were dear to
him are errors, and more, to me :

> Through this desert, day by day,
> Wandered not his steps astray,
> Treading still the royal way.
>
> *Paradisus Animæ.*

Pass we now to

II. The Writings.

It is to be lamented that there is no authentic por-
trait of SOUTHWELL known. DR. HANNAH of Brighton in-
deed has sent me an early etching-like engraving, which,
from the number '89' in the right-hand corner, seems
to have formed one of a series. Beneath is inscribed
'P. Robertvs Sovthvell, Soc. Iesu, Londini, pro Cath.
fide suspensus et sectus 3. mar. 1595' (the date erro-
neous). Above is a cherub reaching out a wreath and
palm : round the neck is '*the* rope,' and in the breast a
sword with blood coming forth in great drops. The face
is a conventional monkish one, self-evidently no Portrait.
We could better have spared other portraits that have
come down for his. I very much mistake if a genuine
Portrait of him would not have shown an intellectual,
etherealised Face, thin and worn no doubt, but ensouled.
One likes to go to the Writings of a man from a study
of his Face. This we are not privileged to do here; but
I have told his Life-story ill from the extant authorities,
if my Readers have not a '*prejudice*' in his favour—
using my Scottish archaic phrase—if his character have

not won an extrinsic interest and transfiguration for his
books. His Prose I can only very briefly notice; nor
indeed is it their literary value that has kept them
'quick' and potential to this day. It was not for a
literary object they were composed, neither as contri-
buting to literature they were published. They were
the outcome of the Author's own 'inner life' and sym-
pathies with the sad, the unwary, the eager, the tempted,
the doubting, the 'tried.' Hence it is, I take it, that
there never has been a decade of years since their ori-
ginal issue, that something bearing the name of SOUTH-
WELL has not been in living circulation and prized by
'weary' and sorrowful spirits.

The Bibliographies (e. g. Hazlitt's) place at the head
of his Writings 'A Supplication to Queen Elizabeth'
(1593): but this was probably his father's Petition. I
have failed to discover a copy. The next—really the first
—is 'An Epistle of Comfort to the Reverend Preistes,
and to the honourable, worshipful, and other of the lay
sorte restrayned in durance for the Catholike faith. Im-
printed at Paris [1593?],' 8vo, 214 leaves: a copy in
the British Museum. Following this was 'A Short
Rule of Good Life: to direct the devout Christian in a
regular and ordinary course, n.p. or d. 8vo: a copy in
the Bodleian. DR. OLIVER (as before) has stated that
these were all 'printed at his private press,' mentioned
in our Memoir. But in such case the date of the 'Epistle
of Comfort' usually filled in, viz. 1593, must be a mis-
take, as SOUTHWELL from 1592 was a 'prisoner.' The
imprint of Paris may have been a blind. Another edi-
tion of this treatise—for it really is such—bears date
'1605' (in the Bodleian). DODD (as before) gives the

imprint of Doway to the 'Short Rule.' His 'Epistle
to his Father to forsake the World' is also assigned to
the 'private press,' and so must have been printed prior
to 1592. I have not been able to trace an early copy.
As we shall find, the Stonyhurst MS. copy of it is dated
1589. The next published prose was the following :
' *The Triumphs ouer Death :* or A Consolatorie Epistle
for afflicted minds, in the affects of dying friends. *First
written for the consolation of one: but nowe published for
the generall good of all, by R. S. the Authour of S. Peters
Complaint, and Mœoniœ his other Hymnes.* London,
Printed by *Valentine Simmes* for *Iohn Busbie,* and are to
be solde at *Nicholas Lings* shop at the West end of
Paules Church. 1596. (4to).' By the liberality of the
authorities of Jesus College, Oxford, I have been allowed
the leisurely use of their very fine copy of this excessively
scarce book. There was a previous edition in 1595.

John Trussell, author of 'Raptvs I Helenæ. The
first Rape of faire Hellen. Done into a Poeme by I. T.'
(1595), appears to have been Editor of the 'Triumphs.'
The Epistle-dedicatory in verse to the SACKVILLES we
have already given in the preceding Memoir, and now
the Verses *in memoriam* of SOUTHWELL by TRUSSELL
must here find successive place ; the former an acrostic,
and neither, so far as I am aware, hitherto reprinted.

I. [OF SOUTHWELL AND HIS BOOK.]

R   Reade with regarde, what here with due regarde,
O   Our second Ciceronian *Southwell* sent :
B   By whose perswasiue pithy argument,
E   Ech well disposèd eie may be preparde
R   Respectiuely their griefe for friends decease
T   To moderate without all vaine excesse.

S Sith the worke is worthie of your view,
O Obtract not him which for your good it pend :
V Vnkinde you are if you it reprehend,
T That for your profit it presented you :
H He pend, I publish this to pleasure all,
E Esteeme of both then, as we merite shall.
W Way his workes woorth, accept of my goodwill,
E Else is his labour lost, mine crost, both to no end :
L Lest then you ill deserue what both intend,
L Let my goodwill and small defects fulfill :
      He here his talent trebled doth present,
      I, my poore mite, yet both with good intent ;
      Then take them kindly both, as we them ment.

II. To the Reader.

Chancing to find with Æsope's cocke a stone,
    Whose worth was more than I knew how to prize ;
And knowing if it should be kept vnknowne,
'Twould many skathe, and pleasure few or none :
    I thought it best, the same in publike wise
    I['d] print to publish, that impartiall eyes
Might, reading iudge, and iudging, praise the wight
The which this Triumph ouer Death did write.

And though the same he did at first compose
    For one's peculiar consolation,
Yet will it be commodious vnto those.
Which for some friend's losse, proue their owne selfe-foes:
    And by extreamitie of exclamation
    And their continuale lamentation
Seeme to forget that they at length must tread
The selfe same path which they did that are dead.

But those as yet whom no friend's death doth crosse,
    May by example guyde their actions so,
That when a tempest comes their barke to tosse,
Their passions shall not superate their losse :
    And eke this Treatise doth the Reader show,
    That we our breath to Death by duety owe,
And thereby prooues, much teares are spent in vaine,
When teares can not recall the dead againe.

Yet if perhappes our late sprung Sectaries,
  Or, for a fashion, Bible-bearing hypocrites,
Whose hollowe hearts doe seeme most holy wise,
Do, for the Author's sake, the worke despise,
    I wish them weigh the worke, and not who writes :
    But they that leaue what most the soule delights,
Because the Preacher's no precisian, sure
To reade what *Southwell* writ will not endure.

But leauing them, since no perswades suffise
  To cause them reade, except the Spirit moue,
I wish all other reade, but not despise
This little Treatise : but if Momus' eies
    Espie Death's Triumph, it doth him behoue,
    This Writer, Worke, or me for to reprooue :
But let this pitch-speecht mouth defile but one,
Let that be me, let t' other two alone :
    For if offence in either merite blame,
    The fault is mine, and let me reape the shame.
                     IOHN TRUSSELL.

SOUTHWELL's own prose address of ' The Authour to
the Reader' is well-turned in phrase. A copy of the ' Tri-
umphs,' including this Epistle, corrected in his own auto-
graph, is preserved among the STONYHURST MSS., dated
' The last of September 1591.' In any reprint this Manu-
script will be found of much value. The date there given
(1591) led us to place the ' Triumphs' before ' Marie
Magdalen's Funerall Teares,' although the latter was in
print one year earlier. This was his last published prose.
The title-page is as follows—taken from the unique copy
in the Bodleian : ' Mary Magdalen's Funerall Teares.
Jeremiæ, c. 6, ver. 26. *Auctum unigeniti fac tibi planc-
tum amarum.* London, Printed for A. I. G. C. 1594'
(8vo, 47 leaves). There were editions of the ' Funerall
Teares' in 1602, 1607, 1609, 1630, &c. &c.

Such were the printed and published Prose Writings

of our Poet. Farther : DOLMAN, the late Catholic pub-
lisher, is stated by TURNBULL to have had in his posses-
sion an unpublished (and still so) MS. of his, entitled 'The
Hundred Meditations of the Love of God,' with a Pre-
face-Letter ' To the Right Honble and virtuous Lady,
the Lady Beauchamp.' It must be the same that is quoted
from by WALTER. Besides these ' Hundred Meditations'
among the Stonyhurst MSS., exclusive of holographs of
the already-named ' Triumphs over Death' and Epistle
to his 'loving cosen,' prefixed to St. Peter's Complaint,
with other Poems (as before), and of the Letter to his
Father, and of the Poems, there are a variety of exceed-
ingly characteristic ' weighty and powerful' productions,
chiefly in Latin, and which I would here record. But
with reference to the Letter to his Father it may be stated
that it thus begins in the MS. : ' To the Worshipfull, his
very good father, Mr. Rich. Sou. Esq^e, his dutifull soon
[*sic*] Rob. Sou. wisheth all happines ;' and ends, 'may
finde excuse of my boldnes, I will surcease. This 22 of
October 1589, your most dutifull and lovinge sonne, R. S.'
The date '1589' is important, and confirms our remark,
that if printed at the ' private press' in his own house, it
must have appeared sooner than the known earliest edi-
tion, viz. 1593. The whole of these are included in the
same Volume with the Poems, as described by us.

The additional autograph pieces in Prose are on
separate foldings of paper, and are these : ' Notes on
Theology,' consisting of the usual scholastic-dogmatic
discussions (in Latin). Next, ' Precationes,' as follow :
' Ante orationem precatio,' 'Ante Missam precatio,' ' Ante
studia precatio,' ' Ad omnia accommodata precatio,' ' An-
tequam cum externis &c.,' and two others without head-

ings. Next, 'Meditationes in Adventu'—both the Prayers
and Meditations being in Latin. Next, a ' Discourse on
Mary Maudelyn,' and 'Alas, why doe I lament,' in Eng-
lish prose, both extrinsically valuable from their relation
to the published 'Mary Magdalen's Funerall Teares,' of
which indeed I believe them to have been the first form.
Finally, another Prayer on a separate bit of paper, and
Notes or jottings for the poem of St. Peter's Complaint.

Returning upon the PROSE of SOUTHWELL, as thus
for the first time fully and accurately placed before the
Reader, I feel a difficulty in making representative quota-
tions, seeing—as remarked in the outset—it is not for
their literary but for their ' spiritual' worth we estimate
them highly: while there is this additional element of
difficulty, that the great body of the instruction and con-
solation presented is plain, simple, unadorned, almost
homely, and so unfurnished of those brilliancies that yield
vivid and often untrue ' *quotable bits*.'

Nevertheless, it were probably to disappoint not to
give something from the Prose—published and unpub-
lished.

As we have seen, the earliest-dated prose of our
Worthy is the Letter to his Father. This Letter is
printed *in extenso* by WALTER (as before), and from him
as Appendix No. 1 by TURNBULL. We have very much
more valuable new materials, and hence have not thought
of reprinting it; but it is of rare interest in many ways,
and won the fine praise of ARIS WILLMOTT. His father
seems either to have been inclined to fall in with The Re-
formation, being at least an absentee from Catholic ob-
servances, or to have been 'gay' and ' of the world.' His
marriage with a lady of the Court—formerly, we learn

from MORE (as before), the instructress of QUEEN ELIZA-
BETH in the Latin language—and his wealth led him
among the highest in the Land. His son ROBERT
yearned over him. Thus does he pave the way for counsel
and admonition:[1] 'I am not of so unnatural a kind, of
so wild an education, or so unchristian a spirit, as not to
remember the root out of which I branched, or to forget
my secondary maker and author of my being. It is not
the carelessness of a cold affection, nor the want of a due
and reverent respect, that has made me such a stranger
to my native home, and so backward in defraying the
debt of a thankful mind, but only the iniquity of these
days that maketh my presence perilous, and the discharge
of my duties an occasion of danger. I was loth to inforce
an unwilling courtesy upon any, or by seeming offici-
ous to become offensive; deeming it better to let time
digest the fear that my return into the realm had bred in
my kindred than abruptly to intrude myself, and to pur-
chase their danger, whose good-will I so highly esteem.
I never doubted but that the belief, which to all my
friends by descent and pedigree is, in a manner, heredi-
tary, framed in them a right persuasion of my present
calling, not suffering them to measure their censures of
me by the ugly terms and odious epithets wherewith
heresy hath sought to discredit my functions, but rather
by the reverence of so worthy a sacrament and the sacred
usages of all former ages. Yet, because I might easily
perceive by apparent conjectures that many were more

---

[1] As most easily got at by Readers desiring to see the whole,
I take my quotations from this Letter from TURNBULL, without
in this instance going back on the old spelling. In WALTER it
occupies pp. 106-125, and was taken from a MS. in the Bodleian.

willing to hear of me than from me, and readier to praise
than to use my endeavours, I have hitherto bridled my
desire to see them by the care and jealousy of their safety ;
and banishing myself from the scene of my cradle in my
own country, I have lived like a foreigner, finding among
strangers that which, in my nearest blood, I presumed
not to seek' (pp. xliii.-iv.). Then follow most wistful
and anxious arguments taking the form of entreaties: *e.g.*
'Surely for mine own part, though I challenge not the
prerogative of the best disposition, yet am I not of so
harsh and churlish a humour, but that it is a continual
corrective and cross unto me, that whereas my endea-
vours have reclaimed many from the brink of perdition,
I have been less able to employ them where they were
most due ; and was barred from affording to my dearest
friends that which hath been eagerly sought and bene-
ficially obtained by mere strangers' (p. xlvi.). More pas-
sionately : 'Who hath more interest in the grape than he
who planted the vine ? who more right to the crop than
he who sowed the corn ? or where can the child owe so
great service as to him to whom he is indebted for his
very life and being ? With young Tobias I have tra-
velled far, and brought home a freight of spiritual sub-
stance to enrich you, and medicinable receipts against
your ghostly maladies. I have with Esau, after long toil
in pursuing a long and painful chase, returned with the
full prey you were wont to love ; desiring thereby to in-
sure your blessing. I have in this general famine of
all true and Christian food, with Joseph, prepared abund-
ance of the bread of angels for the repast of your soul.
And now my desire is that my drugs may cure you, my
prey delight you, and my provisions feed you, by whom

I have been cured, enlightened, and fed myself; that
your courtesies may, in part, be countervailed, and my
duty, in some sort, performed. Despise not, good Sire,
the youth of your son, neither deem your God measureth
His endowments by number of years. Hoary senses are
often couched under youthful locks, and some are riper
in the spring than others in the autumn of their age'
(pp. xlvi.-vii.). That '*you were wont to love*' from the
old Story was exceedingly ingenious and is ingenuously
put. There follow superabundant Scriptural defences of
his ' youth' as no bar to addressing his Father, neither
his subordination as ' son' an argument for silence, nor
' counsels' an accusation, as though his father were unin-
structed in such matters. Again, very finely: ' The full
of your spring-tide is now fallen, and the stream of your
life waneth to a low ebb; your tired bark beginneth to
leak, and *grateth oft upon the gravel of the grave;* there-
fore it is high time for you to strike sail and put into
harbour, lest, remaining in the scope of the winds and
waves of this wicked time, some unexpected gust should
dash you upon the rock of eternal ruin' (p. lix.). And
so the ' sharp arrow' is at last sent home. ' Now there-
fore, to join issue and to come to the principal drift of
my discourse : most humbly and earnestly I am to be-
seech you, that, both in respect of the honour of God,
your duty to His Church, the comfort of your children,
and the redress of your own soul, you would seriously
consider the terms you stand on, and weigh yourself
in a Christian balance, taking for your counterpoise the
judgments of God. Take heed in time, that the word
Thekel, written of old against Balthazar, and interpreted
by young Daniel, be not verified in you ; remember the

exposition, " you have been weighed in the balance and
found wanting." Remember that you are in the balance,
that the date of your pilgrimage is well-nigh expired, and
that it now behoveth you to look forward to your country.
Your strength languisheth, your senses become impaired,
and your body droopeth, and on every side the ruinous
cottage of your faint and feeble flesh threateneth a fall.
Having so many harbingers of death to pre-admonish
you of your end, how can you but prepare for so dread-
ful a stranger? The young may die quickly, but the
old cannot live long. The young man's life by casualty
may be abridged; but the old man's life can by no phy-
sic be long augmented. And therefore, if green years
must sometimes think of the grave, the thoughts of sere
age should continually dwell on the same. The prero-
gative of infancy is innocency; of childhood, reverence;
of manhood, maturity; and of age, wisdom; and seeing
that the chief property of wisdom is to be mindful of
things past, careful of things present, and provident of
things to come, use now the privilege of Nature's talent
to the benefit of your soul, and show hereafter to be wise
in well-doing, and watchful in foresight of future harms.
To serve the world you are now unable, and though you
were able, you have little wish to do so, seeing that it
never gave you but an unhappy welcome, a hurtful enter-
tainment, and now doth abandon you with an unfortunate
farewell. You have long sowed in a field of flint, which
could bring you nothing forth but a crop of cares and
afflictions of spirit; rewarding your labours with re-
morse, and for your pains repaying you with eternal
damages. It is now more than a seasonable time to alter
your course of so unthriving a husbandry, and to enter

into the field of God's Church' (pp. xlix.-li.). The se-
quel is intensely, almost awfully in earnest in its calls for
recovery—'*return* to His Church'—and to 'consider' be-
fore it be 'too late;' and he urges: 'I have expressed not
only my own, but the earnest desire of your other chil-
dren, whose humble wishes are here written with my pen.
For it is a general grief that filleth all our hearts, whom
it hath pleased God to shroud under His merciful wing,
to see our dearest father, to whom both nature hath
bound and your merits fastened our affection, dismem-
bered from the body to which we are united, to be in
hazard of a farther and more grievous separation' (p. lx.).

I know nothing comparable with the mingled affec-
tion and prophet-like fidelity, the wise 'instruction, correc-
tion, reproof,' the full rich scripturalness and quaint ap-
plications, the devoutness, the insistence, the pathos of
this Letter. Even the noble Letter of the late Bishop of
Exeter (PHILLPOTTS) to Lord Chancellor ELDON on his
deathbed—the gem of the 'Life' of ELDON by TWISS—
looks chill and meagre beside it. A shorter Letter to
his Brother (not named), similarly preserved, is of the
same character, and of as urgent and eager intensity for
'decision.' Here is one 'cry' out of it: 'I would I
might send you the sacrifice of my dearest veins, to try
whether nature could awake remorse, and prepare a way
for grace's entrance.'[1]

The 'Triumphs over Death' is a panegyric on the
lady of the family of the HOWARDS noticed in the Me-
moir [Lady Mary Sackville]. It seeks to check over-
grief, and in so doing lacks the gentleness, the softness

[1] WALTER, as before, p. 127: TURNBULL from WALTER,
p. lxiv.

of his other Letters, being severe to sternness in its re-
pression. His 'character' of the 'fair lady' is drawn with
the firm lines of a Painter and the glow of a Poet. It
may serve as an example of the elegance of his style, and
so I adduce it here : 'She was by birth second to none
but vnto the first in the realme ; yet she measured onely
greatnesse by goodnes, making nobility but the mirrour
of vertue, as able to shewe things worthie to be seene, as
apte to draw many eies to beholde it ; shee suted her be-
hauior to her birth, and enobled her birth with her piety,
leauing her house more beholding to her for hauing hon-
oured it with the glorie of her vertues, then she was to
it for the titles of hir degree. She was high-minded in
nothing but in aspiring to perfection and in the disdaine
of vice ; in other things couering her greatnes with hu-
militie among her inferiors, and showing it with curtesie
among hir peeres. Of the carriage of her selfe, and her
sober gouernement [it] may be a sufficient testimony, that
Enuy hirself was dumbe in her dispraise, finding in her
much to repine at, but naught to reproue. The clearenes
of hir honor I neede not to mention, she hauing alwaies
armed it with such modestie as taught the most vntem-
perate tongues to be silent in her presence, and answered
their eyes with scorne and contempt, that did but seeme
to make her an aime to passion ; yea, and in this behalfe,
as almost in all others, shee hath the most honourable
and knowen ladies of the Land so common and knowen
witnesses, that those that least loued her religion were in
loue with her demeanour, deliuering their opinions in
open praises. How mildely she accepted the checke of
fortune fallen vpon her without desert, experience hath
bin a most manifest proofe ; the temper of her mind being

so easie that she found little difficultie in taking downe her thoughts to a meane degree, which true honour not pride hath raised to her former height; her faithfulnes and loue, where she found true friendship, is written with teares in many eies, and will be longer registred in grateful memories.'[1] Scattered up and down the 'Triumphs' are felicitous conceits and most ingenious applications of Bible facts and names: *e.g.* 'Would Saul have thought it friendship to have wept for his fortune in hauing found a kingdome by seeking of cattel? or Dauid account it a curtesie to have sorowed at his successe, that from folowing sheep came to foyle a giant and receiue in fine a royall crowne for his victorie? Why then should her loss bee lamented?' Again : 'Wee moisten not the ground with pretious waters. They were stilled to nobler endes, eyther by their fruits to delight our sences, or by their operation to preserue our healths. Our teares are water of too high a price to be prodigally poured in the dust of any graues. If they be teares of loue, they perfume our prayers.' Once more : 'When Moses threw his rod from him, it became a serpent, redy to sting, and affrighted him, insomuch as it made him to flee; but being quickly taken vp, it was a rod againe, seruiceable for his vse, no way hurtful. The crosse of Christ and rod of every tribulation seem to threaten stinging and terrour to those that shunne and eschew it, but they that mildely take it up and embrace it with patience may say with David (Psalme xxiii.), " Thy *rod* and Thy staffe

---

[1] Our text is the edition of 1596, which being unpaged, references are not easy : but being short the Reader will readily find our quotations. Sir Egerton Brydges reprinted the 'Triumphs.'

have been my comfort." '   Yet again : ' She stood vpon
too lowe a ground to take view of her Sauior's most de-
sired countenance, and forsaking the earth, with Zacheus,
she climed vp into the tree of life, there to giue her soule
a full repast on His beauties. . . . shee departed, with
Jepthae's daughter from her father's house, but to passe
some moneths in wandring about the mountaynes of this
troublesome world. . . . and to ascend out of this desart
like a stemme [= steam] of perfume out of burned
spices.' WILLMOTT appositely (as before, first edition of
' Lives,' p. 13) reminds us in relation to the closing image,
that the voice of the ' Lady' in Comus is described as
rising ' like a steam of rich distilled perfumes.' The fol-
lowing seems to me to contain in brief a very famous paper
of ADDISON in *The Spectator* : ' If men should lay all
their evilles together, to be afterwards by equall portions
divided among them, most men would rather take that
they brought than stand to the diuision.' I close with three
sentences (' golden' the Puritans would have called them)
that you inevitably note in reading : ' That which dieth
to our loue is always aliue to our sorrow.' ' The termes
of our life are like the seasons of the yeare, some for sow-
ing, some for growing, and some for reaping : in this
only different, that as the heauens keepe their prescribed
periods, so the succession of times have their appointed
changes ; but in the seasons of our life, which are not the
laws of necessarie causes, some are reaped in the seed,
some in the blade, some in the vnripe eares, all in the
end : the haruest depending vpon the Reaper's wil.' ' The
dwarfe groweth not on the highest hill, nor the tall man
looseth not his height in the lowest valley.'

   ' Mary Magdalene's Funerall Teares' was in part

reprinted by Dr. Isaac Watts along with his own
Hymns; and it has never, I suppose, been 'out of print.'
I confess, that it has a morbid sentimentalism about
it not at all pleasing—after the type of a good deal
of Father Faber's otherwise striking and suggestive
Prose—an over-dwelling upon and over-valuation of
'weeping' *per se*, that repells. And yet ever and anon
one is arrested by a quaint fancy, an odd metaphor, as
of a gargoyle or cathedral-stall oaken carving. Thus
of Mary, as she stood at the empty tomb in her sor-
row, he says, ' Alas, how vnfortunate is this woman, to
whom neither life will afoord a desired farewell, nor
death allow any wished welcome ! She hath abandoned
the liuing, and chosen the company of the dead; and
now it seemeth that euen *the dead have forsaken her,*
since the coarse she seeketh is taken away from her.'[1]
Again: ' Though teares were rather oyle than water to
her flame, apter to nourish than diminish her griefe, yet
now being plunged in the depth of paine, she yeelded
herselfe captiue to all discomfort.' Once more: ' Re-
member [Lord] that Thou saidst to her sister, that " Mary
had chosen the better part, which should not be taken
from her." That she chose the " best part" is out of
the question, sith she made choice of nothing but only of
Thee. But how can it be verified, that this part shall
not be taken from her, sith Thou that art this part art
already taken away?' Here and elsewhere, without au-
thority, Southwell assumes ' Mary Magdalene' to have
been Mary of Bethany : but the argument is lovingly

---

[1] As with the ' Triumphs,' our text (1630) is unpaged, and
hence we can't give references for our quotations; but again
the treatise is brief.

dexterous on the (erroneous) assumption. Reasoning
that is now commonplace, through familiarity, is notice-
able in its early occurrence in our Worthy: *e. g.* ' Would
any theefe, thinkest thou, haue beene so religious, as to
haue stolen the body and left the clothes? yea, would
he haue beene so vertuous as to haue stayed the vn-
shrouding of the coarse, the well-ordering of the sheets,
and folding vp the napkins? Thou knowest that the
myrrh maketh linnen cleaue as fast as pitch or glue:
and was a theefe at so much leasure, as to dissolue the
myrrh and vncloath the dead?' and so on.   Once more:
' If thou [Mary] seest anything that beareth colour of
mirth, it is vnto thee like the rich spoiles of a van-
quished kingdome in the eye of a captiue prince, which
puts him in mind what he had, not what he hath, and
are but vpbraidings of his losse and whetstones of sharper
sorrow.'   Again: ' Loue is no gift except the giuer be
giuen with it;' and ' Loue is not ruled with reason, but
with loue.'   Yet again: ' If sorrow at the crosse did not
make thee as deafe as at the tombe, it maketh thee for-
getfull, thou diddest in confirmation hereof heare Him-
selfe say to one of the theeues, that the same day he
should be *with Him* in Paradise.'   Finally: on the words
' she taking Him to be a gardener,' there is this odd
expostulation passing into genuine exposition: ' Hath
thy Lord liued so long, laboured so much, died with such
paine, and shed such showers of bloud, to come to no
higher preferment, than to be a gardener?   And hast
thou bestowed such cost, so much sorrow and so many
teares, for no better man than a silly gardener?   Alas,
is the sorry garden the best inheritance that thy loue
can afoord Him, or a gardener's office the highest dig-

nitie that thou wilt allow Him? It had beene better He
had liued to haue beene lord of thy castle [Magdala],
than with His death so dearely to haue bought so small
a purchase. But thy mistaking hath in it a further
mysterie. Thou thinkest not amisse, though thy sight
be deceiued. For as our first father, in the state of grace
and innocency, was placed in the garden of pleasure,
and the first office allotted him was to be a gardener; so
the first man that euer was in glory, appeareth first in
a garden, and presenteth Himselfe in a gardener's like-
nesse, that the beginnings of glorie might resemble the
entrance of innocencie and grace. And as the gardener
was the fall of mankinde, the parent of sinne, and au-
thor of death, so is this gardener the raiser of our ruines,
the ransome of our offences, and the restorer of life. In
a garden Adam was deceiued and taken captiue by the
deuill. In a garden Christ was betrayed and taken pri-
soner by the Jewes. In a garden Adam was condemned
to earne his bread with the sweat of his browes. And
after a free gift of the bread of angels in the Last Sup-
per, in a garden Christ did earne it vs with a bloudy
sweat of His whole body. By disobedient eating the
fruit of a tree, our right to that garden was by Adam
forfeited; and by the obedient death of Christ vpon a
tree, a farre better right is now recouered. When Adam
had sinned in the garden of pleasure, he was there ap-
parelled in dead beasts' skinnes, that his garment might
betoken his graue, and his liuery of death agree with
his condemnation to die. And now to defray the debt
of that sinne, in this garden Christ lay clad in the dead
man's shrowd and buried in his tombe, that as our harmes
began, so they might end; and such places and meanes

as were the premises to our misery, might be also the
conclusions of our misfortune;' and so on, after the
manner of ST. BERNARD. 'Mary Magdalen's Funerall
Teares' supplies also words of SOUTHWELL used in his
Poems, *e. g.* sindon, wrecke as = wreak, demurres, and
the like.

The 'Short Rules' are in many respects admirable
and 'charitable,' but offer nothing very remarkable. The
instructions concerning 'children' and 'servants' are
good.[1]

With relation to the STONYHURST MSS. I must express
an earnest hope that some one capable will make them
the basis of an adequate edition of the Prose Writings
of SOUTHWELL, and that the MS. 'Meditations,' formerly
in possession of WALTER and lately of DOLMAN, will be
forthcoming. The 'Precationes' and 'Meditationes' and
'Notes on Theology' most certainly ought not to remain
in MS. only.

Passing now to the POETRY of our Worthy, from its
greater extent, St. Peter's Complaint claims perhaps first
thought. When we come to examine it, to 'search' it
—the old (English) Bible word—it is discovered to par-
take very much of the character of the shorter poems.
That is to say, that while a thread of unity runs through
it, it really is rather a succession of separate studies on
the sad Fall of St. Peter than a single rounded poem;
so much so, that were it divided into portions and given

---

[1] Originally issued as 'A Shorte Rule,' the little tractate grew
to the 'Short Rules' of the collective edition of 1630. Kerslake
of Bristol had an autograph MS. of the earlier form, 'A shorte
Rule of Good Lyfe to direct the devoute Christian in a regular
and orderlie course.' (Catal. Feb. 1860, No. 449, 4*l.* 14*s.*)

headings, as with the minor pieces in the 1616 edition, we should discern no abruptness, and no distinction as between them and the others. As we have found in the Memoir, the STONYHURST MSS. contain only 12 out of the 131 stanzas (see page 2); and in this form it exists in various contemporary and later copies. Again, in ELIZABETH GRYMESTON's Miscellanea, Meditations Memoratiues (1604), '*sixteene* staves' are taken from the long Poem, which it is said 'she usually sung and played on winde instruments.' Each 'stave' or stanza is prefaced by prose 'meditations' or prayers, simple, sweet, and affectionate. Thus it would seem St. Peter's Complaint extended beyond its Author's original design. That it cost him no little thought and 'pains' and prayer, the fragmentary MSS. of Stonyhurst prove. There are separate stanzas written and re-written, and corrected and re-corrected: *e.g.* a heading is 'The Peeter Playnt' (*sic*) with 'The' erased; and then as follows:

    peer
' That sturdy peter   *did boaste*
 The champion stout which did with othe avowe
 Amyds a thousand pykes and blody blades
 At his deare masters syde to yeld the ghoast
 Perceyvyng that he conquered of two mades when dasht
      his credit *distayne* with dread
 Even at the pinch from premiss did retyre and cowardyce
       angry smart he fades, and
 The shame, the pitye and the gryping griefe at the pinch
           f(ayth)
 Loth of his falt and of his maysters paynes his loyalty doth
 A thousand daggers stabbed in his hart [erased] stayne.
did with puniardes *pushes* [erased] stabbe
 A thousand *woundes* prickyns [erased] pearce [erased] his
  hart.'

So throughout. There are also prose-jottings of ideas and metaphors for the poem: *e.g.* commencing with verse and going on *ad interim* in prose:

' Ech eie of Chryst a running tunge did seeme
        ech lyk a listning
And peters eis so many eagre eares [' s' erased]   Eche ey of pe-
Prest to recyve the voyce and it esteame   ter like a list-
                                                    ninge eare.
According to that sense that it should beare.
More fierce he seemed to say ar thy eis
Then the impious hands which shall naile me on the crosse
Nether feele I any blow [sic] which do so annoy me
Of so many which this gylty
rable doth on me lay
As that blow which came out of thy mouth.
None faythful found I, none courteous
Of so many that I have vochsafned to be myne
But thow in whome my   was more kyndled
And faythlesse and ungratefull above all other
All other with there (cowardly) flyght did only offend
me   my
But thou hast denyed and now with the other (foes) [sic] ghilty
Standest feedynd thy eies with my damage (and sorowes)
As though part of this pleasur belonged unto the.'

These specimens must suffice; and the critical Reader
will delight to compare them with the ultimate published
Poem.[1]

In the Note to St. Peter's Complaint (page 2) I ven-
ture to assign it a foremost place only on the ground of its
being longer than the others. I adhere to the verdict, inas-
much as there are in ' Mæoniæ' and our ' Myrtæ' shorter
pieces that attain a reach and sweep, and which gleam
with a dove-neck or peacock-crest splendour of colour, only
now and again paralleled in the 'Complaint.' At the same
time, regarded as so many distinct Studies of the tragic
Incident, it is ignorance, not knowledge, glance-and-run
reading, not insight, that will pronounce it tedious or idly

---

[1] As these variations and studies are peculiarly interesting
I give the remainder (not extensive) in Additional Notes and Il-
lustrations at close of the Volume.

paraphrastic. BISHOP HALL, among the many mis-esti-
mates of his passionate youth, in his ' Satires' (Book I.
viii.) has one mocking line on the ' Complaint:'

> ' Now good St. Peter weeps pure Helicon,'

with a gibe at ' Mary's Funerall Teares;' and GERVASE
MARKHAM's ' Lamentations of Mary Magdalene' (reprinted
in our Fuller Worthies' Miscellanies):

> ' And both the Marys make a music moan.'

But MARSTON repaid the Satirist with compound interest:

> ' Come daunce, ye stumbling Satyres, by his side,
> If he list once the Syon Muse deride.
> Ye Granta's white nymphs come, and with you bring
> Some sillabub, whilst he does sweetly sing
> 'Gainst Peter's Teares and Marie's mouing Moane,
> And, like a fierce enragèd boare doth foame.'[1]

LODGE and NASH have kindly allusions to the ' Funerall
Teares' and SOUTHWELL: the former in his ' Prosopopeia,
containing the Teares of the holy, blessed, and sancti-
fied Marie, the mother of God' (see Shakespeare Society
Papers, ii. 157); and so too in ' Pierce's Supererogation.'

But it is from the shorter Poems the vitality of SOUTH-
WELL's memory as a Singer has sprung and will abide.
Our Memoir establishes that some of the tenderest and
sweetest must have been composed after the anguish of
his ' *thirteen* rackings' and other prison tortures. The poor
Canary continuing to sing in the darkness of its artificial
and cruel sightlessness (for the eyes are put out on pur-
pose to secure ' singing' at night as during the day) is an
imperfect symbol of our Poet continuing to utter out
the music that was in him under such conditions. Pro-

---

[1] Reactio, sat. iv. Hall's Works (1839), vol. xii. pp. 169-170.

bably his entire Poems were produced in prison; and I
must reiterate that this inevitableness surely determines
that his most quaint and affected-seeming Verse was na-
tural, spontaneous, truthful. The man is a pretender who
can really 'ponder' ' Myrtæ' and ' Mæoniæ' and the rest,
and not recognise a born-poet in SOUTHWELL; not supreme,
high-soaring, imaginative, grand, but within his own self-
chosen lowly sphere pure and bright, well-languaged and
memorable and thought-packed.[1] I name and only name
' Tymes goe by Turnes;' ' Look Home;' ' Scorne not the
Least;' ' A Child my Choyce;' ' Content and Riche;'
' Love's Servile Lott;' ' Life is but Losse,' and those
related; ' Lewd Loue is Losse;' ' Dyer's Phansie turned
to a Synner's Complaynte;' and the whole series on the
Lord and His Mother, with every abatement that we, who
are Protestants, must make in respect of the uttermost
recognition of her as the God-bearer (Θεοτόκος.) The
Latin Poems—printed by us for the first time—have, as
our few notes show, certain superficial metrical defects;
but apart from other things, as their subjects, which are
of special interest, I must regard the long poem on the
Assumption of the Virgin as bold, original, unforgettable;
while that on the Prodigal has a pre-Raphaelite realism
that is taking. Altogether, in recollection of their (early)
date and of the circumstances of their composition, it
were a loss to our small body of English Sacred Poetry
to lose SOUTHWELL. The hastiest Reader will come on
' thinking' and ' feeling' that are as musical as Apollo's
lute, and as fresh as a spring-budding spray; and the
wording of all (excepting over-alliteration and inversion

---

[1] Cf. the Preface-Epistle to his ' loving cosen' for his humble
self-estimate, as onward.

occasionally) is throughout of the 'pure well of English undefiled.' When you take some of the 'Myrtæ' and 'Mæoniæ' pieces, and read and re-read them, you are struck with their condensation, their concinnity, their polish, their *élan*, their memorableness. Holiness is in them not as scent on love-locks, but as fragrance in the Great Gardener's flowers of fragrance. His tears are pure and white as the 'dew of the morning.' His smiles —for he has humour, even wit, that must have lurked in the burdened eyes and corners o' mouth—are sunny as sunshine. As a whole his Poetry is healthy and strong, and I think has been more potential in our Literature than appears on the surface. I do not think it would be hard to show that others of whom more is heard drew light from him, as well early as more recent, from BURNS to THOMAS HOOD. For example, limiting us to the latter, I believe every Reader who will compare the two deliberately, will see in the 'Vale of Tears' the source of the latter's immortal 'Haunted House'—dim, faint, weak beside it, as the earth-hid bulb compared with the lordly blossom of hyacinth or tulip or lily—nevertheless really carrying in it the original of the mightier after-poem.

It only remains that I bring before our Readers certain SHAKESPEREANA out of SOUTHWELL. And in the outset here, while I am not one of those who find allusions to SHAKESPEARE in contemporary writings when the writers were not thinking of him—though I believe that his scenic realities were more suggestive to his brother authors than is commonly supposed—and while I do not think that he alone is alluded to in the Epistle to his 'loving cosen' as preface to St. Peter's Complaint, I yet

must discern thought of the Poet of ' Venus and Adonis'
and ' Lucrece' in these words, which I give from the
Stonyhurst autograph in the original spelling, *not* as in
our reprint (in its place) from 1596 : ' The devill as he
affecteth deitye, and seeketh to have all the complementes
of divine honor applied to his service, so hath he amonge
the reste possessed also most Poetes with his idle phancies;
for in liew of solemne and devoute matter, to which in
dutye they owe their abilities, they now busy themselves
in expressing such passions as onely serve for testimo-
nies to howe unworthy affections they have wedded their
willes.   And because the best course to lett them see the
error of their workes is to weave a newe webb in their
owne loome, I have here laid a fewe course thredds to-
gether to invite some skilfuller wittes to goe forward in
the same or to beginne some fyner peece, wherein it maye
be seene how well verse and vertue suite together.' Then
in St. Peter's Complaint (The Author to the Reader) we
have this more express allusion :

> ' Still finest wits are 'stilling Venvs' rose,
> In Paynim toyes the sweetest vaines are spent.'

We shall produce internal and external evidence imme-
diately ; but at this point I observe that in ' Mary Mag-
dalen's Funerall Teares' there is like lamentation over
the ' finest wits' given up to mere ' idle' love-verse, yet
with a very clear recognition of the loftiest genius: *e. g.*
in the Epistle-dedicatory, ' The *finest wits* are now giuen
to write passionate discourses;' and in ' To the Reader,'
' It may be that courteous skill will reckon this though
course in respect of others' *exquizite labours*, not unfit to
entertaine well-tempered humours.'

Be it remembered farther that at the period ' St. Pe-

ter's Complaint' was written, ' Venus and Adonis' was
one of *the* poems of the day, tabled and learnt by the
gallants, and applied by them in complimentary address
to their mistresses: also, that the stanza-form of the two
poems is identical, and that ' Venus' is mentioned by
name. Then more specifically in the next stanza (ll. 2-4)
and st. vi. of the ' Complaint' itself, reference is intended
to the same chiefest Poets (and it need hardly be said
that the modern theory of the non-appreciation of Shake-
speare by his contemporaries is a baseless and ignorant
vision); and that at a time when epithets were fixed upon
each author of mark, and when ' *sweet*' was a recognised
appellative of the silver-tongued Melicert—coming up later
in MILTON to the perplexity of the present Archbishop of
Dublin (Trench), through his forgetfulness of the love
and intensity that went as elements in the word 'sweet,' as
then and even still in the rapture of fellowship with the
Lord Jesus. Hence I conclude that SHAKESPEARE's ' ex-
quizite labours' and ' finest wit' were included in ' the
heavenly sparks of wit who spend their sweetest veins in
Paynim toys.'

Nor is this all. Turning to St. Peter's Complaint,
st. lvii.-ix. and part of the next, and especially the first
two lines of the stanza next but one (st. lxii.), and st.
lxv. ' Oh eyes, whose glances !'—let the Shakesperean
student compare them with the thesis maintained by
Biron in Love's Labour Lost (iv. 3):

> ' From women's eyes this doctrine I derive :—
> They *sparkle* still the right Promethean *fire ;*
> They are the *books*, the arts, the *academies*,
> That *show, contain, and nourish* all the world.'

Biron's speech being a humorously sophistical mainten-

ance of a thesis in scholastic form—not noticing which
the Commentators have gone astray. In our Notes and
Illustrations I furnish other SHAKESPEARE-parallels and
(probable or possible) allusions and elucidations : and I
invite attention to them.

By the way, it is worth recording that one unusual
use of a word ('*vaunt*,' page 90) by SOUTHWELL, has a
near parallel in the Prologue to Troilus and Cressida,
'leaps o'er the *vaunt*.' Then, as noted in the place (p. 49),
'the cold brook *candied* with ice' (Timon, act iv. sc. 3);
if SHAKESPEARE'S, was not improbably borrowed from
our Poet, for Timon in its present state is several years
later than 1595. On the other hand, the words may be
those of the older Play. Farther, in 'Of the Blessed
Sacrament of the Aulter' = as we have seen, 'The Chris-
tian's Manna,' stanza iii., smacks of Cupid's prologue
in the same Timon (i. 2). It is allowable to indulge in
the 'pleasures of imagination' that the mightier Poet read
the lesser, and that the lesser recognised the coming
effulgence of England's supremest genius. One sentence
in the Epistle to his 'loving cosen' reveals that play or
stage-fetched metaphors were not accounted unhallowed
by our Worthy, inasmuch as he applies such to the Tra-
gedy and Pageant of Calvary. From SOUTHWELL'S pos-
session in (necessarily) MS. of Sir Edward Dyer's 'Phansie'
(turned by him characteristically into a 'Sinner's Plaint'),
it is plain he had access to circles where such Manuscripts
were circulated, and it may be even Shakespeare's 'copies
in MS.' of his 'sweet' poems similarly reached him. It
does not appear that he had seen LORD BROOKE'S deeper
original of DYER'S 'Phansie.' We have also pleasantly
to remember that in his 'Conversations' with DRUMMOND

of Hawthornden, BEN JONSON thus spoke of SOUTHWELL
and one of his poems : ' That Southwell was hanged ; yet
so he [Jonson] had written that piece of his, the Burning
Babe, he would have been content to destroy many of
his' (Laing's edit. p. 13) : and if JONSON ' read' SOUTH-
WELL, equally may ' gentle Will' have done so.

Regarding the ' wording' of Southwell's poetry, it
seems to me very pure English for the time, which is the
more noticeable in that a Latinate style might have been
expected. Occasionally there is a poetic-archaic word—of
one or two of which he is extremely fond—and also in-
tended or accidental provincialisms. In pronunciation
the liquid syllables are generally elided, as is ' ow,' and
words like ' orient' and ' period' are trisyllabic, ' spirit'
gener-ally read as ' sprite,' ' haven' ' heaven,' ' even' (as
adv.-verb, and in ' uneven') always monosyllabic, and
' evil' nearly always so—all as pointed out in our Notes
and Illustrations. Now and then, by license and *metri
gratiâ*, -ions and -ion are made dissyllables. He also
makes over-use of a poetic license and affectation, and
mars the sound of his verse by the too frequently recur-
ring -èd. His sentences are short, especially so as com-
pared with many writers of the period, and rhythmical,
and he adds to the latter by a marked alliterativeness.
In construction he is generally clear and English, and as
with his words, less Latinate than might have been sup-
posed, except that there is a great omission of the arti-
cle, a great use of ellipses both regular and irregular,
and far too frequent inversions, which sometimes obscure
the sense, and in one instance imparts a dash of the
ludicrous, *e.g.* ' of pearl the purest mother,' as = mother-
of-pearl. As examples of irregular ellipses, we find ' thy

trespass' [being], which has to be taken out of ' be' (p.
11, line 17); fray [was] (p. 18, line 2); part [me from
Christ] (p. 20, line 13); keep [me] (p. 29, line 2). The
' blind in seeing what' [was present] (p. 14, line 2) pro-
bably comes rather under the head of a colloquial ellipse,
and one of those many phrases in the old writers which
are more or less obscure, because the Writers have writ-
ten too much as they would have spoken, not allow-
ing for the absence of other language, and for that sym-
pathy and consentaneous knowledge which generally
exist between the speaker and listener. Hence we find
a difficulty at times in referring the pronoun to its pro-
per noun, because the writer does not think so much of
the word-construction as of the main idea or subject
of his discourse, and writes too colloquially. Thus, at
p. 39, lines 19-20, 'whose' refers to 'parts,' not to
'gripes;' and at p. 119, line 8, 'he' is not Joseph,
but God; and at p. 68, the 'they' of line 5 of ' Scorne
not the Leaste' refers not to higher powers, but to
' feebler part.'

There is another obscurity common to Southwell and
writers of his day, in connection with the possessive pro-
noun and case, which is dependent on the causes spoken
of above, but which has sometimes been mis-explained.
'My injuries' meant, according to the context, either the
injuries done by another to me, or the wrongs that I do
or did to others; in the one case the other person or
persons are mainly thought of and considered agental ;
in the other case I am the chief subject of my ideas and
the agent. In such phrases as ' this box is my gift,' or
' this box is his gift,' the other circumstances alone in-
terpret whether it is meant 'this box is the gift bestowed

on me' (or him), or 'this box is the gift bestowed by me' (or him). ' Angels' bread' might be, bread prepared by or brought by angels, or it might be the bread given to angels—according to whatever the context determines to be the agent. So in 'God is my gift' (p. 128, line 17), it is only the context that shows that 'gift' is that which God gave, and has only become mine through His agency, and that the 'God's gift am I' means ' I have given myself as a gift to God.'

I cannot close these inadequate remarks on SOUTH-WELL without expressing the profound regret and pain —in common with many of his warmest admirers—with which I read PROFESSOR LOWELL's verdict on his Poetry, in his charming ' My Study Windows' (on Smith's ' Library of old Authors'). It seems to me harsh to brutality on the man (meet follower of Him ' the first true gentleman that ever breathed'); while on the Poetry it rests on self-evidently the most superficial acquaintance and the hastiest generalisation. To pronounce ' St. Peter's Complaint' a ' drawl' of thirty pages of ' maudlin repentance, in which the distinctions between the north and north-east sides of a [sic] sentimentality are worthy of Duns Scotus,' shows about as much knowledge—that is ignorance—of the Poem as of the Schoolman, and as another remark does of St. Peter: for, with admitted tedium, St. Peter's Complaint sounds depths of penitence and remorse, and utters out emotion that flames into passion very unforgettably, while there are felicities of metaphor, daintinesses of word-painting, brilliancies of inner-portraiture scarcely to be matched in contemporary Verse. The ' paraphrase' of David (to wit, ' David's Peccavi') is a single short piece, and the ' punning' con-

ceit, ' fears are my feres,' is common to some of Eng-
land's finest wits, and in the meaning of ' fere' not at all
to be pronounced against. If we on this side the Atlantic
valued less the opinion of such a unique genius as Pro-
fessor LOWELL's, if we did not take him to our inner-
most love, we should less grieve over such a vulgar affront
offered to a venerable name as his whole paragraph on
SOUTHWELL. I shall indulge the hope of our edition
reaching the ' Study,' and persuading to a real ' study'
of these Poems; and if so, I do not despair of a volun-
tary reversal of the first judgment. ARIS WILLMOTT pro-
nounced SOUTHWELL to be the GOLDSMITH of our early
poets; and ' Content and Rich' and ' Dyer's Phansie
turned to a Sinner's Complaint' warrant the great praise.
But beneath the manner recalling GOLDSMITH, there is a
purity and richness of thought, a naturalness, a fineness
of expression, a harmony of versification, and occasionally
a tide-flow of high-toned feeling, not to be met with in
him.

Nor will Prof. LOWELL deem his (I fear) hasty (mis)
judgment's reconsideration too much to count on, after the
present Archbishop of Dublin's well-weighed words in his
notes to his ' Household Book of English Poetry' (1868):
' Hallam thinks that Southwell has been of late praised at
least as much as he deserves. This may be so; yet, tak-
ing into account the finished beauty of such poems as this
(' Lewd Love is Loss') and No. 2 (' Times go by Turns')
of this collection, poems which, as far as they go, leave
nothing to be desired, he has scarcely been praised *more*
than he deserves. How in earlier times he was rated,
the fact that there were twenty-four editions of his poems
will sufficiently testify; though probably the creed which

he professed, and the death which he died, may have had something to do with this. Robert Southwell was a seminary priest, and was executed at Tyburn in the reign of Queen Elizabeth, in conformity with a law, which even the persistent plottings of too many of these at once against the life of the Sovereign and the life of the State must altogether fail to justify or excuse' (pp. 391-2).

To Archbishop TRENCH's I add, as equally weighty and worthy, the fine and finely sympathetic yet discriminative judgment of DR. GEORGE MACDONALD in 'Antiphon,' as follows : ' I proceed to call up one WHO WAS A POET INDEED, although little known as such, being a Roman Catholic, a Jesuit even, and therefore, in Elizabeth's reign, a traitor, and subject to the penalties according [accruing ?]. Robert Southwell, "thirteen times most cruelly tortured," could "not be induced to confess anything, not even the colour of the horse whereon on a certain day he rode, lest from such indication his adversaries might conjecture in what house, or in company of what Catholics, he that day was." I quote these words of LORD BURLEIGH, lest any of my readers, discovering weakness in his verse, should attribute weakness to the man himself.' I intercalate, that any ' weakness in his verse' will be ' discovered' only here and there, as a withered leaf on a green bough, and rather in the Catholic sensuism of sentiment—as a Protestant thinks—than in the ' verse' itself. He proceeds : ' It was, no doubt, on political grounds that these tortures, and the death that followed them, were inflicted. But it was for the truth *as he saw it*, that is, for the sake of duty, that Southwell thus endured. We must not impute all the evils of a system to every individual who holds by it. It may be

found that a man has, for the sole sake of self-abnega-
tion, yielded homage, where, if his object had been perso-
nal aggrandisement, he might have wielded authority.
Southwell, if that which comes from within a man may
be taken as the test of his character, was a devout and
humble Christian. In the choir of our singers we only
ask, " Dost thou lift up thine heart?" Southwell's song
answers for him : " I lift it up unto the Lord."

' His chief poem is called *St. Peter's Complaint.* It
is of considerable length—a hundred and thirty-two
stanzas. It reminds us of the Countess of Pembroke's
poem [' Our Saviour's Passion']; but is far more ar-
ticulate and far superior in versification. Perhaps its
chief fault is, that the pauses are so measured with the
lines as to make every line almost a sentence, the effect
of which is a considerable degree of monotony. *Like all
writers of the time,* he is of course fond of antithesis, and
abounds in conceits and fancies; whence he attributes a
multitude of expressions to St. Peter, of which never
possibly could the substantial ideas have entered the
Apostle's mind, or probably any other than Southwell's
own. There is also a good deal of sentimentalism in the
poem; a fault from which I fear modern Catholic verse
is rarely free. Probably the Italian poetry with which
he must have been familiar in his youth, during his re-
sidence in Rome, accustomed him to such irreverences
of expression as this sentimentalism gives occasion to,
and which are very far from indicating a correspondent
state of feeling. Sentiment[alism] is a poor ape of love;
but the love is true, notwithstanding.' There follow six
stanzas from St. Peter's Complaint, and 'two little stanzas
worth preserving,' and 'New Prince, New Pomp,' the last

thus introduced: 'The following poem, in style almost as
simple as a ballad, is at once of the quaintest and truest.
Common minds, which must always associate a certain
conventional respectability with the forms of religion,
will think it irreverent. I judge its reverence profound,
and such none the less that it is pervaded by a sweet and
delicate tone of holy humour. The very title has a glim-
mer of the glowing heart of Christianity.' He continues:
'Another, on the same subject, he calls *New Heaven, New
War*. It is fantastic to a degree. One stanza, however,
I like much :

> This little babe, so few days old, &c.

There is profoundest truth in the symbolism of this.' I
again intercalate, that BEN JONSON's insight was disclosed
in his love for the kindred Burning Babe, and its mag-
nificent as simple symbolism. Dr. Macdonald concludes
with the latter half of *St. Peter's Remorse* and *Content
and Rich*.[1]

I believe, then, I shall not appeal in vain to Prof.
LOWELL to give a few hours behind his 'Study Win-
dows' to a re-perusal of some of the poems of SOUTHWELL
named by us and these sufficiently-qualified Critics.

And so I take from 'The Lady of La Garaye' a por-
trait of a Prior, for which I fancy FATHER SOUTHWELL
might have sate :

> He sits by Gertrude's couch and patient listens
> To her wild grieving voice ; his dark eye glistens
> With tearful sympathy for that young wife,
> Telling the torture of her broken life ;
> And when he answers her she seems to know
> The peace of resting by a river's flow.'

---

[1] Pp. 96-103.

Tender his words, and eloquently wise;
Mild the pure fervour of his watchful eyes;
Meek with serenity of constant prayer
The luminous forehead, high and broad and bare;
The thin mouth, though not passionless, yet still;
With a sweet calm that speaks an angel's will,
Resolving service to his God's behest,
And ever musing how to serve Him best.
Not old, nor young; with manhood's gentlest grace;
Pale to transparency the pensive face,
Pale not with sickness but with studious thought,
The body tasked, the fine mind overwrought;
With ·something faint and fragile in the whole,
As though 'twere but a lamp to hold a soul.[1]

ALEXANDER B. GROSART.[2]

---

[1] By Hon. Mrs. Norton (1863), pp. 120-1.
[2] At end of our Volume I add a few farther Notes and Illustrations on points touched on in their places.

I.

ST. PETER'S COMPLAINT.

NOTE.

WE place St. Peter's Complaint first, simply because it is the longest verse-production of its author, not at all as being his best. The only complete MS. of this poem known, is that of Addl. MSS. 10.422 in British Museum; but while furnishing a few good readings, it is, in common with the whole Manuscript, sorrowfully careless and corrupt; as fully shown in our Preface. The STONYHURST MS. and HARLEIAN MS. 6921 unfortunately contain only 12 stanzas out of the 132; viz. 10, 11, 28, 29, 14, 17, 30, 21, 22, 20, 23, and 131 of the completed poem. So that we have been obliged to fall back on the printed editions. Again, unfortunately, we have most unsatisfactory texts to work on, even the original edition of 1595 and that assigned by us to 1596 being extremely faulty; as also shown in our Preface. After an anxious collation of MSS. and editions, we have taken for basis the edition of 1596; and in Notes and Illustrations at the close of the poem, record corrections and various readings, with their several authorities in MS. and print. Opposite is the title-page of 1596. It is placed within an engraved border of quaint device, and having in the centre an open book with an hour-glass set on it, and the motto, ' I line to dy: I dy to liue' (in Jesus College, Oxford, copy there is this in a contemporary hand, ' Vt moriar vivo: vt vivā morior'), and underneath a winged death's-head and a globe; all as reproduced in fac-simile in our illustrated quarto edition. For more on this edition, and certain significances in its ornaments, and others, see our Preface.

The Notes and Illustrations are placed at the close of St. Peter's Complaint, and of each of the others, as throughout. Our Memorial-Introduction sheds light on the formation of the ' Complaint:' and thither the reader is referred. G.

SAINT

PETERS COM-

PLAINT,

Newly augmented

With other Poems.

I liue	I dy
to	to
dy	liue

LONDON,

Printed by H. L. for *William Leake:* and
are to be sold at his shop in Paules Church-
yard, at the signe of the holy
Ghost.

[N.D. 1596? 4to.]

THE AUTHOR TO HIS LOUING COSIN.[1]

POETS, by abusing their talent, and making the follies
and faynings of loue the customarie subiect of their
base endeuours, haue so discredited this facultie, that
a poet, a louer, and a lyer, are by many reckoned but
three words of one signification. But the vanitie of
men cannot counterpoyse the authoritie of God, Who
deliuering many parts of Scripture in verse, and, by
His Apostle willing vs to exercise our deuotion in
hymnes and spiritual sonnets, warranteth the art to
be good, and the vse allowable. And therefore not
onely among the heathen, whose gods were chiefely
canonized by their poets, and their paynim diuinitie
oracled, in verse, but euen in the Olde and Newe
Testament, it hath beene vsed by men of greatest

---

[1] This forms the Author's preface to the volume of 1595,
and is repeated in that of 1596 and after-editions. On the
STONYHURST MS. of this Epistle-dedicatory see our Memorial-
Introduction. These corrections of TURNBULL's text may be
noted: line 8, 'deliuering' for 'delivered:' line 10, 'sonnets'
for 'songs :' line 22, 'and footed' dropped out: line 40, 'com-
mend it' for 'he commended:' line 47, 'the meane' for 'let
them.' These readings are all in 1616, 1620 and 1630, as well
as 1595 and 1596. G.

pietie, in matters of most deuotion. Christ Himselfe, by making a hymne the conclusion of His Last Supper, and the prologue to the first pageant of His Passion, gaue His Spouse a methode to imitate, as in the office of the Church it appeareth; and to all men a patterne, to know the true vse of this measured and footed stile.

But the deuill, as he affecteth deitie and seeketh to haue all the complements of diuine honour applyed to his seruice, so hath he among the rest possessed also most Poets with his idle fansies. For in lieu of solemne and deuout matter, to which in duety they owe their abilities, they now busie themselues in expressing such passions as onely serue for testimonies to what unworthy affections they haue wedded their wills. And, because the best course to let them see the errour of their works is to weaue a new webbe in their owne loome, I haue heere laide a few course threds together, to inuite some skilfuller wits to goe forward in the same, or to begin some finer peece; wherein it may be seene how well verse and vertue sute together.

Blame me not (good Cosin) though I send you a blame-worthy present; in which the most that can commend it is the good will of the Writer; neither arte nor invention giuing it any credite. If in me this be a fault, you cannot be faultlesse that did importune me to commit it, and therefore you must beare part of the penance when it shall please sharp censures to impose it. In the meane time, with many good wishes, I send you these fewe ditties; adde you the tunes, and let the Meane, I pray you, be still a part in all your musicke.

THE AVTHOVR TO THE READER.[1]

Deare eye that doost peruse my Muses stile,   1
With easie censure deeme of my delight :
Giue sobrest countenance leaue sometime to smile,
And grauest wits to take a breathing flight :
Of mirth to make a trade, may be a crime,   5
But tyrèd spirits for mirth must haue a time.

The loftie eagle soares not still aboue,
High flights will force her from the wing to stoupe ;
And studious thoughts at times men must remoue,
Least by excesse before their time they droupe.   10
In courser studies 'tis a sweet repose,
With poets pleasing vaine to temper prose.

Profane conceits and faining fits I flie,
Such lawlesse stuffe doth lawlesse speeches fit :
With Dauid, verse to Vertue I apply,   15
Whose measure best with measured words doth fit :
It is the sweetest note that man can sing,
When grace in Vertue's key tunes Nature's string.

---

[1] This and the next poem belong to the whole volume, and
not merely to St. Peter's Complaint. G.

NOTES AND ILLUSTRATIONS.

St. i. line 2, ' deeme' is = pronounce judgment, as in ' deems-ter,' Dempster. ' Deemed' as a participial is similarly used in ' Life is but Losse' (line 5), ' where death is deemèd gaine,' for adjudged or pronounced ' gain ;' at least this gives a stronger and better sense than if it be taken as merely = thought or considered, or than if ' is deemed' be taken as a verb.

St. ii. line 1, ' still' is = constantly, without reference, as now, to any particular moment of time. Such use was not unfrequent contemporarily.

St. ii. line 4, TURNBULL misprints ' the' for ' their,' and in st. iii. line 1, ' feignèd' for ' feigning.' G.

THE AVTHOVR TO THE READER.[1]

DEARE eye, that daynest to let fall a looke
On these sad memories of PETER'S plaints :
Muse not to see some mud in clearest brooke ;
They once were brittle mould that now are saints.
Their weaknesse is no warrant to offend ;   5
Learne by their faults what in thine owne to mend.

If Equitie's even-hand the ballance held,
Where Peter's sinnes and ours were made the weights,
Ounce for his dramme, pound for his ounce we'd yield
His ship would grone to feele some sinners' freights: 10
So ripe is Vice, so green is Vertue's bud :
The world doth waxe in ill, but wane in good.

This makes my mourning Muse resolue in teares,
This theames my heauie penne to plaine in prose ;
Christ's thorne is sharpe, no head His garland weares ;
Stil finest wits are 'stilling Venvs' rose,   16
In Paynim toyes the sweetest vaines are spent ;
To Christian workes few haue their talents lent.

Licence my single penne to seeke a pheere ;
You heauenly sparkes of wit shew natiue light ;   20

<hr>

¹ In 1630 and later editions, and repeated by TURNBULL,
this is headed ' RVRSVS ad EVNDEM.' G.

Cloud not with mistie loues your orient cleere,

Sweet flights you shoote, learne once to leuell right.

Fauour my wish, well-wishing workes no ill ;

I moue the sute, the graunt rests in your will.

NOTES AND ILLUSTRATIONS.

St. ii. line 1, TURNBULL has ' Justice :' it is ' Equitie's' in 1595, 1596 and 1630.

Lines 1-4. If we read these lines as punctuated in 1596 and by TURNBULL, the line ' Ounce . . . . . yield' must be parenthetical, and the sense and sentence ends at ' freights.' But (*meo judicio*) this sense is very like non-sense, and not in SOUTHWELL'S manner. The same punctuation, viz. in 1596, a comma (,) after ' held,' and colon (:) after ' weights,' and comma (,) after ' yeeld,' and period (.) after ' freights.' Or as in TURNBULL, comma after ' held' and ,— after ' weights,' and ,— after ' yield,' mingles metaphors, and represents one end of the balance with its weights as in St. Peter's ship, which seems a somewhat ludicrous combination ; and the more so, that the difference of weight is given so exactly. But if we end with ' yield' (; or even :), and read ' we'd yield' instead of ' we yield,' and then suppose that the Poet's remembrance of St. Peter's draught and exclamation led him on to ' His ship . . . freights (:)' as a second and allied thought, we get clear sense and sentences, and a stanza after SOUTHWELL'S wont. I have punctuated accordingly, and read ' we'd.'

Line 6. In Addl. MSS. 10.422, for ' ill' the reading is ' evill,' on which see onward on the frequent occurrence of ' evil' for ' ill' and its pronunciation (St. Peter's Complaint, st. ii. line 5 : relative note).

St. iii. line 2, TURNBULL spoils the sense by misreading ' too' for ' to.' The reference in line 1 is to the Author's verse, in line 2 to his prose, *e. g.* his ' Mary Magdalen's Funerall Teares.' ' Theames'=gives a theme or subject.

Lines 4-5, on a probable allusion to SHAKESPEARE here— one of several—see our Memorial-Introduction.

St. iv. line 1, ' phere'= husband or companion : line 4, Addl. MSS. 10.422 reads ' fleghts ;' query ' arrows'? G.

SAINT PETER'S COMPLAINT.

I.

LAUNCH forth, my soule, into a maine of teares,
    Full fraught with griefe, the trafficke of thy mind;
Torn sailes will serue, thoughts rent with guilty feares :
    Giue Care the sterne, vse sighs in lieu of wind :
Remorse, thy pilot ; thy misdeede thy card ;
Torment thy hauen, shipwrack thy best reward.

II.

Shun not the shelfe of most deseruèd shame ;
    Sticke in the sands of agonizing dread ;
Content thee to be stormes' and billowes' game ;
    Diuorct from grace, thy soule to pennance wed ;
Fly not from forraine euils, fly from thy hart ;
Worse then the worst of euils is that thou art.

III.

Giue vent vnto the vapours of thy brest,
    That thicken in the brimmes of cloudie eyes ;
Where sinne was hatcht, let teares now wash the nest,
    Where life was lost, recouer life with cryes.
Thy trespasse foule, let not thy teares be few,
Baptize thy spotted soule in weeping dew.

IV.

Fly mournfull plaints, the ecchoes of my ruth
    Whose screeches in my frighted conscience ring;
Sob out my sorrowes, fruites of mine vntruth,
    Report the smart of sinne's infernall sting;
Tell hearts that languish in the sorriest plight,
There is on Earth a farre more sorry wight.

V.

A sorrie wight, the object of disgrace,
    The monument of feare, the map of shame,
The mirrour of mishap, the staine of place,
    The scorne of Time, the infamy of Fame,
An excrement of Earth, to heauen hatefull,
Iniurious to man, to God vngratefull.

VI.

Ambitious heads, dreame you of Fortune's pride,
    Fill volumes with your forgèd goddesse' prayse;
You Fancie's drudges, plung'd in Follie's tide,
    Devote your fabling wits to louers' lays :
Be you, O sharpest griefes that euer wrung,
Text to my thoughts, theame to my playning tung.

VII.

Sad subiect of my sinne hath stoard my minde,
    With euerlasting matter of complaint;
My threnes an endlesse alphabet doe finde,
    Beyond the pangs which Ieremie doth paint.
That eyes with errors may iust measure keepe,
Most teares I wish, that haue most cause to weepe.

VIII.

All weeping eyes resigne your teares to me,
    A sea will scantly rince my ordur'd soule;
Huge horours in high tides must drownèd be :
    Of euery teare my crime exacteth tole.
These staines are deepe: few drops take out no such;
Euen salue with sore, and most is not too much.

IX.

I fear'd with life, to die, by death to liue ;
    I left my guide,—now left, and leauing God.
To breath in blisse, I fear'd my breath to giue ;
    I fear'd for heauenly raigne an earthly rod.
These feares I fear'd, feares feeling no mishaps :
O fond! O faint! O false! O faultie lapse!

X.

How can I liue, that thus my life deni'd ?
    What can I hope, that lost my hope in feare ?
What trust to one, that Truth it selfe defi'd ?
    What good in him, that did his God forsweare?
O sinne of sinnes! of euils the very worst :
O matchlesse wretch! O catiffe most accurst!

XI.

Vaine in my vaunts, I vowd, if friends had fail'd,
    Alone Christ's hardest fortunes to abide :
Giant in talke, like dwarfe in triall quaild :
    Excelling none, but in vntruth and pride.
Such distance is betweene high words and deeds :
In proofe, the greatest vaunter seldome speeds.

XII.

Ah, rashnes! hastie rise to murdering leape,
    Lauish in vowing, blind in seeing what :
Soone sowing shames that long remorse must reape:
    Nursing with teares that ouer-sight begat ;
Scout of Repentance, harbinger of blame,
Treason to wisedome, mother of ill name.

XIII.

Iohn 9. The borne-blind begger, for receivèd sight,
    Fast in his faith and loue to Christ remain'd ;
He stoopèd to no feare, he fear'd no might,
    No change his choice, no threats his truth distain'd :
One wonder wrought him in his dutie sure,
I, after thousands, did my Lord abiure.

XIV.

Could seruile feare of rendring Nature's due,
    Which growth in yeeres was shortly like to claime,
So thrall my loue, that I should thus eschue
    A vowèd death, and misse so faire an ayme ?
Die, die disloyall wretch, thy life detest :
For sauing thine, thou hast forsworne the best.

XV.

Ah, life! sweet drop, drownd in a sea of sowres,
    A flying good, posting to doubtfull end,
Still loosing months and yeeres to gaine few howres:
    Faine, time to haue and spare, yet forc't to spend :
Thy growth, decrease ; a moment all thou hast :
That gone, ere knowne ; the rest, to come, or past.

XVI.

Ah, life! the maze of countlesse straying waies,—
    Open to erring steps and strew'd with baits,—
To winde weake senses into endlesse strayes,
    Aloofe from Vertue's rough, vnbeaten straights;
A flower, a play, a blast, a shade, a dreame,
A liuing death, a never-turning streame.

XVII.

And could I rate so high a life so base?
    Did feare with loue cast so vneven account,
That for this goale I should runne Iudas' race,
    And Caiphas' rage in crueltie surmount?
Yet they esteemèd thirtie pence His price;
I, worse then both, for nought denyd Him thrice.   Mat. 26.

XVIII.

The mother-sea, from ouerflowing deepes,
    Sends forth her issue by diuided vaines,
Yet back her ofspring to their mother creepes,
    To pay their purest streames with added gaines;
But I, that drunke the drops of heauenly flud,
Bemyr'd the Giuer with returning mud.

XIX.

Is this the haruest of His sowing-toyle?
    Did Christ manure thy heart to breede Him briers?
Or doth it neede, this vnaccustom'd soyle,
    With hellish dung to fertile heauen's desires?
No, no, the marle that periuries do yeeld,
May spoyle a good, not fat a barraine field.

XX.

Was this for best deserts the duest meede?
    Are highest worths well wag'd with spitefull hire?
Are stoutest vowes repeal'd in greatest neede?
    Should friendship, at the first affront, retire?
Blush, crauen sot, lurke in eternall night;
Crouch in the darkest caues from loathèd light.

XXI.

Mat. 16. Ah, wretch! why was I nam'd sonne of a doue,
    Whose speeches voyded spight and breathèd gall?
No kin I am unto the bird of loue:
    My stonie name much better sutes my fall:
My othes were stones, my cruell tongue the sling,
My God the mark at which my spight did fling.

XXII.

Were all the Iewish tyranies too few
    To glut thy hungrie lookes with His disgrace?
That thou more hatefull tyrannies must shew,
    And spet thy poyson in thy Maker's face?
Didst thou to spare His foes put vp thy sword,
Iohn 16. To brandish now thy tongue against thy Lord?

XXIII.

Ah! tongue, that didst His prayse and Godhead sound,
    How wert thou stain'd with such detesting words,
That euerie word was to His heart a wound,
    And launct Him deeper then a thousand swords?
What rage of man, yea what infernall spirit,
Could haue disgorg'd more loathsome dregs of spite?

XXIV.

Why did the yeelding sea, like marble way,   Mat. 14.
     Support a wretch more wauering then the waues?
Whom doubt did plunge, why did the waters stay?
     Vnkind in kindnesse, murthering while it saues :
Oh that this tongue had then been fishes' food,
And I deuour'd, before this cursing mood !

XXV.

There surges, depths and seas, vnfirme by kind,
     Rough gusts, and distance both from ship and shoare,
Were titles to excuse my staggering mind ;
     Stout feet might falter on that liquid floare :
But heer no seas, no blasts, no billowes were,
A puffe of woman's wind bred all my feare.

XXVI.

O coward troups, far better arm'd then harted !
     Whom angrie words, whom blowes could not prouoke ;   Iohn 15.
Whom thogh I taught how sore my weapon smarted,
     Yet none repaide me with a wounding stroke.
Oh no ! that stroke could but one moity kill ;
I was reseru'd both halfes at once to spill.

XXVII.

Ah ! whether was forgotten loue exil'd ?
     Where did the truth of pledgèd promise sleepe?
What in my thoughts begat this vgly child,
     That could through rented soule thus fiercely creepe?
O viper, feare their death by whom thou liuest;
All good thy ruine's wreck, all euils thou giuest.

XXVIII.

Threats threw me not, torments I none assayd :
    My fray with shades ; conceits did make me yeeld,
Wounding my thoughts with feares ; selfely dismayd,
    I neither fought nor lost, I gaue the field :
Infámous foyle ! a maiden's easie breath
Did blow me downe, and blast my soule to death.

XXIX.

Mat. 16.   Titles I make vntruths : am I a rocke,
    That with so soft a gale was ouerthrowne ?
 Am I fit pastor for the faithfull flocke,
    To guide their soules that murdred thus mine owne ?
Mark 9.   A rocke of ruine, not a rest to stay,
A pastor, not to feede but to betray.

XXX.

Fidelitie was flowne, when feare was hatched,
    Incompatible brood in Vertue's neast :
Courage can lesse with cowardise be matched,
    Prowesse nor loue lodg'd in diuided breast.
O Adam's child, cast by a sillie Eue,
Heire to thy father's foyles, and borne to grieue !

XXXI.

Mat. 17.   In Thabor's ioyes I eger was to dwell :
Iohn 21.
Mat. 16.   An earnest friend while pleasures' light did shine,
But when eclipsèd glorie prostrate fell,
    These zealous heates to sleepe I did resigne ;
And now, my mouth hath thrise His name defil'd,
That cry'd so loude three dwellings there to builde.

XXXII.

When Christ, attending the distressefull hower,
    With His surchargèd breast did blesse the ground,
Prostrate in pangs, rayning a bleeding shower,
    Me, like myselfe, a drowsie friend He found,
Thrice, in His care, sleepe clos'd my carelesse eye ;
Presage how Him my tongue should thrise denie.

XXXIII.

Parted from Christ, my fainting force declin'd,
    With lingring foot I followed Him aloofe ;
Base feare out of my hart His love vnshrin'd :   Mark 14.
    Huge in high words, but impotent in proofe,   Luke 22.
My vaunts did seeme hatcht vnder Sampson's locks,
Yet woman's words did giue me murdring knocks.

XXXIV.

So farre lukewarm desires in crasie loue,
    Farre off, in neede with feeble foote they traine ;
In tydes they swim, low ebbes they scorne to proue ;
    They seeke their friends' delights, but shun their
Hire of a hireling minde is earnèd shame :   [paine :
Take now thy due, beare thy begotten blame.

XXXV.

Ah, coole remisnes ! Virtue's quartane feuer,
    Pyning of loue, consumption of grace ;
Old in the cradle, languor dying euer,
    Soule's wilfull famine, sinne's soft-stealing pase ;
The vndermining euill of zealous thought,
Seeming to bring no harmes, till all be brought.

XXXVI.

Iohn 18. O portresse of the doore of my disgrace,
  Whose tongue vnlockt the truth of vowèd minde ;
 Whose words from coward's hart did courage chase,
  And let in deathfull feares my soule to blinde ;
 O hadst thou been the portresse to my toome,
 When thou wert portresse to that cursèd roome !

XXXVII.

Yet loue was loath to part, feare loath to die ;
  Stay, danger, life, did counterplead their causes ;
 I, fauouring stay and life, bad danger flie,
  But danger did except against these clauses :
 Yet stay and liue I would, and danger shunne,
 And lost myselfe while I my verdict wonne.

XXXVIII.

I stayde, yet did my staying farthest part ;
  I liv'd, but so, that sauing life, I lost it ;
 Danger I shunn'd, but to my sorer smart ;
  I gaynèd nought, but deeper damage crost it.
 What danger, distance, death, is worse then his
 That runnes from God and spoyles his soule of blisse ?

XXXIX.

Iohn 18, O Iohn, my guide vnto this earthly hell,
v. 16.
  Too well acquainted in so ill a Court,
 (Where rayling mouthes with blasphemies did swell,
  With taynted breath infecting all resort,)
 Why didst thou lead me to this hell of euils,
 To shew myselfe a fiend among the deuils ?

XL.

Euill president ! the tyde that wafts to vice ;
 Dumme orator, that wooes with silent deeds,
Writing in works lessons of ill aduise ;
 The doing-tale that eye in practise reedes ;
Taster of ioyes to vnacquainted hunger,
With leauen of the old seasoning the younger.

XLI.

It seemes no fault to doe that all haue done ;
 The number of offenders hides the sinne ;
Coach drawne with many horse, doth easely runne,
 Soone followeth one where multitudes beginne.
O had I in that Court much stronger bin,
Or not so strong as first to enter in.

XLII.

Sharpe was the weather in that stormie place,
 Best suting hearts benumd with hellish frost,   Iohn 18.
Whose crusted malice could admitte no grace :
 Where coales were kindled to the warmers' cost ;
Where feare my thoughts canded with ysie cold,
Heate did my tongue to periuries vnfold.

XLIII.

O hateful fire (ah ! that I euer saw it) !
 Too hard my hart was frozen for thy force ;
Farre hotter flames it did require to thaw it,
 Thy hell-resembling heate did freeze it worse.
O that I rather had congeal'd to yse,
Then bought thy warmth at such a damning price !

XLIV.

Mat. 26.
Mark 14. O wakefull bird ! proclaimer of the day,
      Whose pearcing note doth daunt the lion's rage ;
Thy crowing did myselfe to me bewray,
      My frights and brutish heates it did asswage :
But O in this alone, vnhappy cocke,
That thou to count my foyles wert made the clocke !

XLV.

O bird ! the iust rebuker of my crime,
      The faithfull waker of my sleeping feares,
Be now the daily clocke to strike the time,
      When stinted eyes shall pay their taske of teares ;
Vpbraide mine eares with thine accusing crowe,
To make me rew that first it made me knowe.

XLVI.

O milde Reuenger of aspiring pride !
      Thou canst dismount high thoughts to low effects ;
Thou mad'st a cocke me for my fault to chide,
      My lofty boasts this lowely bird corrects.
Well might a cocke correct me with a crowe,
Whom hennish cackling first did ouerthrowe.

XLVII.

1 Reg. 17. Weake weapons did Goliah's fumes abate,
      Whose storming rage did thunder threats in vaine :
His bodie huge, harnest with massie plate,
      Yet Dauid's stone brought death into his braine :
With staff and sling as to a dog he came,
And with contempt did boasting furie tame.

XLVIII.

Yet Dauid had with beare and lyon fought,
    His skilful might excus'd Goliah's foile :
The death is eas'd that worthy hand hath wrought,
    Some honour lives in honourable spoyle ;
But I, on whom all infamies must light,
Was hist to death with words of woman's spight.

XLIX.

Small gnats enforst th' Egyptian king to stoupe,
    Yet they in swarmes, and arm'd with pearcing stings ; Exod. 8.
Smart, noyse, annoyance, made his courage droupe ;
    No small incombrance such small vermine brings :
I quaild at words that neither bit nor stung,
And those deliuerèd from a woman's tongue.

L.

Ah, Feare ! abortiue impe of drouping mind ;
    Selfe-ouerthrow, false friend, roote of remorse :
Sighted, in seeing euils ; in shunning blind :
    Foil'd without field, by fancie not by force ;
Ague of valour ; phrensie of the wise ;
True honour's staine ; loue's frost, the mint of lies.

LI.

Can vertue, wisdome, strength, by women spild
    In Dauid's, Salomon's, and Samson's falls,
With semblance of excuse my errour gild,
    Or lend a marble glosse to muddy walls ?   2 Reg. 11.
O no ! their fault had shew of some pretence :   3 Reg. 11.
No veyle can hide the shame of my offence.   Iudg. 16.

LII.

The blaze of beautie's beames allur'd their lookes ;
    Their lookes, by seeing oft, conceiuèd loue ;
Loue, by affecting, swallowed pleasure's hookes ;
    Thus beautie, loue, and pleasure them did moue.
These Syrens' sugred tunes rockt them asleepe :
Enough to damne, yet not to damne so deepe.

LIII.

But gracious features dazled not mine eyes ;
    Two homely droyles were authors of my death ;
Not loue, but feare, my senses did surprize :
    Not feare of force, but feare of woman's breath ;
And those vnarm'd, ill grac't, despis'd, vnknowne :
So base a blast my truth hath ouerthrowne.

LIV.

O women ! woe to men ; traps for their falls ;
    Still actors in all tragicall mischances ;
Earth's necessarie euils, captiuing thralls,   [glances ;
    Now murdring with your toungs, now with your
Parents of life, and loue, spoylers of both,
The theeues of harts ; false do you loue or loth.

LV.

In time, O Lord ! Thine eyes with mine did meete,
Luke 22.   In them I read the ruines of my fall ;
Their chearing rayes, that made misfortune sweet,
    Into my guiltie thoughts pourd floods of gall :
Their heauenly looks, that blest where they beheld,
Darts of disdaine and angrie checks did yeeld.

LVI.

O sacred eyes ! the springs of liuing light,
    The earthly heauens where angels ioy to dwell,
How could you deigne to view my deathfull plight,
    Or let your heauenly beames look on my hell ?
But those vnspotted eyes encountred mine,
As spotlesse sunne doth on the dunghil shine.

LVII.

Sweet volumes, stoard with learning fit for saints,
    Where blissfull quires imparadize their minds;
Wherein eternall studie neuer faints,
    Still finding all, yet seeking all it finds :
How endlesse is your labyrinth of blisse,
Where to be lost the sweetest finding is !

LVIII.

Ah wretch ! how oft haue I sweet lessons read
    In those deare eyes, the registers of truth !
How oft haue I my hungrie wishes fed,
    And in their happy ioyes redrest my ruth !
Ah ! that they now are heralds of disdaine,
That erst were euer pittiers of my paine !

LIX.

You flames diuine, that sparkle out your heats,
    And kindle pleasing fires in mortall harts ;
You nectar'd aumbryes of soule-feeding meates;
    You gracefull quiuers of loue's dearest darts ;
You did vouchsafe to warme, to wound, to feast,
My cold, my stony, my now famisht breast.

LX.

The matchlesse eyes, matcht onely each by other,
    Were pleas'd on my ill matchèd eyes to glaunce;
The eye of liquid pearle, the purest mother,
    Broach't teares in mine to weepe for my mischance;
The cabinets of grace vnlockt their treasure,
And did to my misdeed their mercies measure.

LXI.

These blazing comets, light'ning flames of loue,
    Made me their warming influence to knowe;
My frozen hart their sacred force did proue,
    Which at their looks did yeeld like melting snowe:
They did not ioyes in former plentie carue,
Yet sweet are crums where pinèd thoughts doe starue.

LXII.

O liuing mirrours! seeing Whom you shew,
    Which equal shadows worths with shadowed things,
Yea, make things nobler then in natiue hew,
    By being shap't in those life-giuing springs;
Much more my image in those eyes was grac't,
Then in myselfe, whom sinne and shame defac't.

LXIII.

All-seeing eyes, more worth then all you see,
    Of which one is the other's onely price;
I worthlesse am, direct your beames on mee,
    With quickning vertue cure my killing vice.
By seeing things, you make things worth the sight,
You seeing, salue, and being seene, delight!

LXIV.

O pooles of Hesebon; the baths of grace,
 Where happie spirits diue in sweet desires,
Where saints reioyce to glasse their glorious face,
 Whose banks make eccho to the angels' quires;
An eccho sweeter in the sole rebound,
Then angels' musick in the fullest sound!

Cant. 7,
v. 3.

LXV.

O eyes! whose glaunces are a silent speach,
 In cipherd words high mysteries disclosing;
Which, with a looke, all sciences can teach,
 Whose textes to faithfull harts need little glosing;
Witnesse vnworthie I, who in a looke
Learn'd more by rote, then all the Scribes by book.

LXVI.

Though malice still possest their hardned minds,
 I, though too hard, learn'd softnes in Thine eye,
Which yron knots of stubborne will vnbinds,
 Offring them loue, that loue with loue wil buy.
This did I learne, yet they could not discerne it;
But woe, that I had now such neede to learne it!

LXVII.

O sunnes! all but yourselues in light excelling,
 Whose presence, day, whose absence causeth night;
Whose neighbour-course brings Sommer, cold expelling,
 Whose distant periods freeze away delight.
Ah! that I lost your bright and fostring beames,
To plung my soule in these congealèd streames!

LXVIII.

O gratious spheres ! where loue the center is,
    A natiue place for our selfe-loaden soules ;
The compasse, loue,—a cope that none can mis,
    The motion, loue,—that round about vs rowles :
O spheres of loue, whose center, cope, and motion,
Is loue of us, loue that inuites deuotion !

LXIX.

O little worlds ! the summes of all the best,
    Where glorie, heauen; God, sunne; all vertues, stars;
Where fire,—a loue that next to heauen doth rest;
    Ayre,—light of life that no distemper marres ;
The water,—grace, whose seas, whose springs, whose
Cloth Nature's earth with euerlasting flowers. [showers,

LXX.

What mixtures these sweet elements do yeeld,
    Let happie worldlings of these worlds expound ;
Best simples are by compounds farre exceld,
    Both sute a place where all best things abound;
And if a banisht wretch ghesse not amisse,
All but one compound frame of perfect blisse !

LXXI.

I, out-cast from these worlds, exilèd rome ;
    Poore saint, from heauen, from fire, cold salamander,
Lost fish, from those sweet waters' kindly home,
    From land of life stray'd pilgrim still I wander.
I know the cause : these worlds had neuer hell,
In which my faults haue best deseru'd to dwell.

LXXII.

O Bethelem-cesterns ! Dauid's most desire,
    From which my sinnes like fierce Philistims keep ;
To fetch your drops what champion should I hire,
    That I therein my witherèd hart may steepe ?
I would not shed them like that holy king :
His were but types, these are the figurèd thing.

2 Reg. 23.

LXXIII.

O turtle-twins ! all bath'd in virgins milke,
    Vpon the margin of full-flowing banks,
Whose gracefull plume surmounts the finest silke,
    Whose sight enamoureth heauen's most happy ranks :
Could I forsweare this heauenly payre of doues,
That cag'd in care, for me were groning loues !

Cant. 5, v.
11, 12.

LXXIV.

Twise Moses' wand did strike the stubborne rock,
    Ere stony veynes would yeeld their crystall blood;
Thine eyes' one looke seru'd as an onely knocke,
    To make my hart gush out a weeping flood ;
Wherein my sinnes, as fishes, spawne their frie,
To shew their inward shames, and then to die.

Exod. 17,
v. 6.

LXXV.

But O how long demurre I on His eyes !
    Whose look did pearce my hart with healing wound,
Launcing imposthumd sore of periur'd lyes,
    Which these two issues of mine eyes have found;
Where runne it must, till death the issues stop,
And penall life hath purg'd the finall drop.

LXXVI.

Like solest swan, that swims in silent deepe,
    And neuer sings but obsequies of death ;
Sigh out thy plaints, and sole in secret weepe,
    In suing pardon, spend thy periur'd breath ;
Attire thy soul in sorrowe's mourning weede,
And at thine eyes let guiltie conscience bleede.

LXXVII.

'Still in the limbecke of thy dolefull brest
    These bitter fruits that from thy sinnes doe grow ;
For fuell, selfe-accusing thoughts be best ;
    Vse feare as fire, the coals let penance blow ;
And seeke none other quintessence but teares,
That eyes may shed what entred at thine eares.

LXXVIII.

Come sorrowing teares, the ofspring of my griefe,
    Scant not your parent of a needfull ayde ;
In you I rest the hope of wisht reliefe,
    By you my sinnefull debts must be defrayd :
Your power preuailes, your sacrifice is gratefull,
By loue obtaining life to men most hatefull.

LXXIX.

Come good effects of ill-deseruing cause,
    Ill-gotten impes, yet vertuously brought forth ;
Selfe-blaming probates of infringèd lawes,
    Yet blamèd faults redeeming with your worth ;
The signes of shame in you each eye may read,
Yet, while you guiltie proue, you pittie plead.

LXXX.

O beames of mercie ! beate on sorrowe's clowd,
   Poure suppling showres vpon my parchèd ground;
Bring forth the fruite to your due seruice vowde,
   Let good desires with like deserts be crownd :
Water young blooming Vertue's tender flower,
Sinne did all grace of riper growth deuoure.

LXXXI.

Weepe balme and myrrhe, you sweet Arabian trees,
   With purest gummes perfume and pearle your ryne ;
Shed on your honey-drops, you busie bees ;
   I, barraine plant, must weepe vnpleasant bryne,
Hornets I hyue, salt drops their labour plyes,
Suckt out of sinne, and shed by showring eyes.

LXXXII.

If Dauid, night by night, did bathe his bed,
   Esteeming longest dayes too short to mone ;   Ps. 6, v. 7.
Inconsolable teares if Anna shed,
   Who in her sonne her solace had forgone ;   Tob. 10.
Then I to dayes and weekes, to monthes and yeeres,
Do owe the hourely rent of stintless teares.

LXXXIII.

If loue, if losse, if fault, if spotted fame,
   If danger, death, if wrath, or wreck of weale,
Entitle eyes true heyres to earnèd blame,
   That due remorse in such euents conceale
Then want of teares might well enroll my name,
As chiefest saint in calender of shame.

LXXXIV.

Loue, where I lou'd, was due, and best deseru'd ;
    No loue could ayme at more loue-worthy marke ;
No loue more lou'd then mine of Him I seru'd ;
    Large vse He gaue, a flame for euerie sparke.
This loue I lost, this losse a life must rue ;
Yea, life is short to pay tho ruth is due.

LXXXV.

I lost all that I had, who had the most,
    The most that will can wish, or wit deuise :
I least perform'd, that did most vainely boast,
    I staynd my fame in most infámous wise.
What danger then, death, wrath, or wreck can moue
More pregnant cause of teares then this I proue ?

LXXXVI.

Gen. 3,v. 7. If Adam sought a veyle to scarfe his sinne,
    Taught by his fall to feare a scourging hand ;
If men shall wish that hils should wrap them in,
    When crimes in finall doome come to be scand ;
What mount, what caue, what center can conceale
My monstrous fact, which euen the birds reueale ?

LXXXVII.

Come shame, the liuerie of offending minde,
    The vgly shroude that ouershadoweth blame ;
The mulct at which foule faults are iustly fin'd ;
    The dampe of sinne, the common sluce of fame,
By which imposthum'd tongues their humours purge ;
Light shame on me, I best deserue the scourge.

LXXXVIII.

Caine's murdering hand imbrude in brother's blood,   Gen. 4.
     More mercy then my impious tongue may craue ;
He kild a riuall with pretence of good,
     In hope God's doubled loue alone to haue.
But feare so spoyld my vanquisht thoughts of loue,
That periurde oathes my spightfull hate did proue.

LXXXIX.

Poore Agar from her pheere enforc't to flye,
     Wandring in Bersabeian wildes alone,
Doubting her child throgh helples drought would die,
     Layd it aloofe, and set her downe to moane :
The heauens with prayers, her lap with teares she fild ;
A mother's loue in losse is hardly stild.

XC.

But Agar, now bequeath thy teares to me ;
     Feares, not effects, did set afloate thine eyes.
But, wretch, I feele more then was feard of thee ;   Gen. 22.
     Ah! not my sonne, my soule it is that dyes.
It dyes for drought, yet hath a spring in sight :
Worthie to die, that would not liue, and might.

XCI.

Faire Absalon's foule faults, compar'd with mine,
     Are brightest sands to mud of Sodome Lakes ;   2 Reg. 15.
High aymes, yong spirits, birth of royall line,
     Made him play false where kingdoms were the stakes :
He gaz'd on golden hopes, whose lustre winnes,
Sometime the grauest wits to greeuous sinnes.

XCII.

But I, whose crime cuts off the least excuse,
    A kingdome lost, but hop't no mite of gaine ;
My highest marke was but the worthlesse vse
    Of some few lingring howres of longer paine.
Vngratefull child, his parent he pursude,
I, gyants' warre with God Himselfe renude.

XCIII.

Mat. 22. Ioy, infant saints, whom in the tender flower
    A happie storm did free from feare of sinne !
Long is their life that die in blisfull hower ;
    Ioyfull such ends as endlesse ioyes begin :
Too long they liue that liue till they be nought :
Life sau'd by sinne, base purchase dearely bought !

XCIV.

This lot was mine ; your fate was not so fearce,
    Whom spotlesse death in cradle rockt asleepe ;
Sweet roses, mixt with lilies, strow'd your hearce,
    Death virgin-white in martyrs' red did steepe ;
Your downy heads, both pearles and rubies crownd
My hoarie locks, did female feares confound.

XCV.

You bleating ewes,—that wayle this woluish spoyle
    Of sucking lambs new-bought with bitter throwes,—
T' inbalme your babes your eyes distill their oyle,
    Each hart to tombe her child wide rupture showes :
Rue not their death, whom death did but reuiue,
Yeeld ruth to me that liu'd to die aliue.

XCVI.

With easie losse sharpe wrecks did he eschew,
    That sindonlesse aside did naked slip :
Once naked grace no outward garment knew ;
    Riche are his robes whom sinne did neuer strip.
I, that in vaunts, displaid Pride's fayrest flags,
Disrob'd of grace, am wrapp'd in Adam's rags.

XCVII.

When, traytor to the Sonne in mother's eyes
    I shall present my humble sute for grace,
What blush can paint the shame that will arise,
    Or write my inward feelings on my face ?
Might she the sorrow with the sinner see,
Though I despisde, my griefe might pittied bee !

XCVIII.

But ah! how can her eares my speech endure,
    Or sent my breath, still reeking hellish steeme ?
Can Mother like what did the Sonne abiure,
    Or hart deflowr'd a virgin's love redeeme ?
The mother nothing loues that Sonne doth loath :
Ah, lothsome wretch! detested of them both.

XCIX.

O sister nymphes, the sweet renownèd payre,
    That blesse Bethania bounds, with your aboade !
Shall I infect that sanctifièd ayre,
    Or staine those steps where Iesus breath'd and trode?
No ; let your prayers perfume that sweetned place ;
Turne me with tygers to the wildest chase.

C.

Iohn 11. Could I reuiuèd Lazarus behold,
        The third of that sweet trinitie of saints,
    Would not astonisht dread my senses hold?
        Ah yes! my hart euen with his naming, faints:
    I seeme to see a messenger from hell,
    That my preparèd torments comes to tell.

CI.

Mat. 16. O John! O James! wee made a triple cord
Luke 8.   Of three most louing and best louèd friends;
    My rotten twist was broken with a word,
        Fit now to fuell fire among the fiends.
    It is not euer true though often spoken,
    That triple-twisted cord is hardly broken.

CII.

    The dispossessèd devils, that out I threw
        In Jesvs' name,—now impiously forsworne,—
    Triumph to see me cagèd in their mew,
        Trampling my ruines with contempt and scorne:
    My periuries were musick to their daunce,
    And now they heape disdaines on my mischaunce.

CIII.

    Our rocke (say they) is riuen; O welcome howre!
        Our eagle's wings are clipt that wrought so hie; *raught*
    Our thundring cloude made noyse, but cast no showre:
        He prostrate lyes that would haue scal'd the skie;
    In woman's tongue our runner found a rub,
    Our cedar now is shrunke into a shrub.

CIV.

These scornefull words vpbraid my inward thought,
    Proofes of their damnèd prompters' neighbour-voice :
Such vgly guests still wait vpon the nought :
    Fiends swarm to soules that swarue from Vertue's
For breach of plighted truth this true I trie;   [choise :
Ah, that my deed thus gaue my word the lie !

CV.

Once, and but once, too deare a once to twice it !
    A heauen in earth, saints neere myselfe I saw :
Sweet was the sight, but sweeter loues did spice it,
    But sights and loues did my misdeed withdraw.
From heauen and saints, to hell and deuils estrang'd,
Those sights to frights, those loues to hates are chang'd.

CVI.

Christ, as my God, was templed in my thought,
    As man, He lent mine eyes their dearest light ;
But sinne His temple hath to ruine brought,
    And now He lighteneth terrour from His sight.
Now of my lay vnconsecrate desires,
Profanèd wretch ! I taste the earnest hires.

CVII.

Ah, sinne ! the nothing that doth all things file,   *defile*
    Outcast from heauen, Earth's curse, the cause of hell;
Parent of death, author of our exile,
    The wrecke of soules, the wares that fiends doe sell ;
That men to monsters, angels turnes to deuils,
Wrong of all rights, self-ruine, roote of euils.

CVIII.

A thing most done, yet more then God can doe ;
    Daily new done, yet euer done amisse ;
Friended of all, yet unto all a foe ;
    Seeming a heauen, yet banishing from blisse ;
Seruèd with toyl, yet paying nought but paine,
Man's deepest losse, though false-esteemèd gaine.

CIX.

Shot, without noyse ; wound, without present smart ;
    First, seeming light, prouing in fine a lode ;
Entring with ease, not easily wonne to part,
    Far, in effects from that the showes abode ;
Endorct with hope, subscribèd with despaire,
Vgly in death, though life did faine it faire.

CX.

O, forfeiture of heauen ! eternall debt,
    A moment's ioy ending in endlesse fires ;
Our nature's scum, the world's entangling net,
    Night of our thoughts, death of all good desires :
Worse then al this, worse then all tongues can say ;
Which man could owe, but onely God defray.

CXI.

This fawning viper, dum till he had wounded,
    With many mouthes doth now vpbraid my harmes ;
My sight was vaild till I myselfe confounded,
    Then did I see the disinchanted charmes :
Then could I cut th' anatomie of sinne,
And search with linxes' eyes what lay within.

CXII.

Bewitching euill, that hides death in deceits,
　　Still borrowing lying shapes to maske thy face,
Now know I the deciphring of thy sleights;
　　A cunning, dearely bought with losse of grace :
Thy sugred poyson now hath wrought so well,
That thou hast made me to myselfe a hell.

CXIII.

My eye, reades mournfull lessons to my hart,
　　My hart, doth to my thought the greefes expound ;
My thought, the same doth to my tongue impart,
　　My tongue, the message in the eares doth sound ;
My eares, back to my hart their sorrowes send ;
Thus circling griefes runne round without an end.

CXIV.

My guiltie eye still seemes to see my sinne,
　　All things characters are to spell my fall ;
What eye doth read without, hart rues within,
　　What hart doth rue, to pensiue thought is gall,
Which when the thought would by the tongue digest,
The eare conueyes it backe into the brest.

CXV.

Thus gripes in all my parts doe neuer fayle,
　　Whose onely league is now in bartring paines ;
What I ingrosse they traffique by retayle,
　　Making each others' miseries their gaines :
All bound for euer prentices to care,
Whilst I in shop of shame trade sorrowe's ware.

CXVI.

Pleasd with displeasing lot, I seek no change ;
　　I wealthiest am when richest in remorse ;
To fetch my ware no seas nor lands I range ;
　　For customers to buy I nothing force :
My home-bred goods at home are bought and sold,
And still in me my interest I hold.

CXVII.

My comfort now is comfortlesse to liue
　　In orphan state, deuoted to mishap :
Rent from the roote that sweetest fruite did giue,
　　I scorn'd to graffe in stock of meaner sap ;
No iuyce can ioy me but of Iesse flower,
Whose heavenly roote hath true reuiuing power.

CXVIII.

At Sorrowe's dore I knockt : they crau'd my name :
　　I aunswered, one unworthy to be knowne :
What one ? say they.　One worthiest of blame.
　　But who ? A wretch, not God's, nor yet his owne.
A man ? O no ! a beast ; much worse : what creature ?
A rocke : how call'd ? The rocke of scandale, Peter !

CXIX.　　　　　　　　[there ?

From whence ? From Caiaphas' house. Ah ! dwell you
　　Sinne's farme I rented there, but now would leaue it.
What rent ? My soule. What gaine ? Vnrest, and feare.
　　Deare purchase ! Ah, too dear ! will you receiue it ?
What shall we giue ? Fit teares and times to plaine mee :
Come in, say they : Thus Griefes did entertaine me.

CXX.

With them I rest true prisoner in their Iayle,
　Chayn'd in the yron linkes of basest thrall;
Till Grace, vouchsafing captiue soule to bayle,
　In wonted See degraded loues enstall.
Dayes pass in plaints, the night without repose;
I wake to weepe, I sleepe in waking-woes.

CXXI.

Sleepe, Death's allye, obliuion of teares,
　Silence of passions, balme of angry sore,
Suspence of loues, securitie of feares,
　Wrath's lenitue, heart's ease, storme's calmest shore;
Senses' and soules' reprieuall from all cumbers,
Benumning sense of ill, with quiet slumbers!

CXXII.

Not such my sleepe, but whisperer of dreames,
　Creating strange chymeras, fayning frights;
Of day-discourses giuing fansie theames,
　To make dum-shewes with worlds of anticke sights;
Casting true griefes in fansie's forging mold,
Brokenly telling tales rightly foretold.

CXXIII.

This sleepe most fitly suteth Sorrowe's bed,
　Sorrow, the smart of euill, Sinne's eldest child;
Best, when vnkind in killing who it bred;
　A racke for guiltie thoughts, a bit for wild;
The scourge that whips, the salue that cures offence:
Sorrow, my bed and home, while life hath sense.

CXXIV.

Here solitarie Muses nurse my griefes,
    In silent lonenesse burying worldly noyse ;
Attentiue to rebukes, deafe to reliefes,
    Pensiue to foster cares, carelesse of ioyes ;
Ruing life's losse, vnder death's dreary roofes
Solemnizing my funerall behoofes.

CXXV.

A selfe-contempt the shroude, my soule the corse,
    The beere, an humble hope, the herse-cloth, feare ;
The mourners, thoughts, in blacks of deepe remorse,
    The herse, grace, pitie, loue and mercie beare :
My teares, my dole, the priest, a zealous will,
Penance, the tombe, and dolefull sighes the knill.

CXXVI.

Christ ! health of feuer'd soule, heauen of the mind,
    Force of the feeble, nurse of infant loues,
Guide to the wandring foote, light to the blind,
    Whom weeping winnes, repentant sorrow moues ;
Father in care, mother in tender hart,
Reuiue and saue me, slaine with sinnefull dart !

CXXVII.

If King Manasses, sunke in depth of sinne,
    With plaints and teares recouered grace and crowne :
A worthlesse worme some mild regard may winne,
    And lowly creepe, where flying threw it downe.
A poore desire I haue to mend my ill,
I should, I would, I dare not say, I will.

CXXVIII.

I dare not say, I will, but wish I may;
   My pride is checkt, high words the speaker spilt.
My good, O Lord, Thy gift, Thy strength my stay!
   Give what Thou bidst, and then bid what Thou wilt.
Worke with me what Thou of me doos't request,
Then will I dare the most and vow the best.

CXXIX.

Prone looke, crost armes, bent knee and contrite hart,
   Deepe sighs, thick sobs, dew'd eyes and prostrate
Most humbly beg release of earnèd smart,   [prayers,
   And sauing shroud in Mercie's sweet repaires.
If iustice should my wrongs with rigor wage,
Feares would despaires, ruth, breed a hopelesse rage.

CXXX.

Lazar at Pitie's gate I vlcer'd lye,
   Crauing the reffuse crums of childrens' plate;
My sores I lay in view to Mercie's eye,
   My rags beares witnes of my poore estate:
The wormes of conscience that within me swarme,
Proue that my plaints are lesse then is my harme.

CXXXI.

With mildnes, Iesu, measure mine offence;
   Let true remorse Thy due reuenge abate;
Let teares appease when trespasse doth incense;
   Let pittie temper Thy deseruèd hate;
Let grace forgiue, let loue forget my fall:
With feare I craue, with hope I humblie call.

CXXXII.

Redeeme my lapse with raunsome of Thy loue,

    Trauerse th' inditement, rigor's doome suspend ;

Let frailtie fauour, sorrowes succour moue,

    Be Thou Thyselfe, though changeling I offend.

Tender my sute, cleanse this defilèd denne,

Cancell my debts, sweet Iesu, say Amen !

The ende of Saint Peter's Complaint

NOTES AND ILLUSTRATIONS.

St. i. line 1, *maine* = sea. Addl. MS. 10.422 spells 'maigne.'
Line 4. TURNBULL modernises ' in lieu' into 'instead.'

  ,,   5. *Card.* Some have said that the ' card' or *carta* is a chart, others that it is the ' card' of the mariner's compass, and hence put for the compass itself. While, however, the former sense, or rather that of map, is the more usual, there are passages which demand some one, and some the other, of these senses, and HALLIWELL is right in giving both. In FLORIO'S World of Words (1611) we find ' Carta ; any paper, a leafe of a book. Also a carde, a map. Also a plaing card. Also &c.' Other dictionaries give the same, and *Carte marine, Carta da nauicáre* (Fl.), *Carta de marear* (Minsheu), a sailing or sea-card. Sometimes, of course, the determinative adjective is omitted, as in Sylvester's translation of Du Bartas, quoted by Dyce in his Shakespeare Glossary :

> ' Sure, if my *card and compass* doe not fail
> W'are neer the Port.'   (*The Triumph of Faith.*)

Here the original is ' mon Quadrant et ma Carte marine,' and ' quadrant' answers to ' compass ;' for though Quadrant is not found in COTGRAVE, yet *Boussole* is given as ' a Pilot's Dyall, Compass, or Quadrant.'   See also quotations from Hakluyt and Sir H. Mainwaring in Hunter's New Illustrations of Shakespeare. On the other hand, though I cannot find that the word is used for the card of the compass or compass itself, in Italian, French, or Spanish, or that it has these meanings attached to it in any English dictionary, or in the English part of any dictionary, yet there are passages which admit of no other. Nares quotes from Beaumont and Fletcher's Chances (i. 11),

> ' We're all like sea cards,
> All our endeavours and our motions,
> As they do to the north, still point at beauty.'

And in Fletcher's Loyal Subject we find (iii. 2),

> 'I send ye . . . . .
> With your own virtues season'd and my prayers ;
> The *card* of goodness in your minds, that shews ye
> When ye sail false ; the needle touched with honour,
> That through the blackest storms still points at happiness.
> Your bodies,' &c.

And elsewhere, in Southwell ('Our Ladie's Natiuitye'),

> 'Loadstarr of all engolfd in worldly waues,
> The *card and compasse* that from shipwracke saues ;'

where the allusion to one person, the determining context 'loadstar,' and the verb in the singular, show that the words mean the compass-card and needle. In some passages the author's meaning may be doubtful; as in Macbeth, i. 3, though from the word 'ports,' I am inclined to think that the seaman's card is his chart ; and this will appear, if, as perhaps we ought to do with the text, we transpose the two lines ending 'blow' and 'know.' It may also be doubtful in the present instance ; but as the misdeed is not so much a chart of his haven, or of the places to be avoided, or of his course, as the standing constant guide pointing to torment, his haven, and as 'card' is used by our poet, as above in 'Our Ladie's Natiuitye,' as the compass-card, so I believe it to be the same here. In Hamlet's 'speak by the card' the word is used in a third and very different sense.

St. ii. line 1, *shelfe* = a ledge of rock.

Lines 5-6. Turnbull misprints 'ills' for 'euils.' I call it a misprint ; for throughout in all the mss. and early editions, Southwell writes 'euill' not 'ill ;' and there is something noticeable herein, inasmuch as this constant use by him of 'euill' as a monosyllable seems to prove that the contemporary pronunciation (in verse at least) was as if written 'e'il ;' very much as in Scotland 'devil' is pronounced 'deil,' and as 'spirit' is pronounced 'sprite.' What if, after all the guesses of the Shakesperean commentators, the much-contested 'dram of *eale*' (Hamlet, i. 4) be a misprint for 'dram of e'il' = evil or ill ? It fits in with the context. See our Memorial-Introduction for numerous examples of 'evill' requiring to be read as 'e'il.'

Line 5. Turnbull misprints 'the' for 'thy.'

Line 10, *penance* = penitence, as in st. 77, line 4 ; st. 125, line 6 ; St. Peter's Remorse, st. ii. line 1. So too in one at least of the R. C. versions. WICKLIF (St. Luke xv. 7) and CHAUCER also use it in the same sense. Cf. RICHARDSON, *s. n.*

St. iii. line 5, '*Thy trespasse foule ;*' an irregular ellipse, where (being), or perhaps (is), is taken out of the succeeding ' be.'

St. iv. line 1, '*plaints ;*' taking 'plaints' as the nominative to 'sob,' 'report,' and 'tell,' I have punctuated ruth not ruth, and, sorrows—fruits of mine untruth,.

St. vii. line 3, ' *Threnes ;*' alluding to the 'threnes' or lamentations c. i-iv., where the stanzas (and in c. iii. the lines) commence with a letter of the Hebrew alphabet in succession, as in Psalm cxix. &c. TURNBULL grossly misprints 'themes.'

St. viii. line 6, *euen,* v. act. = equal or equalise.

St. ix. lines 1-4, the construction is somewhat obscure. Is ' and leaving God' part of the second clause, ending with 'give'? In such case God should either be followed by (,) or by no stop at all, while ' give' should have (;). Then ' now left' to be taken as part of this second clause? or should it close the first? Either way there is no essential difference in the sense. If taken as part of the first, the ellipse requires (and am) left &c. I have followed the punctuation of 1595 and 1596 here, though doubting.

Line 4, TURNBULL again badly misprints 'sign' for 'raigne.' *For* = for sake of.

Line 5. ' *These feares ;*' these are ' fears' in their objective sense, the substantival form of the causal verb, to fear, to make to fear = these fear-causing things ; the second fears are fears subjective, or the fears felt and acted on, through the feeling or belief that the cause so determined avoided disaster.

St. x. line 3, TURNBULL misprints ' in' for ' to.'

St. xiv. line 6, *for* = for sake of, as before.

St. xv. line 3, I have ventured to read ' few' for ' new' of 1595 and 1596.

St. xvi. line 1, ' Ah, life !' TURNBULL now over-punctuates and now under and mis-punctuates, *e.g.* he puts (!) after ' Ah' and (,) after ' life ;' and so throughout. I have put (!) after life, and (,) after ' Ah,' *i.e.* after the noun to which the descriptive sentence applies ; and so elsewhere. 1595 and 1596 punctuate simply ' Ah life,'

Line 3, TURNBULL misprints again 'bind' for 'wind' (of
1595 and 1596).

Line 6, 'never-turning' *not* a misprint as might be supposed
for 'ever-turning;' but = never returning, which might have
been written 'ne'er-returning.' Cf. use of 'turning' in quotation
from BATMAN in our next note on st. xviii. lines 1-6.

St. xviii. lines 1-6.   The old philosophy believed that the
ocean filtered back through narrow chinks, and re-appeared in
springs; *e.g.* Jerome saith (when writing on Eccles. i. 7, and
giving an erroneous interpretation), 'Philosophers tell, that
sweete waters that runne into the Sea, be consumpt and wasted
by heat of the sunne, or els they be foode and nourishing of
saltnesse of the sea. But our Ecclesiastes, the maker of waters,
sayeth, That they come agayne by privie veynes of the earth,
to the well-heades, and commeth out of the mother, that is the
Sea, and walmeth and springeth out in well-heades' (BATMAN
upon Bartholome, lib. xiii. cap. 3).   Some, however, if we may
judge from BATMAN'S quotations from ISIDORE, combined the
two views; and this would appear from the word 'added' to have
been that which SOUTHWELL had been taught.   But besides the
mother-sea or main-ocean, there had to be added, according to
early Christian philosophy, the *abyssus*, the 'deep' of SOUTH-
WELL, and of the authorised version, Gen. i. 2 and vii. 11:
but the views as to its nature and position appear to have
been vague and varied. According to some, 'abyssus' is 'deep-
nesse of water unseene, and thereof come and spring wells and
rivers ; for out of the deepnes come all waters, and turne againe
thereto by priuy waies, as to the mother of water,' as ISIDORE
saith, lib. 13: but according to AUGUSTINE, 'abyssus' is the
primordial matter, made of naught, whereof 'all things that
hath shape and forme should be shaped and formed,' and from
which it would appear that either of the elements of earth or
water were according to the ordination gift of God formed.
Neither does it seem to have been settled whether this Abyss
formed part of the general circulation spoken of above, or
whether the hidden veins from the Sea to the well-heads were
subsidiary to the hidden veins from the abyss or overflowing
deep.   Compare BATMAN, lib. xiii. cap. 3, 22 and 23.

St. xix. line 3. The construction may be doubtful. Looking
to the word 'unaccustomed,' and to the parallelism of 'unac-
customed soil and barren field,' it would seem the heart is = the
soil, and the construction, 'doth this unaccustomed soil need it,'

viz. the fertilising with hellish dung. The very frequent inversions in SOUTHWELL favour this view, and assuming it to be correct I have punctuated (,) after need.

St. xx. line 1, TURNBULL misprints 'direst' for 'duest.'

St. xxi. line 1. If 'Ιωνᾶ of St. Matthew xvi. 17 represent the Hebrew Jonah, Bar-Jonah is, as in the text, 'son of a dove;' but by the analogy of the LXX. and the better reading 'Ιωάννου of St. John i. 42 is with greater probability taken to represent Bar-Johannan = son of God's grace.

St. xxii. line 3, 'That *thou*.' TURNBULL confuses all by misprinting 'these' for 'thou.'

St. xxv. line 1, '*There*.' TURNBULL once more loses the antithesis as between 'there' and 'here' by misprinting 'These.'

St. xxvi. line 6, 'both halfes' = body and soul; the 'two mites' of the old Puritans that all may give the Lord.

St. xxvii. lines 3-6. A reference to the myth-simile of the 'viper' rending the womb of its mother shows that the reading is not 'ruines' but 'ruine's :' = all good is the wreck of thy ruin or ruining; just as a rock of ruin in next stanza is a rock of ruining, or rock causing ruin. 'Vipera is a manner kinde of serpents that is full venemous. Of this serpent ISIDORE speaketh lib. xii. and saith, that Vipera hath that name, for she bringeth forth broode by strength: for when hir wombe draweth to the time of whelping, the whelpes abideth not covenable time nor kinde passing, but gnaweth and fretteth the sides of their dam, and they come so into this world with strength, and with the death of the breeder. It is said, that the male doeth his mouth into the mouth of the female . . . . and she wexeth woode [=wud] in lyking of increase, biteth off the head of the male, and so both male and female are slaine.' (BATMAN upon Bartholome, lib. xviii. cap. 117.)

St. xxviii. line 5, 'Infámous,' and so in st. lxxxv. line 4: but 'ínfamy' in st. xlviii. line 5, and elsewhere.

St. xxix. line 5, *rest* = support: ' and he made narrowed *rests* round about, that the beams should not be fastened in the walls of the house' (1 Kings vi. 6). *To stay* = to support restrainingly, as do the 'stays' of a ship's mast: in st. xxiv. l. 3. it has more the simple sense of restraining (from the plunge); for a 'stay' in the sense of a restraining support is properly a side or inclined support, not an under-pinning or under-propping.

St. xxxii. line 5, TURNBULL vexatiously misprints 'by' for 'my.'

St. xxxiii. line 1, Additional MSS. 10.422 reads 'Parted:' and I prefer it to 'Parting' of 1595 and 1596.

St. xxxiv. line 1, 'Farre' TURNBULL obscures by misprinting 'Fare.'

Line 4, TURNBULL again misprints 'suck' for 'seeke.'

St. xxxviii. line 1, 'part' *i.e.* me, from Christ.

Line 4, TURNBULL misprints 'danger' for 'damage:' 1595 spells 'domage.'

Line 5. I have ventured to make two corrections in this line, viz. 'worse' for 'worst,' and 'his' for 'this.' In the latter the rhyme is not so good; but cf. 'he is' and 'bliss' in A Child my Choice, st. v. 'That runnes' can hardly refer to danger or distance or death.

St. xlii. line 5, '*canded*,' as in SHAKESPEARE, 'The cold brook *candied* with ice' (*Timon*, act iv. sc. 3). On this Shakesperean parallel, see our Memorial-Introduction.

St. xliv. line 5, 'alone' = in this only or alone did the 'crowing' assuage, that the cock thereby became his clock to reckon his task-duty of tears.

St. xlv. line 4, '*stinted*.' The sense is not eyes 'stinted' by any one; but eyes in a state of 'stint' (as compared with the remorse due for so supreme a crime). This sense of the participle in -ed, in which it can hardly be called a participle of past time, allows and explains its use in SHAKESPEARE and others, where we would rather employ the participle -ing. Thus BOLINGBROKE uses 'totter'd:'

> 'Let's march without the noise of threatening drums,
> That from the castle's *totter'd* battlements
> Our fair appointments may be well perused.'
>
> *King Richard II.* act iii. sc. 3.

We use the -ed form in a similar sense, but not so frequently; and where the action appears to exist within the thing itself, as in 'stint' and 'totter,' we prefer (though with less truth) to make the noun agental, and speak of 'stint*ing* eyes' and 'totter*ing* walls.' If BOLINGBROKE had battered Flint Castle, he would probably have said 'totter*ing* walls,' as indicative of a newly present result. For more, see relative note on st. cxi. line 4, 'disenchant*ed*.'

St. xlvi. line 1, ' Revenger'=Christ, not the cock, as TURN-BULL's ' revenger' might suggest.

St. xlviii. line 4, ' spoyle.' See general note onward.

Lines 1-3, ' gnats :' Exodus viii. 16-18. The third plague (of lice, Auth. Vers.). The σνίφες and σνίπες of the LXX., and the *cyniphes* and *scyniphes* of the Vulgate—all taken by the Egyptian and African authorities, Philo, Origen, Augustine, &c., to be gnat-like insects.

St. l. line 6, TURNBULL misreads ' Fine' for ' True' of 1595 and 1596. Addl. MSS. 10.422 spells ' Thrue,' the copyist being probably an Irishman.

St. lii. line 3, TURNBULL again obscures by misprinting ' effecting.'

St. liii. line 2, ' droyles'= drudges.

St. liv. line 3, ' captiuing ;' causal use : thralls=taking captive their masters or those who are free.

Line 6, ' false.' By the usual punctuation false, (,) that interpretation is suggested and favoured which would read, ' do you false ones, when you seem to feel either of these emotions, love or loathe ?' Looking to SOUTHWELL's general style and use of inversion, I prefer to interpret false as=*falsa*=do you love or loathe falsehood ? Accordingly comma (,) omitted.

St. lvii. 13 et seqq. On this passage see our Memorial-Introduction for a very remarkable Shakesperean parallel hitherto overlooked, and confirmatory of other Shakespeare allusions found in SOUTHWELL.

St. lix. line 3, ' ambryes,' in TURNBULL ' ambries.' Ambry =almonry, or the place where alms (and as here alms or doles of food) were kept. In Scotland still=a larder or pantry for cold and broken meats, ' aumry,' as in Fergusson's ' Caller Water.'

St. lxi. line 1, I have printed ' light'ning,' not ' lightning-flames :'=the blazing comets lighten flames of love.

St. lxii. line 2, ' shadows worths,' *not*, as TURNBULL misprints, ' shadow worths.' In so doing the ' living mirrors' go beyond what is natural; for in Nature

' No shadow can with shadow'd things compare.'
Lewd Love is Losse, st. 2.

Line 6, ' Then in myselfe, whom sinne and shame defac't.' The thought is drawn from Holy Scripture, and the expression characteristically elliptical. His ' image' showed itself in the eyes of Christ as that of a man before the Fall made in the image of God, whereas in himself it appeared blurred and defaced. ' My image' may in the first line have the ordinary sense of the 'image' of myself; but in the second line it means as (*meo judicio*) in the first also, the image that is in me, much as ' my wrongs' and ' my injuries' might in the older writers be used to mean the wrongs or injuries done to me.

St. lxiv. line 1, ' Hesebon.' I place in margin, from 1595 edition (dropped in 1596), ' Cant. vii. 3.' Oculi tui sicut piscinæ in Hesebon, quæ sunt in portu filiæ multitudinis (Vulg.) : 'Thine eyes like the fish-pools in Heshbon by the gate of Bath-rabbim' (Auth. Vers.), Cant. vii. 4. The ' baths of grace' is a new epithet, and has nothing to do with the pools of Heshbon. Hence I punctuate Hesebon (;) not (,), and (,) not (;) after ' desires.'

Line 3, TURNBULL misreads ' delight' for ' reioyce.'

St. lxv. line 2, TURNBULL again obscures and nonsensifies by misprinting ' works' for ' words.'

St. lxvi. line 1, cf. St. Luke xxii. 61.

St. lxviii. line 3, ' compasse'=circumference.

St. lxix. line 2, 1595 spells ' soone.'
Line 3, TURNBULL misprints ' Whose' for ' Where :' and line 5, ' Whose' for ' The.'

St. lxx. line 3, I have ventured to read ' Best' for ' But.' The previous stanza and the word ' Both' in the next line warrant the emendation.

St. lxxi. lines 1-4. At first sight it seems natural to make a division at salamander, thus reading [exiled] from heaven, [exiled] from fire ; lost fish [I wander]. Perhaps too the rhythm is rather improved thereby. But as heaven=air, fire, water, land of life, reflect the enumeration in the last stanza but one, I have punctuated roam ; [thus ending the general clause, and then giving the elemental similes] .... salamander .... home .... wander. The ellipse is *more* SOUTHWELL, ' Poor saint *from* heaven [I wander] .... *from* land of life I wander, &c.

St. lxxii. line 1, cf. 1 Chronicles ii. 17-18. Bethlehem is the Vulgate form, which SOUTHWELL has contracted. So too with Salomon (st. li. line 2) and Aman, &c.
Line 2, ' keep.' A strangely elliptical omission of the objective [me].

St. lxxiii. line 3, ' surmounts' = over-passes, excels — one sense of the French *surmonter.*

St. lxxiv. line 1, Addl. MSS. 10.422 reads ' Horebb rocke.'

St. lxxv. line 1, ' *demurre :*'=to delay by dwelling on, to dwell on, its primary sense : French *demeurer.*

St. lxxvi. line 1, SOUTHWELL adds to the old myth of the dying swan's ' singing' solitariness or singleness ; a natural and pathetic inference.

St. lxxvii. line 4, ' penance'=penitence, as before.

St. lxxviii. line 4, ' By'=through, by means of, as more frequently in our Poet's day than now. By love is here, through God's love.

St. lxxix. line 3, ' *probates :*'=proofs, or perhaps provings, though it is difficult to understand how this obsolete sense, or its legal sense, was derived from *probatus.*

St. lxxxv. line 4, ' infámous.' See relative note on st. xxviii. line 5.

St. lxxxvi. line 6, ' euen.' Here, like ' heauen,' monosyllabic : but while our pronunciation of ' heaven' does not require ' heav'n,' the fulness of our ' even' requires ' e'en,' and so I note it (see also st. c. line 4). The student will have no difficulty in properly reading such words in their places by attention to the above rule, and so in the full -ed and -'d (apostrophe), *e. g.* ' Cain's murdering hand imbrued in brother's blood' (st. lxxxviii. line 1), ' murdering' needs no more to be printed ' murd'ring' as dissyllabic, than ' heavens' and ' prayers' require to be ' The heav'ns with pray'rs, her lap with tears she fill'd' (st. lxxxix. line 5). In SOUTHWELL, er, en, and on, are almost constantly slurred, though he seizes every opportunity of syllabling -ed. Throughout, with one or two exceptions (duly noted in their places), that might lead to ambiguous readings, I adhere to the STONYHURST MSS. forms.

St. lxxxvii. line 4, ' sluce.' TURNBULL wretchedly misprints ' slime.'

St. lxxxix. line 1, ' pheare :' spelled in 1595 ' phere'= husband (Abraham).

Line 2, TURNBULL misprints ' In wilds Barsabian wandering alone'=the desert of Beth-sheba, Auth. Vers. ; Βηρσαβεὲ, Sept., Bersabe, Vulg. *passim :* in accord with which I read Ber- not Bar-.

Line 3, 'doubting'=in the old sense of suspecting=dreading.

St. xc. line 3, TURNBULL misprints 'by' for ' of.'

St. xciii. line 5, 'Too.' TURNBULL vexatiously misprints 'For.'

Line 6, TURNBULL once more misprints ' is' for 'base.'

St. xcv. line 3, *not* ' embalm,' as in TURNBULL.

Line 4, '*rupture*.' TURNBULL senselessly misreads and misprints ' rapture.' Cf. The Virgin Mary to Christ, for the sense (st. 4).

St. xcvi. line 2, '*sindonless*.' σινδὼν said to be muslin and a garment of muslin; σινδονίτης, the wearer of such a garment: but the σινδὼν βύσσινος, as the embalming-cloths of the Egyptians are called by HERODOTUS, shows that the word was used more generically. It might also be supposed that SOUTHWELL was anticipating, since it was only by Pharaoh that Joseph was endued with a στολὴ βυσσίνη; but the above words of Herodotus, as interpreted by the mummy-wrappings, show that σινδὼν was not necessarily applied to a thin roller either of fine cotton or fine linen.

Line 4, TURNBULL misprints ' Such' for ' Riche;' and line 5 ' rich' for ' that.'

St. ci. line 1, cf. St. Mark iii. 16-17 ; v. 37 : St. Matthew xvii. 1 ; xxvi. 37.

Line 6, cf. Ecclesiastes iv. 12.

St. ciii. line 2, for ' wrought' I have put ' raught' in the margin, such being the meaning. But in this and other words there was a confusion in the old spelling which hardly amounted to error. In Earle's Phil. of Engl. Tongue (p. 142) Coverdale is quoted as spelling ' raught' like SOUTHWELL ' wrought' (Parker Soc. i. 17).

Line 3, referring to the passages in the Gospels under st. ci. line 1, and to the triple cord of friendship there mentioned, it would almost seem that SOUTHWELL considered St. Peter to have been included in the collective name 'Boanerges.' Or have we the Apostolate represented by St. Peter the rock (line 1) and St. John the eagle (line 2)?

Line 5, TURNBULL misprints, with even more than his usual carelessness, ' rubber' for ' runner,' stupidly perpetrating a miserable pun as between ' rubber' and ' rub.'

Line 6, ' cedar.' From the general imagery of the Old Testament, with possibly especial remembrance of Isaiah xxxvii. 22-24.

St. civ. line 4, St. Matthew xii. 43-5.

St. cv. lines 1-4, at the Transfiguration.

St. cvi. line 4. Here is a case where a strict regard to metre would read 'light'neth ;' but I prefer for emphasis' sake to read and pronounce it as demi-trisyllabic.

Line 5, TURNBULL misprints 'late' for 'lay'=unapostolic.

  ,,   6, in Addl. MSS. 10.422 the reading is 'cast' for 'taste.' Query : Is this the proper word, and the reference to Judas *casting* down his blood-money before the priests? (St. Matthew xxvii. 5.) In 1595, as well as in 1596, it is 'taste,' in the former spelled 'tast.' In 1595 for 'earnèd' of 1596 the reading is 'earnest,' which I adopt as=the foretaste, or Scoticè 'earles,' or earl-money, given on the hiring of servants. Cf. 2 Cor. i. 22 ; Ephesians i. 14, and Mr. W. A. Wright's Bible Word-Book, *s.v.*

St. cix. line 4, '*abode*'=foreshow, v. act., as in SHAKESPEARE,

        ' The night-crow cried, *aboding* luckless time.'

                          3 *Henry VI.* v. 6.

St. cxi. line 4, ' disinchanted charmes,' in their [natural] state of disenchantment. (See relative note on st. xlv. line 4.)

St. cxiii. reminds of the soliloquy of Richard II. act ii.

St. cxv. line 2, '*Whose*' refers to parts, as before.

Line 3, ' ingrosse'=engrossier=make greater.

St. cxvi. line 4, '*force*.' Verb intrans.=strive (Webster) ; alluding not so much to pressing things on would-be customers, as to the usual cry of What d'ye lack ?

St. cxvii. line 3, ' *Rent*.' TURNBULL, with unpardonable negligence, makes nonsense of this by misprinting ' but' for ' rent,' which is the word in 1595, 1596, and Addl. MSS. 10.422.

Line 6, TURNBULL further blunderingly reads ' Where' for ' Whose.'

St. cxx. line 6, ' weepe.' TURNBULL yet again misprints bathetically ' sleep' for ' weepe.'

St. cxxi. line 2, ' balme.' TURNBULL once more actually prints ' blame' for ' balme.'

St. cxxii. line 3, = giving themes to fancy.

Line 6, ' foretold,' not predicted, but rightly recounted during the past time of wakefulness.

St. cxxv. line 6, 'penance'=penitence, as before.

St. cxxvii. line 1, 2 Chronicles xxxii. 11-13.

St. cxxviii. line 1, as the construction is not [I dare] wish I may [mend], but I may [that is, it is allowable for me to] wish [to mend], I punctuate wish (,).

    Line 3, '*my stay*,' TURNBULL misprints 'mistay.'

    ,,   4, a reminiscence of the Confessions of St. Augustine.

    ,,   6, so too he misprints 'worst' for 'most,' and 'love' for 'vow.'

St. cxxix. line 3, 'release.'   Addl. MSS. 10.422 reads 're-leafe.'

Line 4, ' sauing shroud:' the ' saving shroud:' prophetically spoken of his martyrdom and with reference to Rev. vi. 9-11, &c. *Repaires*=places whither one goes or repairs.

St. cxxxi. line 3, TURNBULL provokingly misprints 'increase' for ' incense.'

St. cxxxii. line 1, 1595 badly misprints 'thy' for ' my,' and ' my' for 'thy.' G.

II.

MYRTÆ, OR MYRTLE-WREATHS.

'. . . viridi nitidum caput impedire myrto.
                                    HORACE, *Od.* i. 4, 9.

NOTE.

I have given the name 'Myrtæ' to the second division of the Poems of SOUTHWELL for two reasons :

(a) To avoid the commonplace title of 'Miscellaneous Poems.'

(b) To correspond with that already accepted for the third portion ('Mæoniæ').

If those place our singer among the dainty players of Lydia —and something more—these have the vividness and sweet perfume of the classic 'myrtle.'

The whole of the Poems of this part were added to St. Peter's Complaint in 1595, with the exception of those noticed in our Preface. These were first added in 1596.

I have adhered to the arrangement of 1596, except in removing the Natiuity of Christ, and Christ's Childehood, and Joseph's Amazement, to their own places in Mæoniæ, as choice beads in a string of pearls (as old THOMAS BROOKS has it), placed around the supreme Life and that of His Mother.

Throughout, the basis of our text is the STONYHURST MSS. Notes and Illustrations at the end of each poem give various readings, &c. &c. G.

MARY MAGDALEN'S BLUSHE.

I.

THE signes of shame that stayne my blushinge face,
Rise from the feelinge of my ravinge fittes,
Whose joy annoy, whose guerdon is disgrace,
Whose solace flyes, whose sorowe never flittes :
Bad seede I sow'd, worse fruite is now my gayne,
Soone-dying mirth begatt long-living payne.

II.

Nowe pleasure ebbs, revenge beginns to flowe ;
One day doth wrecke the wrath that many wrought ;
Remorse doth teach my guilty thoughtes to knowe
Howe cheape I sould that Christ so dearely bought :
Faultes long unfelt doth conscyence now bewraye,
Which cares must cure and teares must washe awaye.

III.

All ghostly dints that Grace at me did dart,
Like stobbourne rock I forcèd to recoyle ;
To other flightes an ayme I made my hart
Whose woundes, then welcome, now have wrought my
        foyle.
Woe worth the bowe, woe worth the Archer's might,
That draue such arrowes to the marke so right !

IV.

To pull them out, to leave them in is deathe,
One to this world, one to the world to come ;
Woundes may I weare, and draw a doubtfull breath,
But then my woundes will worke a dreadfull dome ;
And for a world whose pleasures passe awaye,
I loost a world, whose joyes are paste decaye.

V.

O sence! O soule! O had! O hopèd blisse!
Yow woe, yow weane; yow draw, yow drive me backe ;
Yow crosse encountring, like their combate is,
That never end but with some deadly wracke ;
When sence doth wynne, the soule doth loose the feilde,
And present happ makes future hopes to yelde.

VI.

O heaven, lament! sense robbeth thee of sayntes,
Lament, O soules! sence spoyleth yow of grace ;
Yet sence doth scarce deserve these hard complayntes,
Love is the theefe, sence but the entringe place ;
Yett graunt I must, sence is not free from synne,
For theefe he is that theefe admitteth in.

NOTES AND ILLUSTRATIONS.

St. i. line 2, 'feelinge' = the sense or perception of.
Line 5, TURNBULL misprints 'seed' for 'fruite.'
St. ii. line 2, similarly he misprints 'work' for 'wrecke' =
wreak, spelled 'wreake' in 1596.
St. iii. line 1, 'dints.' Dint is used as 1. the force or energy
employed; 2. the stroke itself; 3. the effect of the stroke, a

dent (Webster). In the fourth of the passages in which it occurs
in SOUTHWELL (Man to the Wound in Christ's side, st. v. line
2) it is used as 2. the stroke. In the second (Losse in Delaye,
st. vi. line 3) the same sense may be attributed to it. But in
the third (Life is but Losse, st. iv. line 2) it can, of the three
senses, only have 1. the force. And while in this first instance
senses 1. and 3. are clearly inadmissible, the sense which best
agrees with the context (dart and recoil), and which best ex-
plains the second and especially the third passage, is a fourth
sense, that namely of the weapon while in action. From as-
sociating the word 'dint' with a particular kind of weapon, the
spear or dart, as he clearly does in three out of the four in-
stances, the fourth being left indefinite in its expression, he
seems to have been led to employ it as expressing that weapon
in action; just as two lines lower he uses, as is shown by the
words 'whose wounds,' the word 'flight,' the technical or quasi-
technical term for the action of arrows, for arrows in flight or
action. But, as onward, flights may be fleghts = arrows.

St. iii. line 6, I adopt 'draue' = drave, from 1596, in pre-
ference to 'drawe' of our MS.

St. iv. line 6, TURNBULL misprints 'lose' for 'loost.'

St. v. line 1, 'had,' TURNBULL misprints 'hap.'

Lines 2-3. Here only, as a specimen, I give the uncouth
spelling with a *w* for our *u*. I have not repeated it, nor in
'thou.' Cf. Synne's Heavy Loade, st. iv. and v. (p. 106), where
'thou' in our MS. is spelled 'thow.' It is 'thou' in the first and
early-printed editions, and there is no reason for preserving a
barbarism.

Line 2, 'weane' = wean, TURNBULL misprints 'win.'

,,   6, 'Happ:' in 1596 'haps.' It has been said that happi-
ness (like success) has kept only a part of the original sense
of 'hap.' If this be so, SOUTHWELL has here, and also in Love's
servile Lott (st. xiii. line 2) and in What Joye to live (st. ii.
line 4), used 'hap' in a sense reflected from happiness, and equal
to good hap and bad hap severally. See other examples in
Tymes goe by Turnes (st. i. line 6, and st. ii. line 6), and Con-
tent and Rich (st. xiv. line 4).

St. vi. line 4, TURNBULL misprints 'chief' for 'theefe' G.

MARY MAGDALEN'S COMPLAINT AT CHRIST'S DEATH.

Sith my life from life is parted,
 Death come take thy portion;
Who survives when life is murdred,
 Lives by mere extortíon:
All that live, and not in God,
Couche their life in deathe's abode.

Selye starres must nedes leve shyninge
 When the sunne is shadowèd,
Borowed streames refrayne their runninge
 When hed-springes are hinderèd:
One that lives by other's breathe,
Dyeth also by his deathe.

O trewe life! sith Thou hast left me,
 Mortall life is tedious;
Death it is to live without Thee,
 Death of all most odious:
Turne againe or take me to Thee,
Let me dye or live Thou in me!

Where the truth once was and is not,
 Shadowes are but vanitye;

Shewinge want, that helpe they cannot,
    Signes, not salves, of miserye.
Paynted meate no hunger feedes,
Dyinge life eche death exceedes.

With my love my life was nestled
    In the summe of happynes ;
From my love my life is wrested
    To a world of heavynes :
O lett love my life remove,
Sith I live not where I love !

O my soule ! what did unloose thee
    From thy sweete captivitye,
God, not I, did still possesse thee,
    His, not myne, thy libertie :
O too happy thrall thou wert,
When thy prison was His hart.

Spitefull speare that brak'st this prison,
    Seate of all felicitye,
Workinge thus with dooble treason
    Love's and life's deliverye :
Though my life thou dravst awaye,
Maugre thee my love shall staye.

NOTES AND ILLUSTRATIONS.

Our MS., in agreement with 1596, corrects three of TURN-BULL'S characteristic misreadings and misprints : st. v. line 2, ' sun' for ' summe :' st. vi. line 1, ' that' for ' what :' st. vii. line 5, ' draw'st' for ' drav'st.'   Additional MSS. 10.422 has all these

blunders. St. ii. line 1, see relative note on 'sely' in 'I die
without desert.' St. iii. lines 3 and 5: here and throughout, I
print 'Thee,' not 'The' of our MSS.—the latter simply confuses,
and this record is enough for critical purposes.

Consult our Introduction for elucidation of what I regard as
an affecting personal reminiscence in st. i. lines 3-4. Cf. also
'Life is but Losse,' line 1, and st. iv., especially lines 3 and 5.
G.

————————

TYMES GOE BY TURNES.

THE loppèd tree in tyme may growe agayne ;
Most naked plants renewe both frute and floure ;
The soriest wight may finde release of payne,
The dryest soyle sucke in some moystning shoure ;
Tymes go by turnes and chaunces chang by course,
From foule to fayre, from better happ to worse.

The sea of Fortune doth not ever floe,
She drawes her favours to the lowest ebb ;
Her tide hath equall tymes to come and goe,
Her loome doth weave the fine and coarsest webb ;
No joy so great but runneth to an ende,
No happ so harde but may in fine amende.

Not allwayes fall of leafe nor ever springe,
No endlesse night yet not eternall daye ;
The saddest birdes a season finde to singe,
The roughest storme a calme may soone alaye ;
Thus with succeding turnes God tempereth all,
That man may hope to rise yet feare to fall.

A chaunce may wynne that by mischance was lost ;
The nett that houldes no greate, takes little fishe ;
In some thinges all, in all thinges none are croste,
Fewe all they neede, but none have all they wishe ;
Unmedled joyes here to no man befall,
Who least hath some, who most hath never all.

NOTES AND ILLUSTRATIONS.

TURNBULL has once more provoking misprints in this poem :
e.g. st. i. line 3, ' sorest' for ' soryiest :' st. ii. line 3, 'time' for
'tide :' st. iv. line 2, ' web' for ' nett.' 1596 in st. iii. line 2 has
' nor yet' for 'yet not.' 1630 in st. iv. line 5 reads 'vnmingled.'
G.

LOOKE HOME.

RETYRÈD thoughtes enjoy their owne delightes,
As beauty doth in self-behoulding eye ;
Man's mynde a mirrhour is of heavenly sightes,
A breife wherein all marveylls summèd lye,
Of fayrest formes and sweetest shapes the store,
Most gracefull all, yet thought may grace them more.

The mynde a creature is, yet can create,
To Nature's paterns adding higher skill ;
Of fynest workes witt better could the state
If force of witt had equall poure of will :
Devise of man in working hath no ende ;
What thought can thinke an other thought can mende.

Man's soule of endles bewtye's image is,
Drawen by the worke of endles skill and might;
This skillfull might gave many sparkes of blisse,
And to descerne this blisse a native light;
To frame God's image as His worthes requird,
His might, His skill, His worde and will conspir'd.

All that he had His image should present,
All that it should present he could afforde,
To that he coulde afforde his will was bente,
His will was followed with performinge worde;
Lett this suffice, by this conceave the rest,
He should, he could, he would, he did the best.

NOTE.

TURNBULL badly misprints 'This' for 'His' in st. iv. line 4.
G.

FORTUNE'S FALSEHOODE.

IN worldly merymentes lurketh much misery,
Sly fortune's subtilltyes, in baytes of happynes
Shroude hookes, that swallowèd without recoverye,
Murder the innocent with mortall heavynes.

Shee sootheth appetites with pleasing vanityes,
Till they be conquerèd with cloakèd tyrannye;
Then chaunging countenance, with open enmyties
She tryumphes over them, scorninge their slavery.

With fawninge flattery deathe's dore she openeth,
Alluring passingers to blody destinye;
In offers bountifull, in proofe she beggereth,
Men's ruins registring her false felicitye.

Her hopes are fastned in blisse that vanisheth,
Her smart inherited with sure possession;
Constant in crueltye, she never altereth
But from one violence to more oppression.

To those that followe her, favours are measurèd,
As easie premisses to hard conclusions;
With bitter corrosives her joyes are seasonèd,
Her highest benefittes are but illusions.

Her wayes a laberinth of wandring passages,
Fooles' comon pilgrimage to cursèd deityes;
Whose fonde devotion and idle menages
Are wag'd with wearynes in fruitles drudgeries.

Blynde in her favorites' foolish election,
Chaunce is her arbiter in giving dignitye,
Her choyse of vicious, shewes most discretion,
Sith welth the vertuous might wrest from piety.

To humble suppliants tyran most obstinate,
She sutors answereth with contrarietyes;
Proud with peticion, untaught to mitigate
Rigour with clemencye in hardest cruelties.

Like tigre fugitive from the ambitious,
Like weeping crocodile to scornefull enymies,
Suyng for amity where she is odious,
But to her followers forswering curtesies.

No wynde so changeable, no sea so waveringe,
As giddy fortune in reeling varietyes;
Nowe madd, now mercifull, now ferce, now favoring,
In all thinges mutable but mutabilities.

NOTES AND ILLUSTRATIONS.

One of TURNBULL'S most egregious misprints is 'Flye' for
Sly' in st. i. line 2: and again his (;) after 'happiness' instead
of linking it on to 'Shroude hookes,' as in 1596: our MS. has
'shrouds.' Once more, in st. vii. line 2, he confuses all by print-
ing 'in' for 'is.'

'Menage' (in st. vi. line 3) refers to the management of the
horse in giving him studied paces and action, and therefore
may be = studied movements.

Our MS. (in st. x. line 2) by 'varietyes' corrects the lacking
syllable in TURNBULL'S 'vanities:' so too in 1596. Our MS. is
corrected by S. to 'varietyes' from 'vanityes.' G.

SCORNE NOT THE LEASTE.

WHERE wardes are weake and foes encountring, strong,
Where mightier do assult then do defend,
The feebler part putts upp enforcèd wronge,
And silent sees that speech could not amend;
Yet higher poures must think though they repine,
When sunne is sett, the little starres will shyne.

While pyke doth range the seely tench doth flye,
And crouch in privy creekes with smaller fishe;
Yet pikes are caught when little fish go by,
These fleete afloate while those do fill the dish.
There is a tyme even for the worme to creepe,
And sucke the dewe while all her foes do sleepe.

The merlen cannot ever sore on highe,
Nor greedy grayhounde still pursue the chase;
The tender larke will finde a tyme to flye,
And fearefull hare to runne a quiet race.
He that high grouth on cedars did bestowe,
Gave also lowly mushrumpes leave to growe.

In Aman's pompe poore Mardocheus wept,
Yet God did turne his fate upon his foe;
The lazar pynd while Dives' feast was kept,
Yett he to heaven, to hell did Dives goe.
We trample grasse and prize the floures of Maye,
Yet grasse is greene when flowers do fade awaye.

NOTES AND ILLUSTRATIONS.

In st. i. line 2, 'assult' is = assault (as in 1596). Line 4,
that.' It is perhaps worth notice here, that SOUTHWELL con-
stantly uses 'that' where we would use 'what' or 'that that'
or 'that which,' and this, as in the present instance, causes
some obscurity. See other examples in A Child my Choice
(st. i. line 1), What Joy to Live (st. v. lines 2-4, *et alibi*). It is
used also as we should 'who,' as in Christe's Return out of Egypt
(st. i. line 5). In the same, line 5, our MS., like 1596, reads
'must,' not as in TURNBULL 'most,' and a meaning is attain-
able with this correction, *i.e.* the higher powers when fallen

' think' of the ' little stars' shining, while they, represented by
the great ' sun,' are sunk. But query—is ' think' a misprint
for ' sink,' and the meaning ' Yet, higher powers most sink,
though they repine' (*i.e.* the feebler part)? Cf.

> ' Their fall is worst that from the height
> Of greatest honours slide ;'

and for other difficult and somewhat similar pronominal uses,
see our relative notes on St. Peter's Complaint. As ' most' is
simply TURNBULL'S blunder, I prefer the reading of our text.

　　In st. ii. line 5, even is = e'en. In st. iii. line 1, in 1596 is
spelled ' marline,' in Additional MSS. 10.422 ' merlyn,' and mis-
printed ' martin' by TURNBULL. Merlin or marline is the hawk.
In st. iii. line 6, ' mushrumpes' = mushrooms : so in 1596, as
well as Additional MS. 10.422. In st. iv. line 1, in 1596, the
name is Haman : but Aman is in the Vulgate. In = during. G.

A CHILDE MY CHOYSE.

LETT folly praise that phancy loves, I praise and love
　　　　that Childe
Whose hart no thought, whose tongue no word, whose
　　　　hand no dede defilde.
I praise Him most, I love Him best, all prayse and
　　　　love is His ;
While Him I love, in Him I live, and cannot lyve
　　　　amisse.
Love's sweetest mark, lavde's highest theme, man's most
　　　　desirèd light,
To love Him life, to leave Him death, to live in Him
　　　　delighte.

He myne by gift, I His by debt, thus ech to other
    dewe,

First frende He was, best frende He is, all tymes wilł
    try Him trewe.

Though yonge, yet wise, though small, yet stronge ;
    though man, yet God He is ;

As wise He knowes, as stronge He can, as God He loves
    to blisse.

His knowledge rules, His strength defendes, His love
    doth cherish all ;

His birth our joy, His life our light, His death our end
    of thrall.

Alas ! He weepes, He sighes, He pantes, yet do His
    angells singe ;

Out of His teares, His sighes and throbbs, doth bud a
    joyfull springe.

Almighty Babe, Whose tender armes can force all foes
    to flye,

Correct my faultes, protect my life, direct me when I
    dye !

NOTES AND ILLUSTRATIONS.

In our MS. (to which we adhere) there is no division into
stanzas of four short lines each ; nor in 1596.

    Line 2, TURNBULL misprints ' head' for ' hand.'

    ,, 3, our MS. inadvertently reads ' this' for ' His.'

    ,, 5, TURNBULL most unfortunately misprints 'land's' for
'laud's.' This is one of S.'s own corrections in our MS.

    Line 7, TURNBULL, ' Him' for ' His.'

    ,, 8, 1596 reads ' other's' = other is. G.

CONTENT AND RITCHE.

I DWELL in Grace's courte,
   Enrichd with Vertue's rightes;
Faith guides my witt; Love leades my will
   Hope all my mynde delightes.

In lowly vales I mounte
   To Pleasure's highest pitch;
My sely shroud trew honors bringes,
   My poore estate is ritch.

My conscience is my crowne,
   Contented thoughts my rest;
My hart is happy in it selfe,
   My blisse is in my breste.

Enoughe, I recken welthe;
   A meane the surest lott,
That lyes too highe for base contempt,
   Too lowe for envye's shott.

My wishes are but fewe,
   All easye to fullfill,
I make the lymits of my poure
   The bounds unto my will.

I have no hopes, but one,
    Which is of heavenly raigne ;
Effects atteynd, or not desird,
    All lower hopes refrayne.

I feele no care of coyne,
    Well-dooing is my welth ;
My mynd to me an empire is,
    While grace affordeth helth.

I clipp high-clyming thoughtes :
    The winges of swelling pride ;
Their fall is worst, that from the heyghth
    Of greatest honours slyde.

Sith sayles of largest size
    The storme doth soonest teare,
I beare so lowe and smale a sayle
    As freeth me from feare.

I wrastle not with rage,
    While Furie's flame doth burne ;
It is in vayne to stopp the streame
    Untill the tide do turne.

But when the flame is out,
    And ebbing wrath doth end,
I turne a late enragèd foe
    Into a quiett frende.

And taught with often proofe,
    A tempered calme I finde
To be most solace to it self,
    Best cure for angry mynde.

Spare diett is my fare,
    My clothes more fitt then fine ;
I knowe I feede and cloth a foe
    That pampred would repine.

I envye not their happ,
    Whome favour doth advance ;
I take no pleasure in their payne,
    That have lesse happy chaunce.

To rise by others' fall
    I deeme a loosing gaine ;
All states with others' ruyns built,
    To ruyne runne amaygne.

No chaunge of Fortune's calmes
    Can cast my comfortes downe ;
When Fortune smyles, I smile to thinke
    How quickly she will frowne.

And when in froward moode
    She prooves an angry foe,
Smale gayne I found to lett her come,
    Lesse losse to let her goe.

NOTES AND ILLUSTRATIONS.

TURNBULL has some very careless misprints in this poem: *e.g.* st. ii. line 4, 'to' for 'is:' st. ix. line 4, our MS. spells 'freeeth,' the third 'e' inserted by S.: 'attend' for 'atteynd' = attained (as in 1596): st. xvi. line 1, 'chance' for 'chaunge.'

With reference to the line,

'My mynd to me an empire is' (st. vii. line 3),

it is interesting to come on another reminiscence of Sir EDWARD DYER, whose celebrated poem 'My mynde to me a kingdome is' was doubtless in our Poet's mind at the moment. (See our collection of DYER's Poems.) For more on this, and imitations, consult our Memorial-Introduction. G.

LOSSE IN DELAYE.

SHUNNE delayes, they breede remorse ;
    Take thy time while time doth serve thee ;
Creepinge snayles have weakest force,
    Fly their fault lest thou repent thee.
Good is best when soonest wroughte,
Lingred labours come to noughte.

Hoyse upp sale while gale doth last,
    Tyde and winde stay no man's pleasure ;
Seeke not tyme when tyme is paste,
    Sober speede is wisdom's leysure.
After-wittes are deerely boughte,
Lett thy forewytt-guide thy thoughte.

Tyme weares all his lockes before,
　　Take thy hould upon his forehead ;
When he flyes he turnes no morè,
　　And behinde his scalpe is naked.
Workes adjourn'd have many staies,
Long demurres breede new delayes.

Seeke thy salve while sore is grene,
　　Festred woundes aske deeper launcing ;
After-cures are seldome seene,
　　Often sought scarse ever chancinge.
Tyme and place give best advice,
Out of season, out of price.

Crush the serpent in the head,
　　Breake ill egges ere they be hatched ;
Kill bad chekins in the tredd,
　　Fligg, they hardly can be catched.
In the risinge stifle ill,
Lest it growe against thy will.

Droppes do perce the stubborne flynte,
　　Not by force but often fallinge ;
Custome kills with feeble dinte,
　　More by use then strength prevayling.
Single sandes have little weighte,
Many make a drowninge freighte.

Tender twigges are bent with ease,
　　Agèd trees do breake with bending ;

Younge desires make little prease,
  Grouth doth make them past amendinge.
Happy man, that soone doth knocke
  Babell babes againste the rocke !

NOTES AND ILLUSTRATIONS.

TURNBULL reads in st. i. line 2, 'is lent' for 'doth serve;' but
our MS. and Additional MS. 10.422, and 1596 and 1630, have the
latter.

In st. v. line 4, TURNBULL 'improves' the author's own word
'fligg' into 'Fledged;' and in st. vi. line 4, stupidly reads 'and
vailing' for 'prevailing;' and line 6, 'drawing' for 'drowning.'

In st. ii. line 5, 'after-witte' is = wisdom after the fact, not
second-thoughts.

In st. v. line 2, 'ill eggs' = eggs of noxious birds or vermin.
Or is the idea a continuance of that in the previous line, and
the reference to the egg-like casing of the young scorpion, as in
St. Luke xi. 12, 'If he shall ask an egg, will he offer him a ser-
pent (scorpion) ?' I have seen such 'eggs' as you could hardly
distinguish them from a pigeon's. Or combining the two, the
allusion underlying may be to the belief that asps when hatched
kill whatever had sat on the eggs. 'And as he [Plinius] saith,
it happeneth sometime, that a venemous frogge that is called
rubeta, findeth the egge of such an adder [the *aspis*], and sit-
teth on brood thereon, and of such breeding commeth a worme
that slayeth with blast and with sight, as doth the cockatrice.
The worm that sitteth so on brood, and bringeth it forth, feel-
eth first all y⁰ venim of his matter and venime : for when it is
first hatcht, hee beholdeth and seeth him that bringeth him
forth, and slayeth him in that wise, as he sayeth' (BATMAN on
Bartholome, lxix. c. 80).

Line 3, 'tread' = conception.

St. vi. line 3, 'dint.' See relative note on, elsewhere.

Line 4, *Fligg* or flygge, as Bryddys, maturus, volatilis. In
Prompt.Parv., composed by a Norfolk man (as was SOUTHWELL),
WAY says *fligged* is still used there; and HALLIWELL gives it as
used in Cheshire and the North.

St. vii. line 3, prease = pressure. See WRIGHT, *s. v.*
Line 6, TURNBULL misprints 'Babel's.' Babel, as elsewhere
Jesse rod, &c., preferable : = Happy he that destroys wicked
thoughts ere they grow up. 'Filia Babylonis misera ! . . . Beatus
qui tenebit et allidet parvulos tuos ad petram.' Ps. cxxxvi. 8-9.
(Ps. cxxxvii. Auth. Vers.)—the prophecy being in Isaiah xiii.
16. G.

LOVE'S SERVILE LOTT.

LOVE mistres is of many myndes,
 Yet fewe know whome they serve ;
They recken least how little love
 Their service doth deserve.

The will she robbeth from the witt,
 The sence from reason's lore ;
She is delightfull in the ryne,
 Corrupted in the core.

She shroudeth Vice in Vertue's veyle,
 Pretendinge good in ill ;
She offreth joy, affordeth greife,
 A kisse, where she doth kill.

A honye-shoure raynes from her lippes,
 Sweete lightes shyne in her face ;
She hath the blushe of virgin mynde,
 The mynde of viper's race.

She makes thee seeke yet feare to finde,
    To finde but not enjoye;
In many frowns some glydinge smyles
    She yeldes, to more annoye.

She woes thee to come nere her fire,
    Yet doth she drawe it from thee;
Farr off she makes thy harte to frye,
    And yet to freese within thee.

She letteth fall some luringe baytes,
    For fooles to gather upp;
To sweete, to soure, to every taste
    She tempereth her cupp.

Softe soules she bindes in tender twist,
    Small flyes in spynner's webb;
She setts afloate some luring streames,
    But makes them soone to ebb.

Her watery eies have burninge force,
    Her fluddes and flames conspire;
Teares kindle sparkes, sobbes fuell are,
    And sighes do blowe her fier.

May never was the month of love,
    For May is full of floures;
But rather Aprill, wett by kinde,
    For love is full of showers.

Like tyran, crewell woundes she gives,
　　Like surgeon, salve she lends;
But salve and sore have equall force,
　　For death is both their ends.

With soothing wordes enthrallèd soules
　　She cheynes in servile bandes;
Her eye in silence hath a speeche
　　Which eye best understands.

Her little sweete hath many soures;
　　Short happ immortall harmes;
Her loving lookes are murdring darts,
　　Her songes, bewitchinge charmes.

Like Winter rose and Summer yce,
　　Her joyes are still untymelye;
Before her hope, behinde remorse,
　　Fayre first, in fyne unseemely.

Moodes, passions, phancies, jelious fitts,
　　Attend uppon her trayne;
She yeldeth rest without repose,
　　A heaven in hellish payne.

Her house is sloth, her dore deceite,
　　And slippery hope her staires;
Unbashfull bouldnes bidds her guestes,
　　And every Vice repayres.

Her diett is of such delightes
    As please, till they be past;
But then, the poyson kills the hart
    That did entise the tast.

Her sleepe in synne doth end in wrath,
    Remorse rings her awake;
Death calls her upp, Shame drives her out,
    Despayres her uppshott make.

Plowe not the seas, sowe not the sands,
    Leave off your idle payne;
Seeke other mistres for your myndes,
    Love's service is in vayne.

NOTES AND ILLUSTRATIONS.

TURNBULL has some sad errors in this poem: *e.g.* st. iv. line 3, 'virgin's' for 'virgin:' st. vi. line 2, 'she' dropped out; and so in line 4, 'in' for 'within:' st. xi. line 2, 'salves' for 'salve:' st. xii. line 1, 'soothèd' for 'soothing.' In our MS. there is no division into stanzas. As before, with 'thee,' I print 'off,' not 'of,' as in st. vi. line 3, and elsewhere. G.

LIFE IS BUT LOSSE.

By force I live, in will I wish to dye;
    In playnte I passe the length of lingring dayes;
Free would my soule from mortall body flye,
    And tredd the track of death's desyrèd waies:
Life is but losse where death is deemèd gaine,
And loathèd pleasures breed displeasinge payne.

M

Who would not die to kill all murdringe greives?
 Or who would live in never-dyinge feares?
Who would not wish his treasure safe from theeves,
 And quite his hart from pangues, his eyes from teares?
Death parteth but two ever-fightinge foes,
Whose civill strife doth worke our endles woes.

Life is a wandringe course to doubtfull reste,
 As oft a cursèd rise to damninge leape,
As happy race to wynn a heavenly creste;
 None being sure what finall fruites to reape:
And who can like in such a life to dwell,
Whose wayes are straite to heaven, but wide to hell?

Come, cruell death, why lingrest thou so longe?
 What doth withould thy dynte from fatall stroke?
Nowe prest I am, alas! thou dost me wronge,
 To lett me live, more anger to provoke:
Thy right is had when thou hast stopt my breathe,
Why shouldst thoue stay to worke my dooble deathe?

If Saule's attempt in fallinge on his blade
 As lawfull were as eth to putt in ure,
If Sampson's leave a comon lawe were made,
 Of Abell's lott, if all that woulde were sure,
Then, cruell death, thou shouldst the tyran play
With none but such as wishèd for delaye.

Where life is lov'd, thou ready art to kill,
    And to abridge with sodayne pangues their joy;
Where life is loath'd thou wilt not worke their will,
    But dost adjorne their death to their annoye.
To some thou art a feirce unbidden guest,
But those that crave thy helpe thou helpest lest.

Avaunt, O viper! I thy spite defye:
    There is a God that overrules thy force,
Who can thy weapons to His will applie,
    And shorten or prolonge our brittle course.
I on His mercy, not thy might, relye;
To Him I live, for Him I hope to die.

NOTES AND ILLUSTRATIONS.

The lines already referred to ('Mary Magdalen's Complaint at Christ's Death,' st. i.), and the yearning hope of martyrdom expressed at the close of this infinitely pathetic poem, render it most probable that these semi-autobiographic pieces were composed in prison after the Poet's tortures. The same may be said of the next, 'I die alive.' Strange that none of SOUTH-WELL'S biographers have observed these affecting personal allusions. See our Memorial-Introduction.

St. i. line 5, 'deemed.' See relative note on St. Peter's Complaint, in the 'Author to the Reader,' st. i. line 2.

St. iii. line 2, cf. St. Peter's Compl. st. xii. line 1.

Line 3, an allusion to the βραβεῖον and στέφανον of 1 Cor. ix. 24-5; but the form 'crest' (independent of the needed rhyme with 'rest') suggested by the rayed aureole of the pictured representations of saints.

St. v. line 2 = as easily put in use or practice.

Line 3, TURNBULL misprints 'lean.' Cf. Judges xv. 26, where 'leave' is asked and given to 'lean' or 'feel' the temple-pillars. G.

I DYE ALIVE.

O LIFE ! what letts thee from a quicke decease ?
   O death ! what drawes thee from a present praye ?
My feast is done, my soule would be at ease,
   My grace is saide ; O death ! come take awaye.

I live, but such a life as ever dyes ;
   I dye, but such a death as never endes ;
My death to end my dying life denyes,
   And life my living death no whitt amends.

Thus still I dye, yet still I do revive ;
   My living death by dying life is fedd ;
Grace more then nature kepes my hart alive,
   Whose idle hopes and vayne desires are deade.

Not where I breath, but where I love, I live ;
   Not where I love, but where I am, I die ;
The life I wish, must future glory give,
   The deaths I feele in present daungers lye.

NOTES AND ILLUSTRATIONS.

   In our illustrated quarto edition I furnish facsimile of a
portion of the MS. of this poem, showing the Author's auto-
graph-correction in st. iii. line 1, of ' revive' for ' remayne,'
which also agrees with 1596. See our Memorial-Introduction
and Preface. G.

WHAT JOY TO LIVE.

I wage no warr, yet peace I none enjoy ;
   I hope, I feare, I fry in freesing colde ;
I mount in mirth, still prostrate in annoye ;
   I all the worlde imbrace yet nothing holde.
All welth is want where chefest wishes fayle,
Yea life is loath'd where love may not prevayle.

For that I love I long, but that I lacke ;
   That others love I loath, and that I have ;
All worldly fraightes to me are deadly wracke,
   Men present happ, I future hopes do crave :
They, loving where they live, long life require,
To live where best I love, death I desire.

Here love is lent for loane of filthy gayne ;   [shewe ;
   Most frendes befrende themselves with frendshipp's
Here plenty perill, want doth breede disdayne ;
   Cares comon are, joyes falty, shorte and fewe ;
Here honour envyde, meanesse is dispis'd ;
Synn deemèd solace, vertue little prisde.

Here bewty is a bayte that, swallowed, choakes,
   A treasure sought still to the owner's harmes ;
A light that eyes to murdring sightes provokes,
   A grace that soules enchaunts with mortall charmes ;

A luringe ayme to Cupid's fiery flightes,
A balefull blisse that damnes where it delightes.

O who would live so many deaths to trye?
    Where will doth wish that wisdome doth reprove,
Where Nature craves that grace must nedes denye,
    Where sence doth like that reason cannot love,
Where best in shewe in finall proofe is worste,
Where pleasures uppshott is to dye accurste.

NOTES AND ILLUSTRATIONS.

TURNBULL again has vexatious misprints in this poem: *e. g.*
st. i. line 4, 'If' for 'I :' st. ii. line 2, 'other' for 'others :' st.
iii. line 1, nonsensically, 'Here loan is lent for love of filthy
gain :' st. iv. line 2, 'in' for 'to :' line 5, 'gain' for 'ayme,' and
'slights' for 'flightes.' 1596 agrees with our MS. In st. i. line
1, our MS. inadvertently reads 'nowe' for 'none.' G.

LIFE'S DEATH, LOVE'S LIFE.

WHO lives in love, loves lest to live,   *least*
    And longe delayes doth rue,
If Him he love by Whome he lives,
    To Whome all love is dewe.

Who for our love did choose to live,
    And was content to dye;
Who lov'd our love more then His life,
    And love with life did buy.

Let us in life, yea with our life,
    Requite His livinge love ;
For best we live when lest we live,   *least*
    If love our life remove.

Where love is hott, life hatefull is,
    Their groundes do not agree ;
Love where it loves, life where it lives,
    Desyreth most to bee.

And sith love is not where it lives,
    Nor liveth where it loves,
Love hateth life that holdes it backe,
    And death it best approves.

For seldome is He woonn in life
    Whome love doth most desire ;
If woonn by love, yet not enjoyde,
    Till mortall life expire.

Life out of earth hath no abode,
    In earth love hath no place ;
Love setled hath her joyes in heaven,
    In earth life all her grace.

Mourne, therefore, no true lover's death,
    Life onely him annoyes ;
And when he taketh leave of life,
    Then love beginns his joyes.

NOTES AND ILLUSTRATIONS.

In st. i. line 1, 'lest' is=least, as in 1596.   In st. iii. line 3,
TURNBULL misprints 'best' for 'lest' = 'least,' as before. G.

AT HOME IN HEAVEN.

FAYRE soule! how long shall veyles thy graces shroud?
 How long shall this exile withold thy right?
When will thy sunn disperse this mortall cloude,
 And give thy glories scope to blaze their light?
O that a starr, more fitt for angells' eyes,
Should pyne in earth, not shyne above the skyes!

Thy ghostly beauty offred force to God;
 It cheyned Him in the linckes of tender love;
It woonn His will with man to make aboade;
 It staid His sword, and did His wrath remove:
It made the rigour of His justice yelde,
And crownèd Mercy empresse of the feilde.

This lul'd our heavenly Sampson fast asleepe,
 And laid Him in our feeble nature's lapp;
This made Him under mortall loade to creepe,
 And in our flesh His Godhead to enwrapp;
This made Him sojourne with us in exile,
And not disdayne our titles in His style.

This brought Him from the rancks of heavenly quires
 Into this vale of teares and cursèd soyle;
From floures of grace into a world of briers,
 From life to death, from blisse to balefull toyle.
This made Him wander in our pilgrim-weede,
And tast our tormentes to releive our neede.

O soule! do not thy noble thoughtes abase,
 To loose thy loves in any mortall wight;
Content thy eye at home with native grace,
 Sith God Himself is ravisht with thy sight;
If on thy bewty God enamored be,
Base be thy love of any lesse then He.

Give not assent to muddy-mynded skill,
 That deemes the feature of a pleasing face
To be the sweetest bayte to lure the will;
 Not valewing right the worth of ghostly grace;
Let God's and angells' censure wynne beleife,
That of all bewtyes judge our soules the cheife.

Quene Hester was of rare and peerelesse hew,
 And Judith once for bewty bare the vaunt;
But he that could our soules' endowments vew,
 Would soone to soules the crowne of beuty graunt.
O soule! out of thy self seeke God alone:
Grace more then thyne, but God's, the world hath none.

NOTES AND ILLUSTRATIONS.

Turnbull has one of his most careless misprints in st. ii.

l. 5, 'vigour' for 'rigour.' St. v. line 6, in 1596 reads 'is' for 'be.' In st. vii. line 2, 'bare the vaunt,' the sense answers to the saying of the Assyrians in Judith xi. 19 : 'Non est talis mulier super terram in aspectu, in pulchritudine, et in sensu verborum.' It seems clear that 'vaunt' here is=the van or fore-front. Cf. the parallel phrases, 'bear the bell,' and 'bear the mastership.' I have not met before or elsewhere with 'vaunt' as thus used. But see our Memorial-Introduction on Southwell and Shakespeare. G.

LEWD LOVE IS LOSSE.

MISDEEMING eye! that stoopest to the lure
    Of mortall worthes, not worth so worthy love;
All beautye's base, all graces are impure,
    That do thy erring thoughtes from God remove.
Sparkes to the fire, the beames yeld to the sunne,
All grace to God, from Whome all graces runne.

If picture move, more should the paterne please ;
    No shadow can with shadowed thinge compare,
And fayrest shapes, whereon our loves do ceaze,
    But sely signes of God's high beautyes are.
Go, sterving sense, feede thou on earthly maste ;
Trewe love, in heaven seeke thou thy sweete repast.

Gleane not in barrayne soyle these offall-eares,
    Sith reape thou mayst whole harvests of delighte ;
Base joyes with greifes, bad hopes do end in feares,
    Lewd love with losse, evill peace with dedly fighte :

God's love alone doth end with endlesse ease,
Whose joyes in hope, whose hope concludes in peace.

Lett not the luringe trayne of phansies trapp,
    Or gracious features, proofes of Nature's skill,
Lull Reason's force asleepe in Error's lapp,
    Or drawe thy witt to bent of wanton will.
The fayrest floures have not the sweetest smell ;
A seeminge heaven proves oft a damninge hell.

Selfe-pleasing soules, that play with beautye's bayt,
    In shyning shroud may swallowe fatall hooke ;
Where eager sight on semblant faire doth waite,
    A locke it proves, that first was but a looke :
The fishe with ease into the nett doth glyde,
But to gett out the waie is not so wide.

So long the fly doth dally with the flame,
    Untill his singèd winges do force his fall ;
So long the eye doth followe phancie's game,
    Till love hath left the hart in heavy thrall.
Soone may the mynde be cast in Cupide's gaile,
But hard it is imprisoned thoughtes to bayle.

O loath that love whose finall ayme is luste,
    Moth of the mind, eclipse of reason's lighte ;
The grave of grace, the mole of Nature's rust,
    The wrack of witt, the wronge of every right.
In summe, an evill whose harmes no tongue can tell ;
In which to live is death, to die is hell.

NOTES AND ILLUSTRATIONS.

TURNBULL, in st. ii. line 4, misprints ' folly' for ' sely ;' on the latter see our relative note on ' I die without desert' (st. i. line 4). He also makes nonsense of st. ii. line 6, by misprinting ' is' for ' in.' In st. v. line 3, our MS. miswrites ' or' for ' on.'

In st. vii. line 3, ' *mole* of Nature's rust' is not *moles* a heap, nor yet *mole* a body-stain, but the *mola* of Pliny and French *mole*, a false conception, or shapeless, senseless mass of fleshy matter=the moon-calf of our ancestors. MARVELL uses it in the same sense in Appleton House,

> ' What need of all this marble crust
> T' impare the wanton *mole* of dust ;'

and by early medical writers. This poem, in 1616 and 1620 editions, is headed ' S. Mary Magdalen's Traunce.' G.

LOVE'S GARDYNE GREIFE.

VAYNE loves, avaunt ! infamous is your pleasure,
 Your joye deceite ;
Your jewells jestes, and worthles trash your treasure,
 Fooles' common baite.
Your pallace is a prison that allureth
To sweete mishapp, and rest that payne procureth.

Your garden, greif hedgd in with thornes of envye
 And stakes of strife ;
Your allies, errour gravelled with jelosye
 And cares of life ;
Your bancks, are seates enwrapt with shades of sadnes
Your arbours, breed rough fittes of raging madnes.

Your bedds, are sowen with seedes of all iniquitye
    And poysening weedes,
Whose stalkes evill thoughts, whose leaves words full
      of vanitye,
    Whose fruite misdeedes ;
Whose sapp is synn, whose force and operacion,
To banish grace and worke the soule's damnation.

Your trees are dismall plants of pyning corrosives,
    Whose root is ruth,
Whose bark is bale, whose tymber stubborne phantasies,
    Whose pith untruthe ;
On which in liew of birdes whose voyce deliteth,
Of guilty conscience screching note affrighteth.

Your coolest sommer gales are scalding syghinges,
    Your shoures are teares ;
Your sweetest smell the stench of synnfull livinge,
    Your favoures feares ;
Your gardener Satan, all you reape is misery,
Your gayne remorse and losse of all felicitye.

NOTES AND ILLUSTRATIONS.

The heading is = Garden [House] Greife. The Garden-House was the name of the country or suburban retreat of well-to-do citizens or town-dwellers, and was often made a place of assignation and intrigue.

On ' infamous' (st. i. line 1) see relative note on ' St. Peter's Complaint' (st. xxviii. line 5).

In st. ii. line 3, ' allies'=alleys or green embowered walks. TURNBULL, in st. ii. line 5, misprints ' branches' for ' bancks are.' G.

FROM FORTUNE'S REACH.

Lett fickle Fortune runn her blyndest race,
    I setled have an unremovèd mynde ;
I scorne to be the game of Phancie's chase,
    Or fane to shewe the change of every winde.
Light giddy humours, stinted to no rest,
Still change their choyse, yet never choose the best.

My choise was guided by foresightfull heede,
    It was averrèd with approvinge will ;
It shall be followed with performinge deede,
    And seald with vow, till death the chooser kill.
Yea death, though finall date of vayne desires,
Endes not my choise, which with no tyme expires.

To beautye's fading blisse I am no thrall ;
    I bury not my thoughtes in mettall mynes ;
I ayme not at such fame as feareth fall ;
    I seeke and finde a light that ever shynes :
Whose glorious beames display such heavenly sightes,
As yeld my soule the summe of all delightes.

My light to love, my love to life, doth guide,—
    To life that lives by love, and loveth lighte ;
By love of one, to Whome all loves are tyd
    By duest debt, and never-equalld right ;
Eyes' light, harte's love, soule's truest life He is,
Consorting in three joyes one perfect blisse.

NOTES AND ILLUSTRATIONS.

In st. i. line 4, ' vane' (as in 1596) is spelled ' fane' in our MS. and in Addl. MSS. 10.422.

TURNBULL misprints ' in' for ' to' in st. i. line 5, and, worse still, ' light' for ' life' in st. iv. line 1, and line 3, ' to' for ' of.'

The ' mettall mynes' of st. iii. line 2 is a curious (incidental) indication that ' metal mines' began in Elizabeth's reign to be earnestly sought after. Shortly thereafter Sir Hugh Myddleton, to whom was due the New River water-supply, gained much wealth from his silver-lead mines in Wales. SAMUEL SMILES has recently worthily revived the memory of this great Englishman.

DYER'S PHANCY TURNED TO A SINNER'S COMPLAINTE.

He that his myrth hath lost,
    Whose comfort is to rue,
Whose hope is falne, whose faith is cras'd,
    Whose trust is founde untrue;

If he have helde them deere,
    And cannot cease to mone,
Come, lett him take his place by me;
    He shall not rue alone.

But if the smallest sweete
    Be mixt with all his soure;
If in the day, the moneth, the yere,
    He feele one lightninge houre,

Then rest he with him selfe;
    He is no mate for me,
Whose tyme in teares, whose race in ruth,
    Whose life a death must be.

Yett not the wishèd deathe,
    That feeles no plaint or lacke,
That, makinge free the better parte,
    Is onely Nature's wracke:

O no! that were too well;
  My death is of the mynde,
That allwaies yeldes extremest pangues,
  Yet threttens worse behinde.

As one that lives in shewe,
  And inwardly doth dye;
Whose knowledge is a bloodye feilde,
  Where Vertue slayne doth lye;

Whose hart the alter is
  And hoast, a God to move;
From whome my evell doth feare revenge,
  His good doth promise love.

My phancies are like thornes
  In which I go by nighte;
My frighted witts are like a hoaste
  That force hath put to flighte.

My sence is Passion's spie,
  My thoughtes like ruyns old,
Which shew how faire the building was,
  While grace did it upholde.

And still before myne eyes
  My mortall fall they laye;
Whom Grace and Vertue once advauncd,
  Now synne hath cast away.

O thoughtes! no thoughts, but woundes,
    Sometyme the seate of joye,
Sometyme the store of quiett rest,
    But now of all annoye.

I sow'd the soyle of peace ;
    My blisse was in the springe ;
And day by day the fruite I eate,
    That Vertue's tree did bringe.

To nettles nowe my corne,
    My feild is turn'd to flynte,
Where I a heavy harvest reape.
    Of cares that never stynte.

The peace, the rest, the life,
    That I enjoy'd of yore,
Were happy lott, but by their losse
    My smarte doth stinge the more.

So to unhappye menn,
    The best frames to the worste ;
O tyme! O place! where thus I fell ;
    Deere then, but now accurste!

In *was*, stands my delighte,
    In *is* and *shall*, my woe ;
My horror fastned in the *yea ;*
    My hope hang'd in the *noe.*

Unworthy of releife,
    That cravèd it too late,
Too late I finde, (I finde too well,)
    Too well stoode my estate.

Behould, such is the ende
    That pleasure doth procure,
Of nothing els but care and plaint
    Can she the mynde assure.

Forsaken firste by grace,
    By pleasure now forgotten,
Her payne I feele, but Grace's wage
    Have others from me gotten.

Then, Grace where is the joye
    That makes thy tormentes sweete?
Where is the cause that many thought
    Their deathes through thee but meete?

Where thy disdayne of synne,
    Thy secreet sweete delite?
Thy sparkes of blisse, thy heavenly rayes,
    That shynèd erst so brighte?

O that they were not loste,
    Or I coulde it excuse;
O that a dreame of feynèd losse
    My judgement did abuse!

O frayle inconstant fleshe!
   Soone trapt in every gynn!
Soone wrought thus to betray thy soule,
   And plunge thy self in synne!

Yett hate I but the faulte,
   And not the faltye one,
Ne can I rid from me the mate
   That forceth me to mone ;

To moane a synner's case,
   Then which was never worse,
In prince or poore, in yonge or old,
   In blissd or full of curse.

Yett God's must I remayne,
   By death, by wronge, by shame ;
I cannot blott out of my harte
   That grace wrote in His name.

I cannot sett at noughte
   Whome I have held so deare ;
I cannot make Him seeme afarre,
   That is in dede so neere.

Not that I looke henceforthe
   For love that erst I founde ;
Sith that I brake my plighted truth
   To build on fickle grounde.

Yet that shall never fayle
    Which my faith bare in hande ;
I gave my vow; my vow gave me ;
    Both vow and gift shall stande.

But since that I have synnd,
    And scourge none is too ill,
I yeld me captive to my curse,
    My hard fate to fullfill.

The solitarye woode
    My citye shall become ;
The darkest denns shall be my lodge ;
    In which I rest or come :

A sandy plott my borde,
    The woormes my feast shall be,
Wherewith my carcas shall be fedd,
    Untill they feede on mee.

My teares shall be my wyne,
    My bedd a craggy rocke :
My harmonye the serpente's hysse,
    The screeching oule my clocke.

My exercise, remorse
    And dolefull sinners' layes ;
My booke, remembrance of my crymes,
    And faltes of former dayes.

My walke, the pathe of playnte ;
    My prospect into hell,
Where Judas and his cursèd crewe
    In endles paynes do dwell.

And though I seeme to use
    The feyning poet's stile,
To figure forth my carefull plight,
    My fall and my exile :

Yet is my greife not fayn'd,
    Wherein I sterve and pyne ;
Who feeleth most shall thinke it lest,   *least*
    If his compare with myne.

NOTES AND ILLUSTRATIONS.

The title in 1596 is simply 'A Phansie turned to a Sinner's Complaint.' In the HARLEIAN MS. it is 'Maister diers . . . .' DR. HANNAH, in his Courtly Poets from Raleigh to Montrose (1870), has given Southwell's poem, along with Lord Brooke's and Sir Edward Dyer's. Our MS. yields corrections of all previous texts ; and DR. HANNAH will be pleased to find his own confirmed. The difference between a mind of real insight and a mere pretender could not be better illustrated than by a comparison of the poem as given in Courtly Poets and TURNBULL'S : *e.g.* the latter, in st. i. line 3 reads 'salve' for 'falne :' st. iii. line 4, 'lighting' for 'lightninge :' st. iv. line 4, 'in' for 'a :' st. v. line 2, 'in' for 'no :' DR. HANNAH reads here 'pain' for 'plaint ;' but our MS. and HARLEIAN MS. and 1596 agree in reading 'plaint,' which is also a favourite word with our Poet, as in this very piece : st. vi. *et alibi*, I print 'too,' not 'to :' st. xviii. line 2, DR. HANNAH reads 'is' for 'it' by inadvertence : st. xxii. line 3 : so DR. HANNAH misreads 'joys' for 'rayes,' following 1596 ; but 'rayes,' as in our MS. and HARLEIAN, is preferable : st. xxiv. line 2, TURNBULL misprints 'wrapt' for 'trapt :' st. xxv. line 1, ib. 'have' for 'hate :' I have adopted 'Ne' for 'Nor'

from 1596 here: st. xxx. line 2, ib. 'has' for 'bare:' st. xlii. line
3, 'carefull'=full of cares, as in PHINEAS FLETCHER: st. xliii.
line 4=If his [he] compare.

I may be permitted to refer for more on the series of poems
of which this forms one, to my Works of Lord Brooke, vol. iii.
pp. 145-154, and to my collected Poems of Sir Edward Dyer in
Fuller Worthies' Miscellanies, vol. iv. G.

DAVID'S PECCAVI.

In eaves sole sparowe sitts not more alone,
 Nor mourning pelican in desert wilde,
Than sely I, that solitary mone,
 From highest hopes to hardest happ exild :
Sometyme, O blisfull tyme! was Vertue's meede
Ayme to my thoughtes, guide to my word and deede.

But feares now are my pheares, greife my delight,
 My teares my drinke, my famisht thoughtes my
    bredd ;
Day full of dumpes, nurse of unrest the nighte,
 My garmentes gives, a bloody feilde my bedd ;
My sleape is rather death then deathe's allye,
Yet kil'd with murdring pangues I cannot dye.

This is the change of my ill changèd choise,
 Ruth for my rest, for comfortes cares I finde ;
To pleasing tunes succeedes a playninge voyce,
 The dolefull eccho of my waylinge minde ;
Which, taught to know the worth of Vertue's joyes,
Doth hate it self, for lovinge phancie's toyes.

If wiles of witt had overwroughte my will,

    Or sutle traynes misledd my steppes awrye,

My foyle had founde excuse in want of skill,

    Ill deede I might, though not ill dome, denye.

But witt and will muste nowe confesse with shame,

Both deede and dome to have deservèd blame.

I phancy deem'd fitt guide to leade my waie,

    And as I deem'd I did pursue her track,

Witt lost his ayme and will was phancie's pray ;

    The rebell wonne, the ruler went to wracke.

But now sith phancye did with follye end,

Witt bought with losse, will taught by witt, will mend.

NOTES AND ILLUSTRATIONS.

The title in 1620 edition is ' St. Peter's Complaint :' and with it may be compared that poem, st. xxviii. and others.

St. ii. line 1, ' pheares'= companions (as a husband).

Line 4, 1596 spells ' giues,' our MS. ' gives,' Additional MS. 10.422 ' gyves,' 1630 ' gyues.' TURNBULL blunderingly amends by reading ' give,' not seeing that the word is ' gyves'=manacles or chains.

St. iii. line 1, 1596 reads ' chaunce' for ' change;' so 1630.

St. iv. line 2, TURNBULL again provokes us with misprinting ' away' for ' awrie.'

St. v. line 2, ' deem'd'=judged, as before. TURNBULL misprints ' In' for ' I.'

Line 4, 1596 reads ' rebels' and ' rulers.' In such case probably ' fancyes,' not ' fancye,' was the author's word. G.

SYNNE'S HEAVY LOADE.

O LORD ! my sinne doth overchardge Thy breste,
    The poyse thereof doth force Thy knees to bowe ;
Yea, flatt Thou fallest with my faultes oppreste,
    And bloody sweate runnes tricklinge from Thy browe :
But had they not to earth thus pressèd Thee,
Much more they woulde in hell have pestred me.

This globe of earth doth Thy one finger propp,
    The worlde Thou dost within Thy hand embrace ;
Yet all this waight, of sweat drew not a dropp,
    Nor made Thee bowe, much lesse fall on Thy face ;
But now Thou hast a loade so heavye founde,
That makes Thee bowe, yea flatt fall to the grounde.

O Synne ! howe huge and heavye is thy waight,
    That wayest more then all the worlde beside ;
Of which when Christ had taken in His fraighte,
    The poyse thereof His flesh coulde not abide.
Alas ! if God Himself sincke under synne,
What will become of man that dies therein ?

First flatt Thou fellst where earth did Thee receive,
    In closett pure of Marye's virgin breste ;
And now Thou fallst, of earthe to take Thy leave,
    Thou kissest it as cause of Thy unreste :
O loving Lord ! that so dost love Thy foe
As thus to kysse the grounde where he doth goe !

Thou, minded in Thy heaven our earth to woare,
    Dost prostrate now Thy heaven our earth to blisse ;
As God to earth Thou often wert severe,
    As man Thou sealst a peace with bleedinge kisse :
For as of soules Thou common father art,
So is she mother of man's other parte.

She shortly was to drincke Thy dearest bloode,
    And yelde Thy soule awaye to Satan's cave ;
She shortly was Thy cors in tombe to shroude,
    And with them all thy Deitye to have ;
Now then in one Thou joyntly yealdest all,
That severally to earth should shortely fall.

O prostrate Christ ! erect my croked mynde ;
    Lord ! lett Thy fall my flight from earth obtayne ;
Or if I still in Earth must nedes be shrynde,
    Then, Lord ! on Earth come fall yet once againe ;
And ether yelde with me in earthe to lye,
Or els with Thee to take me to the skye !

NOTES AND ILLUSTRATIONS.

St. i. l. 1, Addl. MS. 10.422 reads 'synnes,' as in 1596, &c.

St. ii. line 4, Addl. MS. 10.422 reads 'Nee' for 'Nor,' and 1596 'Ne.' I have adopted it in preference to 'Nor,' as in TURN-BULL and our MS.

St. iii. line 4, 'poyse' is = poize. I note this, as 'poise' in the present day gives rather the idea of balance.

St. v. line 6, our MS. inadvertently reads 'the' for 'she.'

St. vi. line 1, TURNBULL misprints 'the' for 'Thy.'

Line 2, our MS. inadvertently reads 'awaye,' and TURNBULL so misprints. 1596 and 1630 properly have 'a way' = Earth is to yield a way or passage for thy soul to Satan's cave.

Line 6, again TURNBULL misprints 'several' for 'severally.'

St. vii. line 3, 1596 reads 'Or if I needes must still in earth . . . .'

NEW PRINCE, NEW POMPE.

BEHOULD a sely tender Babe,
 In freesing winter nighte,
In homely manger trembling lies;
 Alas, a pitious sighte!

The inns are full, no man will yelde
 This little pilgrime bedd;
But forc'd He is with sely beastes
 In cribb to shroude His headd.

Despise not Him for lyinge there,
 First what He is enquire;
An orient perle is often founde
 In depth of dirty mire.

Waye not His cribb, His wodden dishe,
    Nor beastes that by Him feede ;
Way not His mother's poore attire,
    Nor Josephe's simple weede.

This stable is a Prince's courte,
    The cribb His chaire of State ;
The beastes are parcell of His pompe,
    The wodden dishe His plate.

The parsons in that poore attire
    His royall liveries weare ;
The Prince Himself is come from heaven,
    This pompe is prisèd there.

With joy approch, O Christian wighte !
    Do homage to thy Kinge ;
And highly prise His humble pompe
    Which He from heaven doth bringe.

NOTES AND ILLUSTRATIONS.

Line 9, 1596 reads ' Despise Him not :' line 24, TURNBULL misprints ' praised' for ' prized :' line 27, TURNBULL, after 1630 and 1634, misprints ' praise' for ' prise.' I read ' His' for ' this ;' a frequent misprint.

On ' silly' (line 1) see relative note onward, on ' I die without dessert' (line 4). G.

THE BURNING BABE.

As I in hoary Winter's night stood shiveringe in the
    snowe,
Surpris'd I was with sodayne heat, which made my
    hart to glowe ;
And liftinge upp a fearefull eye to vewe what fire was
    nere,
A prety Babe all burninge bright, did in the ayre ap-
    peare,
Who scorchèd with excessive heate, such floodes of teares
    did shedd,
As though His floodes should quench His flames which
    with His teares were fedd ;
Alas ! quoth He, but newly borne, in fiery heates I frye,
Yet none approch to warme their hartes or feele my fire
    but I !
My faultles brest the fornace is, the fuell woundinge
    thornes,
Love is the fire, and sighes the smoke, the ashes shame
    and scornes ;
The fuell Justice layeth on, and Mercy blowes the
    coales,
The mettall in this fornace wrought are men's defilèd
    soules,

For which, as nowe on fire I am, to worke them to their
        good,
So will I melt into a bath to washe them in My bloode:
With this He vanisht out of sight, and swiftly shroncke
        awaye,
And straight I callèd unto mynde that it was Christmas-
        daye.

NOTES AND ILLUSTRATIONS.

See our Memorial-Introduction for BEN JONSON'S 'Conver-
sation' with Drummond of Hawthornden on this poem.

Line 5, TURNBULL misreads 'exceeding:' line 6, also mis-
reads 'with what' for 'which with.'

NEW HEAVEN, NEW WARRE.

COME to your heaven, yowe heavenly quires!
Earth hath the heaven of your desires;
Remove your dwellinge to your God,
A stall is nowe His beste aboade;
Sith men their homage do denye,
Come, angells, all their fault supply.

His chilling could doth heate require,
Come, seraphins, in liew of fire;
This little ark no cover hath,
Let cherubs' winges His boody swath;

Come, Raphiell, this babe must eate,
Prouide our little Tobie meate.

Let Gabriell be nowe His groome,
That first tooke upp His earthly roome;
Let Michell stand in His defence,
Whome love hath linckd to feeble scnce;
Let Graces rocke, when He doth crye,
And angells singe His lullybye.

The same yow sawe in heavenly seate,
Is He that now suckes Marye's teate;
Agnize your Kinge a mortall wighte,
His borowed weede letts not your sight;
Come, kysse the maunger where He lies;
That is your blisse aboue the skyes.

This little babe so fewe daies olde,
Is come to rifle Satan's foulde;
All hell doth at His presence quake,
Though He Him self for cold do shake;
For in this weake unarmèd wise
The gates of hell He will surprise.

With teares He fightes and wynnes the feild,
His naked breste standes for a sheilde,
His battering shott are babishe cryes,
His arrowes, lookes of weepinge eyes,
His martiall ensignes, colde and neede,
And feeble fleshe His warrier's steede.

His campe is pitchèd in a stall,
His bulwarke but a broken wall,
The cribb His trench, hay-stalkes His stakes,
Of shepeherdes He His muster makes ;
And thus, as sure His foe to wounde,
The angells' trumpes alarum sounde.

My soulo, with Christ joyne thow in fighte ;
Sticke to the tents that He hath pight ;
Within His cribb is sureste warde,
This little babe will be thy garde ;
If thow wilt foyle thy foes with joye,
Then flitt not from this heavenly boye.

NOTES AND ILLUSTRATIONS.

In st. i. line 6, TURNBULL misprints 'faults,' emptying the
expressiveness : st. ii. line 5, Tobit vi. 3-5 : in st. iii. line 6, I
adopt 'his' for 'this' from 1596 : in st. iv. line 3, 'agnize' is
= acknowledge or recognize : line 4, letts not = hinders not :
in st. vii. line 2 there is a B placed opposite in our MS.—why,
I know not : in same, line 3, TURNBULL misprints 'His' for
'The :' ib. stakes = used defensively in the manner of palisades
and the like : in st. viii. line 2, 1596 reads 'dight' for 'pight ;'
the latter = pitched : line 6 in 1596 reads 'the' for 'this.' G.

III.

MÆONIÆ.

NOTE.

The original title-page of Mæoniæ is given opposite this ; and for our exemplar of the exceedingly rare volume, I owe thanks to the authorities of JESUS COLLEGE, OXFORD. For the bibliography of Mæoniæ see our Preface.

As before in Myrtæ, I continue the arrangement of 1596, save that under Mæoniæ will be found certain poems that belong to this division rather than to the other ; as pointed out in relative notes, and in the Epistle below.

The basis of our text is the STONYHURST MS. : and in Notes and Illustrations at the close of each poem, as in the others, are various readings, &c.

The following Epistle from 1595 Mæoniæ will best find place here :

' THE PRINTER TO THE GENTLEMEN READERS.—Hauing beheld (kind Gentlemen) the numberlesse Iudges of not to be reckoned labours, with what kind admiration you haue entertained the Diuine Complaint of holy Peter ; and hauing in my hands certaine especiall Poems and diuine Meditations, full as woorthie, belonging to the same, I thought it a charitable deede to giue them life in your memories, which els should die in an obscure sacrifice. Gently imbrace them, gentle censurers of gentle indeuors : so shall you not be fantastike in diuersity of opinions, nor contradict your resolues by denying your former iudgements, but still bee your selues discreetely vertuous : nor could I other wish but that the courteous reader of these labors, not hauing already bought Peter's Complaint, would not for so small a mite of money loose so rich a treasure of heauenly wisdome as these two treatises should minister unto him, the one so needfully depending vpon the other. One thing amongst the rest I am to admonish thee of, that hauing in this treatise read Marie's Visitation, the next that should follow is Christ's Natiuity ; but being afore printed in the end of Peter's Complaint, we haue heere of purpose omitted : that thou shouldest not be abridged of that and the other like comforts which that other treatise profereth thee. Your's (kind Gentlemen) in all his abilities. I[ohn] B[usbie].'

Collation: title-page and epistle, 4 pp.; Poems, pp. 32 (4to).

Mæoniæ.

OR,

CERTAINE

excellent Poems and Spiri-
tuall Hymnes :

*Omitted in the last Impression of Peters
Complaint ; being needefull there-
vnto to be annexed, as being both Di-
uine and Wittie.*

All composed by R. S.

Printer's ornament.

London

*Printed by Valentine Sims, for
John Busbie.*

1595.

THE CONCEPTION OF OUR LADIE.

OUR second Eve putts on her mortall shrowde,
    Earth breedes a heaven for God's new dwelling-
        place ;
Nowe ryseth upp Elias' little cloude,
    That growing shall distill the shoure of grace ;
Her being now begins, who, ere she ende,
Shall bringe the good that shall our evill amende.

Both Grace and Nature did their force unite
    To make this babe the summ of all their best ;
Our most, her lest, our million, but her mite,   *least*
    She was at easyest rate worth all the reste :
What Grace to men or angells God did part,
Was all united in this infant's hart.

Fower onely wightes bredd without fault are nam'd,
    And all the rest conceivèd were in synne ;
Without both man and wife was Adam fram'd,
    Of man, but not of wife, did Eve beginne ;
Wife without touch of man Christ's mother was,
Of man and wife this babe was bredd in grace.

In 1596 this is headed ' The Virgine Marie's Conception.'

St. i. line 4, TURNBULL misprints ' showers' for ' shoure ;'
and line 6, ' *our* good' for ' the good.'   Cf. on ll. 3-4 :

> Quot latent miracula
> Fiet hæc nubicula
>   In vim magnam pluviæ.
> Hy. Gaudii primordium, used on Nat. B.V.

The themes of each of the next stanzas are contained in two
lines of a later stanza of the same hymn : line 7, ' Tota plena
gratiâ :' line 13, ' Tota sine macula.'

St. iii. line 6, ' bredd :' 1596 reads ' borne.' G.

OUR LADIE'S NATIVITYE.

Joye in the risinge of our orient starr,
That shall bringe forth the Sunne that lent her light ;
Joy in the peace that shall conclude our warr,
And soone rebate the edge of Saton's spight ;
Load-starr of all engolfd in worldly waves,
The card and compasse that from shipwracke saves.

The patriark and prophettes were the floures
Which Tyme by course of ages did distill,
And culld into this little cloude the shoures
Whose gracious droppes the world with joy shall fill ;
Whose moysture suppleth every soule with grace,
And bringeth life to Adam's dyinge race.

For God, on Earth, she is the royall throne,
The chosen cloth to make His mortall weede ;
The quarry to cutt out our Corner-stone,
Soyle full of fruite, yet free from mortall seede ;
For heavenly floure she is the Jesse rodd
The childe of man, the parent of a God.

NOTES AND ILLUSTRATIONS.

St. i. line 1, ' Ave maris stella,' hymn at Vespers of F. of the
Holy Rosary, &c. : ' Stella maris,' of hymn 'Alma Redemptoris:'
' Stella matutina,' Litany of B.V. or Litany of Loretto; the
' stella maris' being = stella matutina, or the morning-star in
the East, with a people who had the sea eastward of them.
　　Line 2, cf.

> Domum quam inhabitet
> Moxe quà nos visitet,
> 　Ornat sol justitiæ,
> Quot micat luminibus
> Suis Deus usibus,
> 　Quod vas fingit gloriæ.
> 　　　　　Hy. Gaudii, &c.

Line 3, cf.

> Funda nos in pace,
> 　Mutans Evæ nomen.
> 　　　Hy. Ave maris stella.

Line 4, ' rebate'=blunt.
　　,,　5, 1596 reads 'inclosed' for ' engolfed:' so 1630 also.
　　,,　6, cf. St. Peter's Complaint, st. i. line 5, and relative
note : 1596 and 1630 misprint ' care' for ' card.'
　　Line 9, see relative note on the Conception of our Ladie,
st. i. lines 3-4.
　　St. ii. line 3, 1630 and 1634 misprint after 1596 ' call'd,'
which TURNBULL repeated.
　　Line 11, cf. St. Peter's Complaint, st. lxxx. line 2.
　　St. iii. line 2, our MS. reads ' this ;' but as ' His' is better,
and is in 1596, I prefer it : 1596 in line 3 reads ' his little.'
　　Line 4, 1634, misreads blunderingly,

> ' Soile full of, yet free from, all mortall seed ;'

and again TURNBULL perpetuates.　Mortal=deadly.

Line 5, in Addl. MSS. 10.422 'Jesse's:' in 1596 and 1630 'Iessa.' Cf. Isaiah xi. It may be noted, that while Auth. Vers. reads here 'Branch,' the Vulg. has 'flower,' —'et *flos* de radice ascendet.'

In 1596 the poem is not divided into stanzas, and so throughout in this series. The heading is simply 'Her Natiuitie.' G.

OUR LADYE'S SPOUSALLS.

WIFE did she live, yet virgin did she die,
    Untowchd of man, yet mother of a sonne;
To save herself and childe from fatall lye,
    To end the webb whereof the thredd was spoone,
In mariage knottes to Josephe she was tyde,
Unwonted workes with wonted veyles to hide.

God lent His paradice to Josephe's care,
    Wherein He was to plante the tree of life;
His Sonne, of Joseph's childe the title bare,
    Just cause to make the mother Josephe's wife.
O blessèd man! betrothd to such a spouse,
More blessd to live with such a childe in house!

Noe carnall love this sacred league procurde,
    All vayne delites were farre from their assent;
Though both in wedlock bands them selves assurde,
    Yet strait by vow they seald their chast entent:
Thus had she virgins', wives', and widowes' crowne,
And by chast childbirth doubled her renowne.

NOTES AND ILLUSTRATIONS.

St. i. line 2, 1596 misreads 'Vntaught' for 'Untowchd.'
Line 6, 1596 misreads 'wiles' for 'veyles,' and so 1630.
St. ii. line 5, 1596 reads badly 'betroth'd too much.'
St. iii. line 1, 1596 reads 'his' for 'this.'
Line 3, 1596 reads 'Though both themselues,' and so 1630.
   ,,   4, 1596, 1630 and 1634 read 'chaste' for 'strait;' and
so TURNBULL.
Line 5, 1596 and 1630 read 'the' for 'she.'
In 1596 the heading is simply 'Her Spousalls.' G.

OUR LADIE'S SALUTATION.

SPELL Eva backe and Ave shall yowe finde,
    The first beganne, the last reversd our harmes;
An angell's witching wordes did Eva blynde,
    An angell's Ave disinchauntes the charmes:
Death first by woeman's weakenes entred in,
In woeman's vertue life doth nowe beginn.

O virgin brest! the heavens to thee inclyne,
    In thee their joy and soveraigne they agnize;
Too meane their glory is to match with thyne,
    Whose chaste receite God more then heaven did prize.
Hayle fayrest heaven, that heaven and earth dost blisse,
Where vertewes starres, God sonne of justice is!   *sun*

With hauty mynd to Godhead man aspird,
  And was by pride from place of pleasure chasd ;
With lovinge mind our manhead God desird,
  And us by love in greater pleasure placd ;
Man labouring to ascend procurd our fall,
God yelding to descend cut off our thrall.

NOTES AND ILLUSTRATIONS.

St. i. line 1, see relative note on Our Ladie's Natiuitie, st. i. line 3, and also Coventry Mysteries, p. 112, line 16 (Shaks. Soc.), ' Here this name Eva is turned Ave,' and Halliwell's note, p. 412. The quotation from Coventry Mysteries is given incorrectly in Collier, Hist. Dram. p. ii. 176. Cf. also Audæni Epigr. iii. 46.

St. ii. lines 1-2, our MS. here and elsewhere reads ' the' for ' thee,' and ' to' for ' too.' Throughout I give the present forms, as in 1596 and other early and later editions.

Line 2, 1596 misreads ' In thee they joy ;' and so 1630 in error. ' Agnize'=acknowledge.

Line 5, 1596, 1630 and 1634 read ' did' for ' dost.'

  ,, 6, our MS. reads ' starres' inadvertently.

St. iii. line 4, TURNBULL misprints 'And *as* by love' for ' us.'

In 1596 the heading is ' The Virgin's Salutation.' This poem bears throughout, as does The Visitation, recollections of the hymn ' Gaudii,' &c. as elsewhere.

JOSEPHE'S AMAZEMENT.

WHEN Christ, by grouth, disclosèd His descent
    Into the pure receite of Marye's breste,
Poore Joseph, straunger yet to God's intent,
    With doubtes of jelious thoughtes was sore opprest ;
And, wrought with divers fittes of feare and love,
He nether can her free nor faultye prove.

Now Sence, the wakefull spie of jelious mynde,
    By stronge conjectures deemeth her defilde ;
But Love, in dome of thinges best lovèd, blynde,
    Thinkes rather Sence deceiv'd then her with child ;
Yet proofes so pregnant were, that no pretence
Could cloake a thinge so cleare and playne to sence.

Then Joseph, daunted with a deadly wounde,
    Let loose the reynes to undeservèd greife ;
His hart did throbb, his eyes in teares were drounde,
    His life a losse, death seem'd his best releife ;
The pleasing relis of his former love   *relish*
In gallish thoughtes to bitter tast doth prove.

One foote he often setteth forth of doore,
    But t'other's loth uncerten wayes to treade ;
He takes his fardell for his needefull store,
    He casts his inn, where first he meanes to bead ;
But still ere he can frame his feete to goe,
Love wynneth tyme till all conclude in noe.

Sometyme, greif addinge force, he doth depart,
    He will, against his will, keepe on his pace ;
But straight remorse so rackes his ruing hart,
    That hasting thoughtes yeld to a pawsing space ;
Then mighty reasons presse him to remayne,
She whome he flyes doth winne him home againe.

But when his thought, by sight of his aboade,
    Presentes the signe of mysesteemèd shame,
Repenting every stepp that backe he trode,
    Teares drowne the guides, the tongue the feete doth
            blame ;
Thus warring with himself, a feilde he fightes,
Where every wounde upon the giver lightes.

And was (quoth he) my love so lightly prysed ?
    And was our sacred league so soone forgott ?
Could vowes be voyde, could vertues be despisd ?
    Could such a spouse be staynd with such a spott ?
O wretched Joseph ! that hast livd so longe,
Of faithfull love to reape so grevous wronge !

Could such a worme breede in so sweete a wood ?
   Coulde in so chast demeanure lincke untruth ?
Could Vice lye hidd where Vertue's image stoode ?
   Where hoary sagenes gracèd tender youthe ?
Where can affyance rest, to rest secure ?
In Vertue's fayrest seat faithe is not sure.

All proofes did promise hope a pledge of grace,
   Whose good might have repaide the deepest ill ;
Sweete signes of purest thoughtes in saintly face
   Assurd the eye of her unstaynèd will.
Yett, in this seeminge lustre, seeme to lye
Such crymes for which the lawe condemns to die.

But Josephe's word shall never worke her woe :
   I wishe her leave to live, not dome to dye ;
Though fortune myne, yett am I not her foe,
   She to her self lesse lovinge, is then I :
The most I will, the lest I can, is this,   *least*
Sithe none may salve, to shunne that is amisse.

Exile my home, the wildes shall be my walke,
   Complainte my joye, my musicke mourninge layes ;
With pensive greives in silence will I talke,
   Sad thoughtes shalbe my guides in sorowe's wayes :
This course best suites the care of curelesse mynde,
That seekes to loose what moste it joy'd to finde.

Like stockèd tree whose braunches all do fade,
    Whose leaves do fall and perisht fruite decaie ;
Like herb that growes in colde and barrayne shade,
    Where darkenes drives all quickninge heate away;
So dye must I, cutt from my roote of joye,
And throwen in darkest shades of deepe annoye.

But who can fly from that his harte doth feele ?
    What chaunge of place can change implanted payne?
Removinge moves no hardnes from the steele ;
    Sicke hartes, that shift no fittes, shift roomes in vayne.
Where thought can see, what helpes the closèd eye ?
Where hart pursues, what gaynes the foote to flye ?

Yett still I tredd a maze of doubtfull end ;
I goe, I come, she drawes, she drives away ;
She woundes, she heales, she doth both marr and mend,
    She makes me seeke and shunn, depart and stay ;
She is a frende to love, a foe to loathe,
And in suspence I hange betwene them both.

NOTES AND ILLUSTRATIONS.

St. i. line 2, 'receite'=place of receipt, as in sitting at the receipt of custom, St. Matthew ix. 9, &c. Cf. The Visitation, st. iii. line 3, and Sinne's Heavy Load, st. iv. line 2. See also with relation to the meaning of 'receipt' and 'brest,' Joseph's Amazement, st. i. line 2.

St. ii. line 3, ' dome' = doom or judgment.

St. iii. line 6, the word 'gallish' shows that our text from our MS., and as in 1596 as well as in Addl. MSS. 10.422, is right, and the emendation in TURNBULL an impertinence and wrong, which reads ' in taste doth bitter prove.' Our Poet was thinking of ' it was in my mouth as sweet as honey, and as soon as I had eaten it, my belly was bitter,'—amaricatus est venter meus. Apoc. x. 10.

St. iv. line 3, fardell = burden.

Line 4, casts = determines in his mind. RICHARDSON *s. v.* derives this sense of it from wrestling; but it is simpler to consider it as either a soothsaying or gaming sense, taken from the *casting* of lots or dice, or from the ' *casting*' of nativities. Bead is = bed, *i.e.* sleep.

St. v. line 3, 1596 reads ' raging' for ' ruing.'

St. vi. line 4, 1596 reads stupidly ' done the guide.'

St. ix. line 5. Our MS. is corrected by S. It originally stood as a word of five letters, probably ' luste,' and is changed to ' lustre' (apparently) as in 1596.

St. x. line 3, perhaps we have here a reference, if not a quotation, from the song ' Fortune my foe, why dost thou frown on me?' and it is the more applicable that this song ' is a sweet sonnet, wherein the lover exclaims against Fortune for the loss of his lady's favour, almost past hope to get it again.'

Line 5, TURNBULL misprints ' less :' lest = least.

St. xii. line 1, to ' stock' a tree is to cut it down, so as to leave a ' stock' on which to graff some other, and the reference here is to that part of the stock and branches so cut off.

Line 5, TURNBULL misreads ' So must I die.' G.

THE VISITATION.

PROCLAYMÈD queene and mother of a God,
   The light of Earth, the soveraigne of saintes,
With pilgrimm foote upp tyring hills she trodd,
   And heavenly stile with handmayds' toyle acquaints :
Her youth to age, her helth to sicke she lends,
Her hart to God, to neighbour hand she bendes.

A prince she is, and mightier prince doth beare,
    Yet pompe of princely trayne she would not have ;
But doubtles heavenly quires attendant were,
    Her child from harme, her self from fall to save :
Worde to the voyce, songe to the tune she bringes,
The voyce her word, the tune her ditye singes.

Eternall lightes inclosèd in her breste
    Shott out such percing beames of burning love,
That when her voyce her cosen's eares possest
    The force thereof did force her babe to move :
With secreet signes the children greete ech other,
But open praise ech leaveth to his mother.

NOTES AND ILLUSTRATIONS.

St. i. line 3, St. Luke i. 39.

Line 5, 1630 and 1634 misread 'her selfe' for 'her helth :' and TURNBULL repeats the blunder.

Line 6, St. Luke i. 56.

St. ii. line 1, '*prince*.' So in the Assumption of our Ladie, st. iii. line 2: a usage not infrequent.

Lines 5 - 6, St. Luke i. 42. She 'themes' or gives the words in which the voice of Elizabeth finds expression, and thus gives articulate song to the joyful time. 'Word' in line 5 is probably used in a double sense—SOUTHWELL being almost as fond of such double uses as SHAKESPEARE—and her 'ditty' is both her song-words and the song about her, or made in her praise.

St. iii. line 1, see relative note on Our Ladie's Salutation, st. i. line 2.

Addl. MSS. 10.422 differs only in orthographic changes. G.

THE NATIVITY OF CHRISTE.

BEHOULD the father is His daughter's sonne,
　　The bird that built tho nest is hatchd therein,
The old of yeres an hower hath not outrunne,
　　Eternall life to live doth nowe beginn,
The Worde is dumm, the Mirth of heaven doth weepe,
Mighte feeble is, and Force doth fayntely creepe.

O dyinge soules ! behould your living springe !
　　O dazeled eyes ! behould your sunne of grace !
Dull eares, attend what word this Word doth bringe !
　　Upp, heavy hartes, with joye your joy embrace !
From death, from darke, from deaphnesse, from des-
　　　　payres,
This Life, this Light, this Word, this Joy repaires.

Gift better then Him self God doth not knowe,
　　Gift better then his God no man can see ;
This gift doth here the giver given bestowe,
　　Gift to this gift lett ech receiver bee :
God is my gift, Him self He freely gave me,
God's gift am I, and none but God shall have me.

Man altred was by synn from man to best ;   *beast*

   Beste's foode is haye, haye is all mortall fleshe ;

Now God is fleshe, and lyes in maunger prest,

   As haye the brutest synner to refreshe :

O happy feilde wherein this foder grewe,

Whose taste doth us from beastes to men renewe !

NOTES AND ILLUSTRATIONS.

In his Epistle ' To the Gentlemen Readers' the printer (John Busbie), introducing Mæoniæ (1595), says, ' One thing amongst the rest I am to admonish thee of, that hauing in this treatise read Marie's Visitation, the next that should follow is Christ's Natuity ; but being afore printed in the end of Peter's Complaint, we have heere of purpose omitted; that thou should-est not be abridged of that and the other like comforts, which that other treatise profereth thee.' TURNBULL so places the present poem ; but in so doing reveals he had never seen, or at least never used, the 1595 edition.

In st. ii. line 2, our MS. inadvertently reads ' summe' for ' sunne' of 1596, &c.

St. iii. lines 17-18, that is the gift bestowed on me—that which is mine now, but is essentially a gift from another ; and so next line—God's gift am I—is, I am the gift which I have given to God. So elsewhere, ' His angels' gifts' = His gifts to angels, as noted in the place.

St. iv. line 2, ' Omnis caro fenum,' Is. xl. 6 and Ps. cii. 15 (ciii. Auth. Vers.), and all the parallel passages, give ' hay,' ex-cept Ps. lxxxix. (xc.) 5, which has ' herba,' as there required.

Line 3, TURNBULL similarly misprints 'lives' for 'lyes.' G.

THE CIRCUMSISION.

THE head is launc'd to worke the bodie's cure,
    With angring salve it smartes to heale our wounde ;
To faltlesse Sonne, from all offences pure,
    The falty vassall's scourges do redounde ;
The judge is cast, the guilty to acquite,
The sonne defac'd, to lende the starre his lighte.

The Vine of life distilleth droppes of grace,
    Our rock gives yssue to a heavenly springe ;
Teares from His eyes, blood runnes from wounded place,
    Which showers, to heaven, of joy a harvest bringe :
This sacred deaw let angells gather upp,
Such deynty droppes best fitt their nectared cupp.

With weeping eyes His mother reu'd His smart,
    If bloode from Him, teares rann from her as fast ;
The knife that cutt His fleshe did perce her hart,
    The payne that Jesus felt did Marye tast ;
His life and her's hunge by one fatall twiste,
No blowe that hitt the Sonne the mother miste.

NOTES AND ILLUSTRATIONS.

St. i. lines 1-4, said, perhaps, with reference to the earthly-royal custom by which a vassal whipping-boy was scourged for the faults of the heir.

St. ii. line 1, 1596 ed. corrects our MS. and 1634—the latter blindly followed by TURNBULL—in reading, as in 1630 also, ' Vine' for ' vein.'

Line 3, 1634, and so TURNBULL, reads ' streames' for ' runnes.'
,,   4, With = whose or which.

St. iii. lines 2-4, in 1596 are very inaccurate, reading ' came' for ' rann,' ' his' for ' her heart,' and ' set' for ' felt.'

Line 5, *fatal.* Latinate, in so far as it contains the sense of appointed (or spun) by destiny.   So in Virgil and Cicero.

In 1596 the heading is ' His Circumcision.' G.

THE EPIPHANYE.

To blase the rising of this glorious sunne,
    A glittringe starre appeareth in the Easte,
Whose sight to pilgrimm-toyles three sages wunne
    To seeke the light they long had in requeste ;
And by this starre to nobler starr they pase,
Whose armes did their desirèd sunne embrace.

Stall was the skye wherein these planettes shynde,
    And want the cloude that did eclipse their rayes ;
Yet through this cloude their light did passage finde,
    And percd these sages' harts by secrett waies,
Which made them knowe the Ruler of the skyes,
By infant tongue and lookes of babish eyes.

Heaven at her light, Earth blusheth at her pride,
 And of their pompe these peeres ashamèd be ;
Their crownes, their robes, their trayne they sett aside,
 When God's poore cotage, clowtes, and crewe, they
All glorious thinges their glory nowe dispise, [see ;
Sith God contempt, doth more then glory prize.

Three giftes they bringe, three giftes they beare awaye ;
 For incense, myrrhe and gould, faith, hope and love ;
And with their giftes the givers' hartes do staye,
 Their mynde from Christ no parting can remove ;
His humble state, his stall, his poore retynewe,
They phansie more then all theire ritch revenewe.

NOTES AND ILLUSTRATIONS.

 In st. i. line 1, *blase* = to blaze, or to blaze abroad or pub-
lish, is probably drawn from the use of beacon-fires and the like
as messengers of news : line 3, 1596 reads 'pilgrims' toile :'
line 7, the transition to this thought is so natural, that SOUTH-
WELL may or may not have had in his mind that legend several
times repeated in the apocryphal Gospels, that a bright light
filled the cave when Jesus was born, especially in the Gospel
of James, where it is said 'a bright cloud overshadowed the
cave . . . and suddenly the cloud withdrew, and there appeared
a great light in the cave, so that their eyes could not bear it.'
As a Protestant, it is noticeable to me that SOUTHWELL is ex-
ceptionally free from references to legends. In st. ii. line 6,
TURNBULL misprints 'infant's :' in st. iv. line 1, ' brought' for
' bringe ;' and line 2, actually ' mirth' for ' myrrhe.' Lines 5-6, ' re-
venewe.' There seem to have been two pronunciations of ' re-
venue' in SOUTHWELL's time, and probably two of ' retinue.' In
Midsummer Night's Dream ' révenue' and ' revénue' occur in the
same scene (i. 1) ; and in the verse of his plays ' revénue' occurs
ten times, and ' révenue' six ; nor is there any change in his

earlier or later usage, nor anything to indicate that one was more courtly or more impressive or poetic than the other. In the one case in which he uses 'retinue' in verse (Lear, i. 4) the emphasis on 'insolent' requires 'retínue' or 'ret'nue.' The penultimate accentuation is from the older and fuller French forms 'revenuë' and 'retenuë,' and both nations in adopting the shorter forms have thrown back the accent. G.

THE PRESENTATION.

To be redeem'd the world's Redeemer brought,
    Two selye turtle-doves, for ransome payes ;
Oh ! ware with empyres worthy to be bought,
    This easye rate doth sounde, not drowne Thy praise !
For sith no price can to Thy worth amounte,
A dove, yea love, dew price Thou dost accounte.

Old Simeon cheap penyworth and sweete
    Obteyn'd, when Thee in armes he did embrace ;
His weeping eyes Thy smyling lookes did meete,
    Thy love his hart, Thy kisses blissd his face :
O eyes ! O hart ! meane sightes and loves avoyde,
'Base not your selves, your best you have enjoy'd !

O virgin pure ! thou dost these doves presente
    As due to lawe, not as an equall price ;
To buy such ware thou would'st thy life have spente ;
    The worlde to reach His worth coulde not suffice ;
If God were to be bought, not worldly pelfe,
But thou, wert fittest price next God Him self.

In st. i. line 3, 1596 reads 'wares :' in st. iii. line 3, 'thy self' for 'thy life.' In st. ii. line 1, 'cheap pennyworth' was an ordinary and usual phrase for a cheap or good cheap bargain. St. i. lines 1-2 = the world's Redeemer brought to be redeemed, payes two selye turtle-doves for ransome. G.

THE FLIGHT INTO EGIPT.

ALAS ! our Day is forc'd to flye by nighte !
　　Light without light, and sunne by silent shade.
O Nature, blushe ! that suffrest such a wighte,
　　That in thy sunne this dark eclipse hath made ;
Day to his eyes, light to his steppes denye,
That hates the light which graceth every eye.

Sunne being fledd the starres do leese their light,
　　And shyninge beames in bloody streames they
A cruell storme of Herod's mortall spite　　[drenche ;
　　Their lives and lightes with bloody shoures doth
The tiran to be sure of murdringe one,　　[quench :
For feare of sparinge Him doth pardon none.

O blessèd babes ! first flowers of Christian Springe,
　　Who though untymely cropt fayre garlandes frame,
With open throates and silent mouthes you singe
　　His praise, Whome age permitts you not to name ;
Your tunes are teares, your instrumentes are swordes,
Your ditye death, and bloode in lieu of wordes !

NOTES AND ILLUSTRATIONS.

In st. i. line 3, 'wight' = Herod. Line 4, 1596 reads
'hast:'. st. ii. line 1, 'loose' for 'leese;' probably therefore =
'lease,' *i. e.* 'to lose,' for in the old philosophy all the stars re-
ceived their light from the sun. The metaphor scarcely applies
if = less: line 4, I have adopted 'do' for 'doth:' st. iii. line 3,
both followed the conceits of their age, but cf. Antony in Julius
Cæsar, iii. 1 and iii. 2. G.

CHRISTE'S RETORNE OUT OF EGIPT.

When Death and Hell their right in Herode clayme,
　　Christ from exile returnes to natyve soyle,
There with His life more deepely Death to mayme,
　　Then Death did life by all the infantes spoyle.
He shewd the parentes that their babes did mone,
That all their lives were lesse then His alone.

But hearing Herod's sonne to have the crowne ;
　　An impious offspring of a bloodye syre ;
To Nazareth (of heaven belovèd) towne,
　　Flower to a floure, He fittly doth retyre ;
For floure He is and in a floure He bredd,
And from a thorne nowe to a floure He fledd.

And well deservd this floure His fruite to vew,
　　Where He invested was in mortall weede ;
Where first unto a tender budd He grewe,
　　In virgin branch unstaynd with mortall seede :

Yonge floure, with floures in floure well may He be,
Ripe fruite, He must with thornes hange on a tree.

NOTES AND ILLUSTRATIONS.

In st. i. line 4, 'spoyle' = rob: line 5, 1596 badly mis-
prints 'the' for 'their:' st. ii. line 2, reads 'The' for 'An:'
line 5, 'For He is a flower:' very badly, and followed by TURN-
BULL, 'throne' for 'thorne:' st. iii. line 3, 'into' for 'unto.' In
our MS. in the margin explanatory of the play on the word
'flower' is this note, 'Nazareth significth a flower.' So Isaiah
xii. in Vulg. as before noted. Nazareth has been supposed to
be derived from some dialectic variation of Nitza or Netzer,
Hebrew for 'flower,' the town being situated in the most fertile
and beautiful part of Judea. The Virgin is called a 'flower' ac-
cording to the name 'Rosa mystica' in the Litany of B.V. G.

CHRISTE'S CHILDHOODE.

TILL twelve yeres' age, how Christ His childhood spent
    All earthly pennes unworthy were to write;
Such actes to mortall eyes He did presente,
    Whose worth not men but angells must recite :
No nature's blottes, no childish faultes defilde,
Where Grace was guide, and God did play the childe.

In springing lockes lay couchèd hoary witt,
    In semblance younge, a grave and auncient port;
In lowly lookes high maiestie did sitt,
    In tender tunge, sound sence of sagest sort :
Nature imparted all that she could teache,
And God supplyd where Nature coulde not reach.

His mirth, of modest meane a mirrhour was,
    His sadnes, tempred with a mylde aspecte ;
His eye, to trye ech action was a glasse,
    Whose lookes did good approue and bad correct ;
His nature's giftes, His grace, His word, and deede,
Well shew'd that all did from a God proceede.

NOTES AND ILLUSTRATIONS.

TURNBULL in st. ii. line 1 wretchedly misprints ' crouched' for ' couched:' line 2, I adopt ' semblance' from 1596 for ' semblant.' G.

CHRIST'S BLOODY SWEATE.

FATT soyle, full springe, sweete olive, grape of blesse,
    That yeldes, that streames, that poures, that dost
        distill,
Untild, undrawne, unstampde, untouchd of presse,
    Deere fruit, clere brookes, fayre oyle, sweete wine at
        will !
Thus Christ unforcd preventes, in shedding bloode,
The whippes, the thornes, the nayles, the speare, and
        roode.

He pelican's, he phœnix' fate doth prove,   [die :
    Whome flames consume, whome streames enforce to
How burneth blood, how bleedeth burninge love,
    Can one in flame and streame both bathe and frye ?
How coulde He joyne a phœnix' fyerye paynes
In faynting pelican's still bleeding vaynes ?

Elias once, to prove God's soveraigne poure,
     By praire procurd a fier of wondrous force,
That blood and wood and water did devoure,
     Yea stones and dust beyonde all Nature's course :
Such fire is love, that, fedd with gory bloode,
Doth burne no lesse then in the dryest woode.

O sacred fire ! come shewe thy force on me,
     That sacrifice to Christe I maye retorne :
If withered wood for fuell fittest bee,
     If stones and dust, yf fleshe and bloode will burne,
I withered am, and stonye to all good,
A sacke of dust, a masse of fleshe and bloode.

NOTES AND ILLUSTRATIONS.

St. i. line 5, ' prevents' = forestalls.

St. ii. line 4. On ' frye,' see our CRASHAW, vol. i. p. 118, and relative note. G.

CHRISTE'S SLEEPING FRENDES.

WHEN Christ, with care and pangues of death opprest,
     From frighted fleshe a bloody sweate did rayne,
And, full of feare, without repose or reste,
     In agonye did praye and watche in payne ;
Three sundry tymes He His disciples findes
With heavy eyes, but farre more heavy myndes.

With milde rebuke He warnèd them to wake,
　　Yet sleepe did still their drowsy sences hould,
As when the sunne the brightest shewe doth make,
　　In darkest shroudes the night-birdes them infold :
His foes did watche to worke their cruell spight,
His drowsye frendes slept in His hardest plighte.

As Jonas saylèd once from Joppe's shoare
　　A boystrous tempest in the ayre did broyle,
The waves did rage, the thundring heavens did rore,
　　The stormes, the rockes, the lightninges threatned
　　　　spoyle ;
The shipp was billowes' game and chaunce's praye,
Yet careles Jonas mute and sleepinge laye.

So now, though Judas, like a blustringe gust,
　　Do stirre the furious sea of Jeweshe ire,
Though storming troopes, in quarrells most unjust,
　　Against the barke of all our blisse conspire,
Yett these disciples sleepinge lie secure,
As though their wonted calme did still endure.

So Jonas once, his weary lymmes to reste,
　　Did shroude him self in pleasant ivy shade,
But loe! while him a heavye sleepe opprest,
　　His shadowy boure to withered stalke did fade ;
A canckered worme had gnawen the roote away,
And brought the glorious braunches to decaye.

O gratious plante! O tree of heavenly springe!
    The paragon for leafe, for fruite and floure,
How sweete a shadow did Thy braunches bringe
      To shroude these soules that chose Thee for their
          boure!
But now while they with Jonas fall asleepe,
To spoyle their plant an envious worme doth creepe.

Awake, ye slumbring wightes! lift upp your eyes,
    Marke Judas, how to teare your roote he strives;
Alas! the glory of your arbour dyes,
    Arise and gard the comfort of your lives;
No Jonas' ivye, no Zacheus' tree,
Were to the world so greate a losse as Hee.

NOTES AND ILLUSTRATIONS.

St. ii. line 4, TURNBULL misprints 'darkness' for 'darkest.'
Line 6, 1596 reads 'night' for 'plight,' and so 1630.

St. iii. line 5. Our MS. misreads 'gaine' for 'game' of 1596: latter adopted.

St. iv. line 4, one of TURNBULL's most vexatious misprints is 'backe' for 'barke.'

St. v. line 1, 1596 reads 'heauy' for 'weary.'

Line 2, 1596 reads 'in iuy pleasant.' Jerome translated Jonah's *kikayon* as *hedera* (though he did not put it forth as an exact rendering), and he thereby raised a storm in one diocese at least, where the older *cucurbita* was upheld as orthodox against the new heretical upstart. However, 'hedera' is retained in the present Vulgate. It is perhaps needless to add that the now commonly received opinion is, that it is the castor-oil plant, or tree as it may be sometimes called.

Line 5, TURNBULL reads 'A canker-worm:' 1596, 'did' for 'had.' G.

THE VIRGIN MARY TO CHRIST ON THE CROSSE.[1]

WHAT mist hath dimd that glorious face? what seas of
    griefe my sun doth tosse?
The golden raies of heauenly grace lies now ecclipsèd
    on the crosse.

Iesus! my loue, my Sonne, my God, behold Thy mother
    washt in teares :
Thy bloudie woundes be made a rod to chasten these
    my latter yeares.

You cruell Iewes, come worke your ire, vpon this worth-
    lesse flesh of mine :
And kindle not eternall fire, by wounding Him which
    is diuine.

Thou messenger that didst impart His first discent into
    my wombe,
Come helpe me now to cleaue my heart, that there I
    may my Sonne intombe.

---

[1] Curiously enough this poem is not in our MS. nor in Addl.
MSS. 10.422 or HARLEIAN MS. 6921. Our text is from 1596. G.

You angels all, that present were, to shew His birth
    with harmonie;
Why are you not now readie here, to make a mourning
    symphony?

The cause I know, you waile alone and shed your teares
    in secresie,
Least I should mouèd be to mone, by force of heauie
    companie.

But waile my soule, thy comfort dies, my wofull wombe,
    lament thy fruit;
My heart, giue teares unto my eies, let Sorrow string
    my heauy lute.

THE DEATH OF OUR LADIE.[1]

WEEPE, living thinges, of life the mother dyes;
    The world doth loose the summ of all her blisse,
The quene of Earth, the empresse of the skyes;
    By Marye's death mankind an orphan is :
Lett Nature weepe, yea, lett all graces mone,
Their glory, grace, and giftes dye all in one.

[1] TURNBULL printed this poem from Addl. MSS. 10.422, but
showed his usual incapacity even to transcribe, by reading st.
iii. line 5,
    ' Such eyed the light thy beams untimely shine ;'
the nonsense of which he discerned not. The MS. 10.422 differs
only orthographically (slightly). I place this poem here, as
belonging to the series on Mary. G.

It was no death to her, but to her woe,
　　By which her joyes beganne, her greives did end ;
Death was to her a frende, to us a foe,
　　Life of whose lives did on her life depende :
Not pray of death, but praise to death she was,
Whose uglye shape seemd glorious in her face.

Her face a heaven, two planettes were her eyes,
　　Whose gracious light did make our clearest day ;
But one such heaven there was and loe! it dyes,
　　Deathe's darke eclipse hath dymmèd every ray :
Sunne, hide thy light, thy beames untymely shine!
Trew light sith wee have lost, we crave not thine.

THE ASSUMPTION OF OUR LADY.[1]

IF sinne be captive, grace must finde release ;
　　From curse of synne the innocente is free ;
Tombe, prison is for sinners that decease,
　　No tombe, but throne to guiltles doth agree :
Though thralles of sinne lye lingring in their grave,
Yet faultles cors, with soule, rewarde must have.

　　[1] TURNBULL printed this from Addl. MSS. 10.422.　Our MS.
differs only in orthography, and st. i. line 5 reads ' their' for
' the.'　As with the preceding, I give this poem here as its fit-
ting place. G.

The daseled eye doth dymmèd light require,
    And dying sightes repose in shrowdinge shades ;
But eagles' eyes to brightest light aspire,
    And living lookes delite in loftye glades :
Faynte wingèd foule by ground doth fayntly flye,
Our princely eagle mountes unto the skye.

Gemm to her worth, spouse to her love ascendes,
    Prince to her throne, queene to her heavenly Kinge,
Whose court with solemne pompe on her attends,
    And quires of saintes with greeting notes do singe ;
Earth rendreth upp her undeservèd praye,
Heaven claymes the right, and beares the prize awaye.

SAINT THOMAS OF AQUINES HYMNE READ
ON CORPUS CHRISTY DAYE.

Lauda Sion Salvatorem.

PRAISE, O Syon ! praise thy Saviour,
Praise thy captayne and thy pastour,
    With hymnes and solemne harmony.
What pour affordes, performe in dede ;   *power*
His worthes all prayses farre exceede,
    No praise can reach His dignitye.

A speciall theme of praise is redd,
A livinge and life-givinge bredd,
  Is on this day exhibitèd ;
Which in the Supper of our Lorde,
To twelve disciples at His borde,
  None doubtes but was deliverèd.

Lett our praise be loude and free,
Full of joye and decent glee,
  With myndes' and voyces' melodye ;
For now solemnize wee that daye,
Which doth with joye to us displaye
  The prime use of this mistery.

At this borde of our newe Ruler
Of newe lawe, newe paschall order
  The auncient rite abolisheth ;
Old decrees by newe anullèd,
Shadowes are in truthes fullfillèd,
  Day former darkenes finisheth.

That at Supper Christ performèd,
To be donne He straightly chargèd
  For His eternall memorye.
Guided by His sacred orders,
Bredd and wyne upon our alters
  To saving hoast we sanctifie.

Christians are by faithe assurèd
That to flesh the bredd is chaungèd,
 The wyne to bloode most pretious :
That no witt nor sence conceiveth,
Firme and grounded faithe beleeveth,
 In strange effects not curious.

Under kyndes two in appearance,
Two in shewe but one in substance,
 Lye thinges beyond comparison ;
Flesh is meate, bloode drinck most heavenly,
Yett is Christe in eche kynde wholye,
 Most free from all division.

None that eateth Him doth chewe Him,
None that takes Him doth devide Him,
 Receivd, He whole persevereth.
Be there one or thowsandes housled,
One as much as all receivèd,
 HE by no eating perisheth.

Both the good and badd receive Him,
But effectes are divers in them,
 Trew life or dewe distruction.
Life to the good, death to the wicked,
Marke how both alike receivèd
 With farre unlike conclusion.

When the preiste the hoaste devideth,
Knowe that in ech parte abideth
 All that the whole hoast coverèd.
Forme of bredd, not Christ is broken,
Not of Christ, but of His token,
 Is state or stature alterèd.

Angells' bredd made pilgrims feedinge,
Trewly bread for childrens eatinge,
 To doggs not to be offerèd.
Signed by Isaake on the alter,
By the lambe and paschall supper,
 And in the manna figurèd.

Jhesu, foode and feeder of us,
Here with mercy, feed and frend us,
 Then graunt in heaven felicity!
Lord of all, whome here Thou feedest,
Fellowes, heyres, guestes with Thy dearest,
 Make us in heavenly companye! Amen.

NOTES AND ILLUSTRATIONS.

In 1596 the title is simply 'A holy Hymne:' in 1630 'An holy Hymne.'

St. i. line 5, 1596 reads 'workes' for 'worthes:' so 1630.

St. ii. line 4, 1596 and 1630 read 'Within' for 'Which in.'

Line 6, ib. read 'As doubtlesse 'twas deliuered.'

St. iii. line 2, 'decent.'

Line 6, 1596 misprints 'priuie' and 1630 'secret' for 'prime use.' TURNBULL strangely reads 'prince.' See below.

St. iv. line 4, 1596 and 1630 spell ' annill'd' and ' annil'd.'
Turnbull misprints ' be' for 'by.'

St. vi. line 6, 1596 spells ' affects.' In 1630 the following
lines are substituted for the next stanzas :

> ' As staffe of bread thy heart sustaines,
> And chearefull wine thy strength regaines,
>   By power and vertue naturall :
> So doth this consecrated food,
> The symbol of Christ' flesh and bloud
>   By vertue supernaturall.
>
> The ruines of thy soule repaire,
> Banish sinne, horrour and despaire,
>   And feed faith, by faith receiued :
> Angels' bread,' &c.

St. vii. line 3, 1596 reads ' Be' for ' Lye.'

St. viii. line 3, ' persevereth' used in a kind of reflective
sense.

Line 4, our ms. reads 'hous'led;' Addl. mss. 10.422 'housled,'
and 1596 'housoled.' Turnbull reads 'hosted'=given the
host. Is 'hous'led'=in the house (of God) and at the Supper?
Or is it parallel (in part) with Shakespeare's 'unhouseled' of
Hamlet (i. 5)?

St. ix. line 3, 1596 reads ' true' for ' dewe.'

St. x. line 2, 1596 inadvertently drops ' in.'

St. xi. line 3, cf. St. Matthew vii. 6 and xv. 27.

Line 4, ' signed'=' præsignatur,' presigned, foreshadowed or
prefigured, just as shadowed and figured are used.

It will be observed that our ms. supplies the lacking syllable
(' but') in st. ii. line 6, and by its reading makes st. iii. line 6
agree with the rest. Turnbull blindly printed the former
' None doubts was deliverèd,' and the latter ' The prince of this
mystery,' to the destruction of the measure and meaning. G.

SAINT PETER'S AFFLICTED MYNDE.[1]

IF that the sicke may grone,
    Or orphane mourne his losse;
If wounded wretch may rue his harmes,
    Or caytif shewe his crosse;

If hart consumd with care,
    May utter signes of payne;
Then may my brest be Sorowe's home,
    And tongue with cause complayne.

My malidye is synne
    And languor of the mynde;
My body but a lazar's couche
    Wherein my soule is pynde.

The care of heavenly kynne,
    Is ded to my releife;
Forlorne, and left like orphane child,
    With sighes I feede my greife.

[1] Copy in Addl. MSS. 10.422, only usual orthographic differences. G.

My woundes, with mortall smarte
    My dying soule tormente,
And, prisoner to myne owne mishapps,
    My follyes I repente.

My hart is but the haunte
    Where all dislikes do keepe ;
And who can blame so lost a wretche,
    Though teares of bloode he weepe ?

SAINT PETER'S REMORSE.

REMORSE upbraides my faultes ;
    Selfe-blaming conscience cries ;
Synn claymes the hoast of humbled thoughtes
    And streames of weeping eyes :

Let penance, Lorde, prevayle ;
    Lett sorowe sue release ;
Lett love be umpier in my cause,
    And passe the dome of peace.

If dome goe by deserte,
    My lest desert is death ;   *least*
That robbes from soule, immortall joyes,
    From bodye, mortall breathe.

But in so highe a God,
   So base a worme's annoy
Can add no praise unto Thy poure,
   No blisse unto Thy joye.

Well may I frye in flames,
   Due fuell to hell-fire !
But on a wretch to wreake Thy wrath
   Cannot be worth Thyne ire.

Yett sith so vile a worme
   Hath wrought his greatest spite,
Of highest treasons well Thou mayst
   In rigour him endite.

Butt Mercye may relente,
   And temper Justice' rodd,
For mercy doth as much belonge
   As justice to a Godd.

If former tyme or place
   More right to mercy wynne,
Thou first wert author of my self,
   Then umpier of my synne.

Did Mercye spynn the thredd,
   To weave in Justice' loome ?
Wert thou a Father, to conclude
   With dreadfull judge's doome ?

It is a small releife
　　To say I was Thy childe,
If, as an evell-deserving foe,
　　From grace I be exilde.

I was, I had, I coulde,
　　All wordes importing wante ;
They are but dust of dead supplies,
　　Where needfull helpes ar scante.

Once to have bene in blisse
　　That hardly can retorne,
Doth but bewray from whence I fell,
　　And wherefore now I mourne.

All thoughtes of passèd hopes
　　Encrease my present crosse ;
Like ruynes of decayèd joyes,
　　They still upbraide my losse.

O mylde and mightye Lorde !
　　Amend that is amisse ;
My synn my sore, Thy love my salve,
　　Thy cure my comfort is.

Confirme Thy former deede,
　　Reforme that is defild ;
I was, I am, I will remayne
　　Thy charge, Thy choise, Thy childe.

NOTES AND ILLUSTRATIONS.

St. i. line 3, 'host'=hostia, sacrifice.

St. iii. line 3, TURNBULL misprints 'souls,' losing the antithesis.

St. iv. line 2, =hurt inflicted by God on the worm.

St. vi. line 3, 1596 'treason.'

St. ix. line 3, TURNBULL misprints 'then' for 'thou.'

St. x. line 3, on 'ill' and 'evill,' see relative note on St. Peter's Complaint, st. ii. line 5.

Line 4, 1596, 'am' for 'be.'

St. xv. l. 1, 1596 'deedes.' On st. xi. 'I was [Thy child], I had [Thy grace,] I could [have been a rock], or I could [have attained to bliss], see St. Matthew xvi. 17. G.

MAN TO THE WOUND IN CHRIST'S SIDE.

O PLEASANT port ! O place of rest !
    O royal rift ! O worthy wound !
Come harbour me, a weary guest,
    That in the world no ease haue found !

I lie lamenting at Thy gate,
    Yet dare I not aduenture in :
I beare with me a troublous mate,
    And cumbred am with heape of sinne.

Discharge me of this heauy loade,
    That easier passage I may find,
Within this bowre to make aboade,
    And in this glorious toomb be shrin'd.

Here must I liue, here must I die,
　　Here would I vtter all my griefe ;
Here would I all those paines descrie,
　　Which here did meete for my releefe.

Here would I view that bloudy sore,
　　Which dint of spiteful speare did breed :
The bloudy woundes laid there in store,
　　Would force a stony heart to bleede.

Here is the spring of trickling teares,
　　The mirror of all mourning wights,
With dolefull tunes for dumpish eares,
　　And solemne shewes for sorrowed sights.

Oh, happie soul, that flies so hie
　　As to attaine this sacred caue !
Lord, send me wings, that I may flie,
　　And in this harbour quiet haue !

NOTES AND ILLUSTRATIONS.

This poem is not in our MS. nor in Addl. MSS. 10.422, nor HARLEIAN MS. 6921. Our text is 1596, which corrects TURN-BULL's unhappy misprint of ' spot' for ' port' (st. i. line 1). We correct ' me' for ' we' (st. vii. line 3). I question if the title given to this poem had SOUTHWELL's authority. The Poet speaks of having ' a troublous mate,' *i.e.* the body, and the poem ends, ' Oh, happie soul :' whence I think the truer title were ' Man's Soul.' Moreover this would be more in accord with the conceits of the time, as the wound was made with intent to let out Christ's life, and the blood and water were deemed emblematic of life given to man, as alluded to in stanza iv., and there, therefore, man's soul would enter and lodge.

St. vi. line 4, 'sorrowed sights,' eyes in a state of sorrow. Cf. St. Peter's Complaint, st. cviii. line 4, 'terror from His sight'=eyes.

VPON THE IMAGE OF DEATH.

BEFORE my face the picture hangs,
　　That daily should put me in mind
Of those cold names and bitter pangs,
　　That shortly I am like to find :
But yet, alas ! full little I
Do thinke hereon, that I must die.

I often looke upon a face
　　Most vgly, grisly, bare and thinne ;
I often view the hollow place,
　　Where eyes and nose, had sometimes bin :
I see the bones acrosse that lie,
Yet little think that I must die.

I reade the labell vnderneath,
　　That telleth me whereto I must ;
I see the sentence eake that saith,
　　Remember, man, that thou art dust :
But yet, alas ! but seldome, I
Doe thinke indeede that I must die.

Continually at my bed's head
    A hearse doth hang, which doth me tel
That I ere morning may be dead,
    Though now I feele my selfe ful well :
But yet, alas ! for all this, I
Haue little minde that I must die.

The gowne which I do vse to weare,
    The knife wherewith I cut my meate,
And eke that old and ancient chaire
    Which is my onely vsuall seate :
All these do tel me I must die,
And yet my life amend not I.

My ancestors are turnd to clay,
    And many of my mates are gone ;
My yongers daily drop away,
    And can I thinke to 'scape alone ?
No, no, I know that I must die,
And yet my life amend not I.

Not Salomon, for all his wit,
    Nor Samson, though he were so strong,
No king nor person euer yet
    Could 'scape, but Death laid him along :
Wherefore I know that I must die,
And yet my life amend not I.

Though all the East did quake to heare
   Of Alexander's dreadfull name,
And all the West did likewise feare
   To heare of Iulius Cæsar's fame,
Yet both by Death in dust now lie ;
Who then can 'scape, but he must die ?

If none can 'scape Death's dreadfull dart,
   If rich and poore his becke obey ;
If strong, if wise, if all do smart,
   Then I to 'scape shall haue no way.
Oh ! grant me grace, O God ! that I
My life may mend, sith I must die.

NOTES AND ILLUSTRATIONS.

   This poem, like the preceding, is not in our MS. nor in Addl.
MSS. 10.422 nor HARLEIAN MS. 6921.   Our text is 1596, which in
st. iii. line 4 corrects TURNBULL's misprint, ' Remember, man,
thou art but dust.'   St. ii. line 4, the cross-bones or thigh-bones,
so called because they were generally put cross-wise beneath
the skull.   St. iv. line 1, ' head'=canopy of the bed.   St. viii.
line 2, Hamlet couples the same names in a similar thought
(v. 1). G.

A VALE OF TEARES.

A vale there is, enwrapt with dreadfull shades,
    Which thicke, of mourning pynes, shrouds from the
        sunne,
Where hanging clyftes yelde shorte and dumpish glades,
    And snowye fludd with broken streames doth runne.

Where eye rome is from rockes to clowdye skye,
    From thence to dales with stony ruyns strowd,
Then to the crushèd water's frothy frye,
    Which tumbleth from the toppes where snowe is
        thowde.

Where eares of other sounde can have no choise,
    But various blustringe of the stubborne wynde
In trees, in caves, in strayts with divers noyse ;
    Which now doth hisse, now howle, now roare by
        kinde.

Where waters wrastle with encountringe stones,
    That breake their streames and turne them into
        fome,
The hollowe cloudes full fraught with thundring grones,
    With hideous thumpes discharge their pregnant
        wome.

And in the horrour of this fearefull quire
    Consistes the musicke of this dolefull place ;
All pleasant birdes their tunes from thence retyre,
    Where none but heavy notes have any grace.

Resort there is of none but pilgrimm wightes,
    That passe with trembling foote and panting hart ;
With terrour cast in colde and shuddring frightes,
    They judge the place to terror framed by art.

Yett Nature's worke it is, of art untowch't,
    So straite in deede, so vast unto the eye,
With such disordred order strangely cowcht,
    And so with pleasing horrour low and hye,

That who it vewes must needes remayne agaste,
    Much at the worke, more at the Maker's mighte ;
And muse how Nature suche a plott coulde caste
    Where nothing seemèd wronge, yett nothinge right.

A place for mated myndes, an onely boure
    Where everye thinge doth sooth a dumpish moode ;
Earth lyes forlorne, the clowdy skye doth lowre,
    The wind here weepes, here sighes, here cryes
        alowde.

The strugling floode betwene the marble grones,
    Then roaring beates uppon the craggy sides ;
A little off, amids the pible stones,
    With bubling streames and purling noyse it glides.

The pynes thicke sett, highe growen and ever greene,
   Still cloath the place with sadd and mourning vayle;
Here gapinge cliffe, there mossy playne is seene,
   Here hope doth springe, and there agayne doth quaile.

Huge massy stones that hange by ticle staye,
   Still threaten fall, and seeme to hange in feare;
Some withered trees, ashamd of their decaye,
   Besett with greene are forc'd gray coates to weare.

Here christall springes crept out of secrete veyne,
   Strait finde some envious hole that hides their
       grace;
Here seared tuftes lament the wante of rayne,
   There thunder-wrack gives terrour to the place.

All pangues and heavy passions here may finde
   A thowsand motives sutely to theire greifes,
To feed the sorrowes of their troubled mynde,
   And chase away dame Pleasure's vayne releifes.

To playninge thoughtes this vale a rest may bee,
   To which from worldly joyes they may retire;
Where Sorowe springes from water, stone and tree;
   Where every thinge with mourners doth conspire.

Sett here, my soule, mayn streames of teares aflote,
   Here all thy synnfull foyles alone recounte;
Of solemne tunes make thou the dollfullst note,
   That, to thy dityes, dolour maye amounte.

When eccho doth repeate thy playnefull cryes,
　　Thinck that the very stones thy synnes bewray,
And nowe accuse thee with their sadd replyes,
　　As heaven and earth shall in the later day.

Lett former faultes be fuell of the fire,
　　For greife, in lymbeck of thy hart, to .'still
Thy pensive thoughtes and dumpes of thy desire,
　　And vapour teares upp to thy eyes at will.

Lett teares to tunes, and paynes to playnts be prest,
　　And lett this be the burdon of thy songe—
Come, deepe Remorse, possesse my synfull brest;
　　Delightes, adiew! I harboured yowe too longe.

<hr>

NOTES AND ILLUSTRATIONS.

In 1596 this poem is not divided into stanzas. Addl. MS. 10.422 and HARLEIAN MS. 6921 agree with our MS. save in usual orthographic differences.

St. i. line 4, in 1596 reads 'flouds. . . . . do.'

St. ii. line 2, ib. misreads 'which stormy ruines shroud:' so 1630.

St. v. line 2, *consists* = agrees with, harmonises with.

St. vi. line 3, I have adopted 'shuddring' from 1596 and 1630 for 'shivering:' but 1596 misreads here 'With terrour cast. . . . And all the place. . .' So also 1630.

Line 4, 'to terror:' Latinate *ad terrorem*, and perhaps as dedicated to terror.

St. vii. line 4, TURNBULL misprints 'with' for 'so.'

St. viii. line 3, 'plot' in a double sense of a conspiracy and plot of ground.

Line 4, 1596 misprints 'her' for 'here' (*bis*).

St. ix. line 2, TURNBULL misprints 'do' for 'doth:' ib. sooth = not allay, but assent to, agree with; and hence soothed is =

flattered by, in st. xiv. line 2 of 'The Prodigall Chyld's Soule Wracke.'

St. x. line 4, 1596 misreads 'a purling:' so 1630.   See on this word relative note in our Henry Vaughan *s. v.*

St. xi. line 4, 1596 reads 'mosse growne :' so 1630.

St. xii. line 2, 1596 and 1630 spell 'foule.'

Line 4, TURNBULL blunderingly amends 'Bereft of' for 'Besett with,' missing the pathos of the blanched trunk ringed with living green trees.

St. xiii. line 3, 1596 misprints 'wants of grace :' so 1630.

St. xvi. line 1, 1596 reads 'Sit' for 'Sett :' so 1630.

St. xvii. line 1, 1596 and 1630 have 'doth' for 'shall.'

St. xix. line 2, 1596 reads 'burthen to.'   See our Memorial-Introduction for the relation of the 'Vale of Tears' to HOOD's 'Haunted House.'   G.

THE PRODIGALL CHYLD'S SOULE WRACKE.

DISANCRED from a blisfull shore,
  And lanch'd into the maygne of cares ;
Groune rich in vice, in vertewe pore,
  From freedome falne in fatall snares ;

I founde my selfe on every syde
  Enwrappèd in the waves of woe,
And, tossèd with a toylsome tyde,
  Could to no port for refuge goe.

The wrastling wyndes with raging blasts,
  Still holde me in a crewell chase ;
They breake my ankers, sayles and mastes,
  Permitting no reposing place.

The boystrous seas, with swelling fludds,
   On every syde did worke theire spyte,
Heaven, overcast with stormy cloudes,
   Deny'd the planets' guyding lyght.

The hellishe furyes laye in wayte
   To wynn my soule into theire poure,
To make me byte at everye bayte,
   Wherein my bane I might devoure.

Thus heaven and hell, thus sea and land,
   Thus stormes and tempests did conspire,
With just revenge of scourging hand,
   To witnesse God's deservèd ire.

I, plungèd in this heavye plyght,
   Founde in my faltes just cause of feare ;
By darkness taught to knowe my light,
   The loss thereof enforcèd teares.

I felt my inwarde-bleeding soares,
   My festred wounds beganne to smart,
Stept farr within deathe's fatall dores,
   The pangues thereof were neere my hart.

I cryèd truce, I cravèd peace,
   A league with death I woulde conclude ;
But vaine it was to sue release,
   Subdue I must or bee subdude.

Death and deceite had pitch'd theire snares,
   And putt theire wicked proofes in ure,
To sincke me in despayring cares,
   Or make me stoupe to pleasure's lure.

They sought by theire bewitching charmes
   So to enchant my erring sense,
That when they sought my greatest harmes,
   I might neglect my best defense.

My dazeled eyes coulde take no vew,
   No heed of theire deceiving shiftes,
So often did they alter hew,
   And practise new-devisèd driftes.

With Syren's songs they fedd my eares,
   Till, lul'd asleepe in Error's lapp,
I found these tunes turn'd into teares,
   And short delightes to long mishapp.

For I entysèd to theire lore,
   And soothèd with theire idle toyes,
Was traynèd to theire prison dore—
   The end of all such flying joyes.

Where cheyn'd in synn I lay in thrall,
   Next to the dungeon of despaire,
Till Mercy raysd me from my fall,
   And Grace my ruines did repaire.

NOTES AND ILLUSTRATIONS.

In 1596 this poem is printed in long lines continuously, not in stanzas.

St. i. line 2, 1596 misprints 'meane' for 'maine.'

St. iii. line 3, I adopt 'breake' from 1596 for 'broke.'

St. ix. line 1, TURNBULL mis-inserts 'a' (*bis*).

St. x. line 2, 'ure' = use.

St. xii. line 2, 1596 misprints 'receiving.'

St. xiii. line 3, 1596 reads 'their' for 'these.' G.

MAN'S CIVILL WARRE.

My hoveringe thoughtes would fly to heaven,
　　And quiet nestle in the skye;
Fayne would my shipp in Vertue's shore
　　Without remove at anker lye;

But mounting thoughtes are halèd downe　　*hauled*
　　With heavy poyse of mortall loade;　　*poise*
And blustringe stormes denye my shipp
　　In Vertue's haven secure aboade.

When inward eye to heavenly sightes
　　Doth drawe my longing hart's desire,
The world with jesses of delightes
　　Would to her perch my thoughtes retyre.

Fonde Phancy traynes to Pleasure's lure,
　　Though Reason stiffly do repine ;
Thoughe Wisdome woe me to the sainte,
　　Yet Sense would wynne me to the shrine.

Wheare Reason loathes, there Phancy loves,
　　And overrules the captive will ;
Foes sences are to Vertue's lore,
　　They drawe the witt their wish to fill.

Need craves consent of soule to sence,
　　Yett divers bents breed civill fraye ;
Hard happ where halves must disagree,
　　Or truce of halves the whole betraye !

O cruell fight ! where fightinge frende
　　With love doth kill a favoringe foe ;
Where peace with sence is warr with God
　　And self-delite the seede of woe !

Dame Pleasure's drugges are steept in synne,
　　Their sugred tast doth breed annoye ;
O fickle Sence ! beware her gynn,
　　Sell not thy soule to brittle joye !

NOTES AND ILLUSTRATIONS.

In 1596 this poem is printed in long continuous lines—a favourite form.

St. ii. line 1, 1596 reads ' mounted' and ' hailed.'

Line 4, our ms. and Addl. ms. 10.422 read ' secure :' the
reading of 1596, ' sure,' is needed by the rhythm, unless ' haven'
be read as one syllable.

St. iii. line 3, 1596 misprints ' lesses.'

St. iv. line 3, 1596 reads here ' Reason' for ' Wisdome,' and
next st. line 1, ' wisdome' for ' reason.'

St. v. line 2, 1596 reads ' euer rules.'

Line 3, 1596 misprints ' and' for ' are.'

St. vi. line 3, happ is here = chance or lot. So in 'Decease,
Release,' st. iii. line 3 ; and ' I die without Desert,' st. ii. line 6.

Line 4, reads ' trust' for ' truce.'

St. viii. lines 9-10. Probably in allusion to a house-dame's
gin, where flies are enticed to sugared and poisoned water. G.

SEEKE FLOWERS OF HEAVEN.

Soare upp, my soule, unto thy reste,
    Cast off this loathsome loade ;
Long is the date of thy exile,
    Too long thy straite aboade.

Grase not on worldly withered weede,
    It fitteth not thy taste ;
The floures of everlastinge Springe
    Do growe for thy repaste.

Their leaves are stayn'd in bewtye's dye,
    And blasèd with their beames,
Their stalkes enameld with delight,
    And lymm'd with glorious gleames.

Life-giving juce of livinge love
  Their sugred veynes doth fill,
And watered with eternall shoures
  They nectared dropps distill.

These floures do spring from fertile soyle,
  Though from unmánur'd feilde ;
Most glittering goulde in lewe of glebe,
  These fragrant flowers, doth yelde.

Whose soveraigne sent surpassing sense
  So ravisheth the mynde,
That worldly weedes needes must he loath
  That can these floweres finde.

NOTES AND ILLUSTRATIONS.

TURNBULL has some annoying misprints in this poem: *e.g.*
st. i. line 3, 'death' for 'date ;' line 4, 'strict' for 'straite' =
narrow, confined : st. ii. line 1, 'wood' for 'weede :' st. iii. line
2, 'her' for 'their' (= the leaves not Beauty). St. v. line 2,
note the accentuation of 'unmánur'd,' on which there has been
recently an exchange of Notes and Queries in N. and Q. While
Dyche's Dictionary (7th edition, 1752) gives 'mánure' sub-
stantive, and 'manúre' verb, and so bears out for that later
date, Mr. Earle's conjecture, our text until farther evidence be
obtained, renders it doubtful whether SOUTHWELL has taken a
poetic license, or whether the word, like revenue, had a double
pronunciation.   Lines 3-4 : construction—gold not glebe does
yield these flowers. The 'do' (of 1596) hitherto printed, which
in part causes the confusion, is 'doth' properly in our MS., the
correction being in S.'s own handwriting. St. vi. line 3 explains
st. ii. line 1, as not worldly-withered but worldly withered. G.

IV.

MELOFOLIA, OR APPLES IN LEAVES.

NOTE.

I bring together here, under the title of Melofolia, such Poems as were not included in 1595, 1596 or any of the early editions. Those printed by WALTER, and with his ineradicable carelessness by TURNBULL, from MSS. in the British Museum, are also preserved among the STONYHURST MSS. and with a superior text. As before, I reproduce the STONYHURST text; but in Notes and Illustrations at close of each poem will be found various readings and authorities for the others. G.

DECEASE, RELEASE. DUM MORIOR, ORIOR.

THE pounded spice both tast and sent doth please,
　　In fading smoke the force doth incense shewe ;
The perisht kernell springeth with increase,
　　The loppèd tree doth best and soonest growe.

God's spice I was, and pounding was my due,
　　In fadinge breath my incense savored best ;
Death was the meane, my kyrnell to renewe,
　　By loppinge shott I upp to heavenly rest.

Some thinges more perfect are in their decaye,
　　Like sparke that going out gives clerest light ;
Such was my happ, whose dolefull dying daye
　　Beganne my joy and termèd Fortune's spite.

Alive a Queene, now dead I am a sainte ;
　　Once Mary called, my name nowe Martyr is ;
From earthly raigne debarrèd by restraint,
　　In liew whereof I raigne in heavenly blisse.

My life my greife, my death hath wrought my joye,
　　My frendes my foyle, my foes my weale procur'd ;
My speedy death hath shortnèd longe annoye,
　　And losse of life an endles life assur'd.

My skaffold was the bedd where ease I founde,
    The blocke a pillowe of eternall reste ;
My hedman cast me in a blisfull swounde,
    His axe cutt off my cares from combred breste.

Rue not my death, rejoyce at my repose ;
    It was no death to me, but to my woe ;
The budd was opened to lett out the rose,
    The cheynes unloos'd to let the captive goe.

A prince by birth, a prisoner by mishappe,
    From crowne to crosse, from throne to thrall I fell ;
My right my ruthe, my titles wrought my trapp,
    My weale my woe, my worldly heaven my hell.

By death from prisoner to a prince enhaunc'd,
    From crosse to crowne, from thrall to throne againe ;
My ruth my right, my trapp my stile advauncd
    From woe to weale, from hell to heavenly raigne.

NOTES AND ILLUSTRATIONS.

WALTER was the first to print this poem from Addl. MS.
10.422, and to entitle it ' On the unfortunate Mary Queen of
Scots :' but his text is mere carelessness. TURNBULL followed,
but in st. ii. line 2 mis-read ' favour'd' for ' savor'd,' &c. &c.
&c. Our MS. corrects in st. v. line 3, by reading ' shortnèd' for
' scornèd,' and line 4 ' an' for ' and.' In our MS. the Poet has
left the name of ' Mary' (st. iv.) unfilled in—a suggestive fact.
The ' Mary' was unquestionably Mary Queen of Scots. See
Notes at close of next poem. In st. i. line 2 =' It is in fading
smoke that incense shows its force' (as in fading life did Mary):
in st. iii. line 4, ' termèd,' causal sense of verb—made a term or
limit of, ended: in st. viii. line 1, ' prince:' see relative note on
' The Visitation,' st. ii. line 1. G.

I DYE WITHOUT DESERT.

If orphane childe, enwrapt in swathing bands,
    Doth move to mercy when forlorne it lyes ;
If none without remorse of love withstands
    The pitious noyse of infante's selye cryes ;
Then hope, my helpelesse hart, some tender eares
Will rue thy orphane state and feeble teares.

Relinquisht lamb, in solitarye wood,
    With dying bleat doth move the toughest mynde ;
The grasping pangues of new engendred brood,
    Base though they be, compassion use to finde :
Why should I then of pitty doubt to speede,
Whose happ would force the hardest hart to bleede ?

Left orphane-like in helpelesse state I rue,
    With onely sighes and teares I pleade my case ;
My dying plaints I daylie do renewe,
    And fill with heavy noyse a desert place :
Some tender hart will weepe to here me mone ;
Men pitty may, but helpe me God alone !

Rayne downe, yee heavens, your teares this case requires;
　　Man's eyes unhable are enough to shedd ;
If sorow could have place in heavenly quires,
　　A juster ground the world hath seldome bredd :
For Right is wrongd and Vertue wagd with blood ;
The badd are blissd, God murdred in the good.

A gracious plant for fruite, for leafe and flower,
　　A peereles gemm for vertue, proofe and price,
A noble peere for prowesse, witt, and poure,
　　A frend to truth, a foe I was to vice ;
And loe, alas ! nowe innocente I dye,
A case that might even make the stones to crye.　　*e'en*

Thus Fortune's favors still are bent to flight,
　　Thus worldly blisse in finall bale doth end ;
Thus Vertue still pursuèd is with spight,
　　But let my fall, though ruefull, none offend :
God doth sometymes first cropp the sweetest floure,
And leaves the weede till Tyme do it devoure.

NOTES AND ILLUSTRATIONS.

WALTER again first printed this from Addl. MS. 10.422, but
again very badly.　So too TURNBULL, who mis-read in st. i. line 5
' cares' for ' eares,' &c. &c.　Our MS. corrects st. iv. line 5, by
reading ' wrongd' for ' wrong;' and in st. vi. line 4, ' fall' for
' fate.'　Probably Mary Queen of Scots is the supposed speaker,
as in the preceding poem. See also the Latin Elegy, first printed
by us, in which the Shade ('Umbra') of Mary laments her hap-
less fate. In st. i. line 3, remorse of love is = loving pity.

' Sely' = silly (st. i. line 4) is so frequently-used a word in

SOUTHWELL, that I gladly avail myself of the present opportunity of bringing together a number of memoranda on it, the more readily that my invaluable friend Dr. Brinsley Nicholson has here specially enriched me from his rare stores. Besides the meaning now attached to 'silly,' there is no question but it had those of innocent, harmless, plain, and simple, and the like, much as simple and innocent have similar shades of meaning at the present time, and, as they are substantively used, not without touch of pathos, for 'silly' persons or idiots. Nor is it necessary to enter into its real or supposed derivation from *selig*, blessed or holy, to understand the connection between these several meanings. SOUTHWELL's 'silly shroud' (Content and Rich, st. ii. line 3) may with SHAKESPEARE's 'silly habit' (Cymbeline, v. 3) mean simple or plain clothing; and the 'silly women' of the Two Gentlemen of Verona (iv. 1), and the 'silly sheep' of 3 Henry VI. (ii. 5), and the 'silly beasts' of 'New Prince, New Pompe' (st. ii. line 3), are so called as innocent, harmless, and inoffensive, as in part at least the doves of 'The Presentation' (st. i. line 2) are silly or innocent.

But there is a now provincial North-country use of 'silly' in the sense of 'sickly' or 'weakly' (HALLIWELL's Ar. Dict. *s. v.*) derived from the stronger sense of sillies, simples, or innocents, because they are not only weakly of mind, but frequently weakly in body and constitution, so much so that from their increased desire for warmth comes the sarcastic proverbial saying—'*Yea, wit enough to keep himself warm.*' Now, as with other provincial words and meanings, this provincialism is but the shrunken remnant of a more widely-spread usage. No other sense can, I think, be given it in Mary Magdalen's Complaynt at Christ's Death in st. ii. line 1, and Lewd Love is Losse (st. ii. l. 4—so stupidly misprinted 'folly' by TURNBULL), nor can the 'silly beggars' of Richard II. (v. 5) be anything but poor beggars; for there is no reason why Richard should call them 'harmless.' Nor could the beggars and vagabonds of Shakespeare's time be as a class so called; the representatives of them give them the very opposite character, and we know that they were hung by thousands in Henry VIII.'s time :

> 'Thoughts tending to content, flatter themselves
> That they are not the first of Fortune's slaves,
> Nor shall not be the last ; like *silly beggars*,
> Who sitting in the stocks, refuge their shame,
> That many have, and others must sit there.'

So in 1 Henry VI. (ii. 3) it is tolerably clear from the context that the Countess does not mean to call Talbot an inoffensive but a 'silly' weakly dwarf:

> 'Alas, this is a child, a *silly* dwarf!
> It cannot be this weak and writheld shrimp
> Should strike such terror to his enemies.'

And in Cymbeline (v. 3) 'poor habit' is a better gloss than plain, both from the context and from the passage (v. 1), where Posthumus says he will 'habit' himself as a Breton peasant, and lead the fashion of less without and more within. From 'weakly' we easily arrive at 'poor' or 'insignificant,' and one of the three meanings must be given to two of the quotations in RICHARD-SON's Dictionary, from HALL's Satires (vi. 1) and BROWNE's Pas-torals, as to the 'silly ant' or other insect compared with an elephant, or silly canoe of wood or bark as compared with builded vessels; while weakly, if not the main sense, is certainly involved in a third quotation from CHAPMAN (Iliad, b. viii.),

> 'O fools, to raise such *silly* forts,' &c.

In other passages also where this sense is not a necessity, it still seems to be involved and to give a much fuller meaning. The 'silly turtle doves' of The Presentation (st. i. line 2) are contrasted with 'empires ware,' and the infant's silly or weakly plaintive cries with the feeble tears of the next and parallel line of 'I die without Desert' (as before). PALSGRAVE also, as quoted by HALLIWELL, gives 'sely' as 'pavoreux;' and with this we may take 'she sighit sely sore,' and, against ELLIS and JAMIESON's 'wonderfully sore,' gloss it as '*piteously* sore,' and regard it as akin to PALSGRAVE's 'sely,' 'wretched' or '*meschant.*' 'Silly' ('sely') in David's Peccavi (st. i. line 3) seems to be best glossed by 'pavoreux,' as indicated by the first line of next stanza.

In st. iv. line 5, wag'd' = 'recompensed. G.

OF THE BLESSED SACRAMENT OF THE
AULTER.

In paschall feast, the end of auncient rite,
    An entraunce was to never-endinge grace ;
Tipes to the truth, dymm glymses to the light ;
    Performinge deed presaging signes did chase :
Christe's final meale was fountayne of our good,
For mortall meate He gave immortall foode.

That which He gaue, He was : O peerelesse gifte !
    Both God and man He was, and both He gaue.
He in His handes Himself did trewlye lifte,
    Farre off they see whome in them selves they have ;
Twelve did He feede, twelve did their feeder eate,
He made, He dressd, He gave, He was their meate.

They sawe, they harde, they felt Him sitting nere,
    Unseene, unfelt, unhard, they Him receivd ;
No diverse thinge, though divers it appeare ;
    Though sences faile, yet faith is not deceiv'd ;
And if the wonder of the worke be newe,
Beleive the worke because His worde is trewe.

Here truth beleefe, beleefe inviteth love,
    So sweete a truth Love never yett enjoy'd ;

What thought can thincke, what will doth best approve,
    Is here obteyn'd where no desire ys voyde :
The grace, the joy, the treasure here is such,
No witt can wishe, nor will embrace so much.

Self-love here cannot crave more then it fyndes ;
    Ambition to noe higher worth aspire ;
The eagrest famyn of most hungry myndes
    May fill, yea farre exceede their owne desire :
In summ here is all in a summ expressd,
Of much the most, of every good the best.

To ravishe eyes here heavenly bewtyes are ;
    To winne the eare sweete musick's sweetest sound ;
To lure the tast the angells' heavenly fare ;
    To sooth the sent divine perfumes abounde ;
To please the touch, He in our hartes doth bedd,
Whose touch doth cure the dephe, the dumm, the dedd.

Here to delight the witt trewe wisdome is,
    To wooe the will—of every good the choise ;
For memory, a mirrhor showing blisse ;
    Here's all that can both sence and soule rejoyce ;
And if to all, all this it do not bringe,
The fault is in the men, not in the thinge.

Though blynde men see no light, the sunne doth shyne ;
    Sweete cates are sweete, though fevered tastes deny it ;
Perles pretious are, though trodden on by swyne ;
    Ech truth is trewe, though all men do not trye it ;

The best still to the badd doth worke the worste ;
Thinges bredd to blisse do make them more accurst.

The angells' eyes, whome veyles cannot deceive,
    Might best disclose that best they do descerne ;
Men must with sounde and silent faith receive
    More then they can by sence or reason lerne ;
God's poure our proofes, His workes our witt exceede,
The doer's might is reason of His deede.

A body is endew'd with ghostly rightes ;
    And Nature's worke from Nature's law is free ;
In heavenly sunne lye hidd eternall lightes,
    Lightes cleere and neere, yet them no eye can see :
Dedd formes a never-dyinge life do shroude ;
A boundlesse sea lyes in a little cloude.

The God of hoastes in slender hoste doth dwell,
    Yea, God and man with all to ether dewe,
That God that rules the heavens and rifled hell,
    That man whose death did us to life renewe :
That God and man that is the angells' blisse,
In forme of bredd and wyne our nurture is.

Whole may His body be in smallest breadd,
    Whole in the whole, yea whole in every crumme ;
With which be one or be tenn thowsand fedd,
    All to ech one, to all but one doth cumme ;
And though ech one as much as all receive,
Not one too much, nor all too little have.

One soule in man is all in everye part ;
　　One face at once in many mirrhors shynes ;
One fearefull noyse doth make a thowsand start ;
　　One eye at once of countlesse thinges defynes ;
If proofes of one in many, Nature frame,
God may in straunger sort performe the same.

God present is at once in everye place,
　　Yett God in every place is ever one ;
So may there be by giftes of ghostly grace,
　　One man in many roomes, yett filling none ;
Sith angells may effects of bodyes shewe,
God angells' giftes on bodyes may bestowe.

What God as auctour made He alter may ;
　　No change so harde as making all of nought ;
If Adam framèd were of slymye claye,
　　Bredd may to Christe's most sacred flesh be wrought :
He may do this that made with mighty hande
Of water wyne, a snake of Moyses' wande.

NOTES AND ILLUSTRATIONS.

　　We give the above poem from our MS. (STONYHURST) with slight exceptions, noted in the places below. TURNBULL printed it with such errors as really turn it into nonsense, and prove him to have been incapable of so much as reading an old MS., even so plain a one as Addl. MS. 10.422. WALTER included it in his volume (1817), pp. 90-95. But a curious circumstance has now for the first time to be mentioned. This poem proves to be none other than 'The Christian's Manna,' which was ori-

ginally published in the edition of 1616, and repeated in that of
1620; but over which Editors and Bibliographers alike shook
their heads doubtfully; 'Mister Park' (to adopt RITSON's form)
pronouncing emphatically against it, and so after-editors and
bibliographers followed blindly.   It is now sufficiently plain
that its presence in the STONYHURST MS. (as before in Addl. MS.
10.422) establishes its authenticity and vindicates the integrity
of the Douai editors.   The texts of 1616 and 1620 present some
various readings that I have adopted, as noted.

Addl. MS. 10.422 differs from our MS. only orthographically,
except in the following: st. i. line 2, 'was' dropped: line 3,
'glymes' (= gleams) for 'glymses;' in 1616 and 1620 'glimpses,'
which gives the lacking syllable, and on which cf. St. John i. 9:
st. iii. line 5, misreads 'workes' for 'worke:' st. v. line 6, mis-
reads 'which' for 'much:' st. vii. line 1, 'will' for 'witt:' st.
xii. line 3, drops 'be' before 'tenn'—all faithfully continued by
TURNBULL, and in the last 'even,' ill supplied by him.   St. i.
contains reminiscences of SOUTHWELL's favourite hymn, 'Lauda
Sion Salvatorem' (st. iv.), with the sequence of the thoughts
reversed.   On another Shakesperean parallel in st. vi. see our
Memorial-Introduction.   In st. x. line 2, 'Nature's work . . . .'
= the wafer of the host: st. xi. line 6, 'angells' gifts'=His gifts
to angels.   I have adopted the following from 1616 and 1620:
st. vii. line 4, 'Here's' for 'Here:' st. x. line 2, 'And' for 'A
Nature's.'   I record, but do not accept, the following: st. iii.
line 6, 'the' for 'His:' st. iv. line 1, 'Here true beliefe of force
inuiteth love:' st. vi. does not appear in either edition : st. x.
line 1, 'indued :' st. xiii. line 2, 'glasses': lines 5-6,

> 'If proofe of one in many, Nature forme,
> Why may not God much more performe the same ?'

St. xv. lines 5-6,

> 'He still doth this, that made with mighty hand
> Of water wine, a snake of Moyses' wand.' G.

LAMENTS FOR A NOBLE LADY.

CLARA Ducum soboles, superis nova sedibus hospes,
 Clausit inoffenso tramite pura diem :
Dotibus ornavit, superavit moribus ortum,
 Omnibus una prior, parfuit vna sibi :
Lux genus ingenio, generi lux inclita virtus,
 Virtutique fuit mens generosa decus.
Mors minuit, properata dies orbamque reliquit,
 Prolem matre, virum conjuge, flore genus.
Occidit, ast alium tulit hic occasus in ortum,
 Vivit, ad occiduas non reditura vices.

Of Howarde's stemm a glorious braunch is dead,
 Sweete lightes eclipsèd were at her decease ;
In Buckhurst' lyne, she gracious yssue spredd,
 She heaven with two, with fower did Earth encrease :
Fame, honour, grace, gave ayre unto her breathe,
Rest, glory, joyes, were sequelles of her deathe.

Death aymd too highe, he hitt too choise a wighte,
 Renownde for birth, for life, for lovely partes ;
He kilde her cares, he brought her worthes to light,
 He robd our eyes, but hath enrichd our hartes :

He lett out of the arke a Noe's dove,
But many hartes are arkes unto her loue.

Grace, Nature, Fortune, did in hir conspire
    To shewe a proofe of their united skill :
Slye Fortune, ever false, did soone retyre,
    But double grace supplid false Fortune's ill :
And though she wrought not to her Fortune's pitch,
In Grace and nature fewe were founde so ritche.

Heaven of this heavenly perle is now possest,
    Whose lustre, was the blaze of Honnor's lighte ;
Whose substance pure, of every good the best,
    Whose price, the crowne of Vertue's highest right ;
Whose praise, to be her self ; whose greatest blisse,
To live, to love, to be where nowe she is.

NOTES AND ILLUSTRATIONS.

I have given a heading to these two poems, which appeared originally at close of SOUTHWELL's prose treatise in the form of ' A consolatorie Epistle,' entitled ' The Triumphs ouer Death.' Our text is that of the Stonyhurst MS., which is superior to that of 1596.

Latin, line 7 in 1596 is ' Mors muta at:' line 9, ' a se alium:' English, in Addl. MS. 10.422, st. i. line 2, ' in' for ' at :' st. ii. line 5, note also the very important reading of ' Hee' for the nonsensical ' Lot' of 1596 blindly repeated by TURNBULL : st. iii. line 5, ' raught' in 1596 = ' wrought' (see relative note on St. Peter's Complaint, st. ciii. line 2): ' her' dropped out by TURN-BULL: line 6, ' nature,' adopted for ' vertue:' st. iv. line 4, ' Vertue's' dropped in 1596, and ill-filled by TURNBULL's ' every.' G.

TO THE CHRISTIAN READER OF 'SHORT RVLES OF GOOD LIFE.'[1]

IF Vertue be thy guide,
    True comfort is thy path,
And thou secure from erring steps,
    That leade to vengeance' wrath.

Not widest open doore,
    Nor spacious wayes she goes ;
To straight and narrow gate and way,
    She cals, she leads, she shewes.

She cals, the fewest come :
    She leades, the humble sprited ;
She shews them rest at race's end,
    Soule's rest to heauen inuited.

'Tis she that offers most ;
    'Tis she that most refuse ;
'Tis she preuents the broad-way plagues,
    Which most do wilfull chuse ;

---

[1] Our text of this and three following is that of 1630. One obvious misprint, 'dog' for ' do,' in st. iv. line 4, is corrected. G.

Doe choose the wide, the broad,
　　The left-hand way and gate :
These Vice applauds, these Vertue loaths
　　And teacheth hers to hate.

Her waies are pleasant waies,
　　Vpon the right-hand side ;
And heauenly-happy is that soule
　　Takes Vertue for her guide.

A Preparatiue to Prayer.

When thou doest talke with God, by prayer I meane,[1]
　　Lift vp pure hands, lay downe all Lust's desires :
Fix thoughts on heauen, present a conscience cleane :
　　Such holy balme, to mercie's throne aspires.
Confesse faults' guilt, craue pardon for thy sinne ;
Tread holy paths, call grace to guide therein.

---

[1] Turnbull grossly misprints 'clear' for ' cleane,' notwith-
standing the rhyme with 'meane,' line 3; and in st. iv. line 2,
'servant' for 'seruants.' I have corrected 'blame' (st. i. line 4)
by ' balme,' which vindicates itself. St. iii. line 6, 'converts,'
verb neut. reflective=turns, changes: st. iv. line 4, 'impeach'
(Fr. empêcher)=hindrance, the literal and, in that day, com-
mon meaning : line 6 seems corrupted—qy. 'salvation's hill
on Mercie's wings'?

I am not sure that I do right in adhering to the divisions
and separate headings of 1630 in what must have been meant
by its Author to be one poem on prayer. In reading let these
separate headings be ignored, and thereby the reader will be

It is the spirit with reuerence must obey
    Our Maker's will, to practise what He taught;
Make not the flesh thy counsell when thou pray :
    'Tis enemie to euery vertuous thought :
It is the foe we daily feed and cloath :
It is the prison that the soule doth loath.

Euen as Elias, mounting to the skie,   *e'er.*
    Did cast his mantle to the Earth behind :
So, when the heart presents the prayer on high,
    Exclude the world from traffike with the mind.
Lips neere to God, and ranging heart within,
Is but vaine babbling and conuerts to sinne.

Like Abraham, ascending vp the hill
    To sacrifice ; his seruants left below,
That he might act the great Commander's will,
    Without impeach to his obedient blow ;
Euen so the soule, remote from earthly things ;
Should mount saluation's shelter, Mercie's wings.

---

relieved of the misconception which otherwise is inevitable as
to ' Oh, fortresse of the faithfull,' &c. (Ensamples, st. ii. line 1).
At present no one, till he reads farther and reconsiders, can
avoid taking it as an epithet of what is now the opening of
the poem and the subject of the first stanza, namely, our Sa-
viour. G.

The Effects of Prayer.

The sunne by prayer did cease his course, and staid ;
 The hungrie lions fawnd vpon their prey ;
A wallèd passage through the sea it made ;
 From furious fire it banisht heat away ;
It shut the heauens three yeares from giuing raine,
It opened heauens, and clouds powrd downe againe.

Ensamples of our Saviour.

Ovr Sauiour, (patterne of true holinesse,)
 Continuall praid, vs by ensample teaching,—
When He was baptized in the wildernesse,
 In working miracles and in His preaching ;
Vpon the mount, in garden-groues of death,
At His Last Supper, at His parting breath.

Oh ! fortresse of the faithfull, sure defence,
 In which doth Christians' cognizance consist ;
Their victorie, their triumph comes from thence,
 So forcible, hell-gates cannot resist :
A thing whereby both angels, clouds and starres,
At man's request fight God's reuengefull warres.

Nothing more gratefull in the Highest eyes,
 Nothing more firme in danger to protect vs,

Nothing more forcible to pierce the skies,

 And not depart till Mercy doe respect vs :

And, as the soule life to the body giues,

So prayer reuiues the soule, by prayer it liues.

NOTES.

St. ii. line 1, 'fortresse' = prayer : st. iii. line 4, 'respect' = to look back upon or again, hold in view, look upon considerately.

Part of one of these (the Preparation to Prayer) was prefixed to Bp. COSIN'S *Horæ:* but with some variations (pp. 16-18, Oxford reprint). Some of the Prayers in that book are taken from Southwell (which rather modifies what is said in the Oxford Preface from Evelyn, p. xii.): for example, on pp. 68-72, which is altered from one in Southwell's Rules of Good Life (latter part of sheet y, ed. 1630). G.

v.

POEMATA LATINA.

FROM THE MSS. OF THE AUTHOR.

Never before printed.

The whole of the following hitherto unprinted Latin Poems by SOUTHWELL are from his own MSS. now preserved in STONY-HURST COLLEGE, near Blackburn. They are written in fasci-culi distinct from the English Poems' MS. (on which see our Preface).

The first two pieces explain themselves—and for remarks on them and the others, reference may be made to our Me-morial-Introduction; but it may be well to note here, that the first of the Fragment of a Series of Elegies seems to relate to some disaster to the Spanish arms, probably the Armada collapse of 1588; that 'Elegia VIII.' is the lament of a husband for the death of his wife, in which there is a conceit running throughout, founded upon the idea of the one being ' *alter ego*' of the other; and that 'Elegia IX.' is historically interesting as being put into the ' fair lips' of the ' Shade' of Mary, Queen of Scots, and so a fitting companion to his English poem, ' Decease, Release. Dum morior, orior.' The shorter sacred poems are elucidated by their headings.

Even with the anxious assistance of the Rev. S. SOLE of St. Mary's College, Oscott, Birmingham, and the coöperation of the Rev. JOSEPH STEVENSON of the same College—to the latter of whom the whole of the SOUTHWELL MSS. of STONYHURST had been sent for calendaring in the Report of the Government Com-mission on (private) Historical MSS.—I cannot hope to have furnished an immaculate text. But no pains have been spared to make out the small and difficult handwriting, and it is believed few or no important errors will be found. Some words have been conformed to classical usage in the orthography. G.

POEMA DE ASSUMPTIONE B.V.M.

CUM cælum et tellus et vasti machina mundi,   1
Ponderibus librata suis, basis inscia, firmas
Sortita est sedes, et legibus omnia certis
In propriis digesta locis jam fixa manerent,
Extremum Deus urget opus, primosque parentes   5
Cunctarum format veluti compendia rerum.
Hos orbis statuit dominos, atque omnibus ornans
Deliciis, sacra paradisi in sede locavit.
Hic locus a primo mundi memorabilis ortu,
Consitus arboribus, leni quas aura susurro   10
Murmureque interflat molli, labensque per herbas
Dulcisonos ciet unda modos, paribusque recurrens
Flexibus, in varios per gramina finditur arcus.
Hic vagus incerto discurrens tramite piscis
Plurimus ignoti generis, dum lusibus instat   15
Decipit, et placide fallendo lumina mulcet.
Per ripas diffusa patet cum floribus herba,
Luxuriansque viget vario lætissima partu,
Quem sponte effudit curvo sine vomere tellus.
Hic rosa cum violis, cum calthis lilia certant ;.   20
Hic casiæ narcissus adest, hyacinthus acantho ;

Hic crocus et mixtis crescunt vaccinia bacis.
Quis dulces avium modulos, genus omne ferarum
Quis memoret, quis cuncta loci miracula narret?
Quicquid in immenso pulchri diffunditur orbe,   25
Et sparsum solumque alias aliasque per oras
Cernitur, hoc uno totum concluditur horto.

    Hæc sedes antiqua fuit, quam Lucifer Adæ
Invidit, tetrumque Erebi detrusus in antrum
Et cælo extorris, diro molimine fraudes   30
Intulit, et tectis veri sub imagine verbis
Lethiferum suasit morsum, cæloque rebelles
Reddidit, et victis Stygiæ cervicibus Aulæ
Imposuit servile jugum, placidisque fugatos
Sedibus, exilio gravibusque doloribus anxit.   35
Hic primum sua signa ferox victricia Pluto
Extulit, hic ultrix morbi mortisque potestas
Cœpit, et humanum genus in sua jura vocavit.

    Mox variis grassata modis mors tempore vires
Colligit, et cunctos nullo discrimine mactans   40
Imperat, et toto late dominatur in orbe.
Non minus heroas, proceres, mundique dynastas
Sceptrigerumque genus, quam vili stirpe creatos
Abripit, atque omnes vincens invicta triumphat;
Donec virgo, suæ vindex generosa parentis,   45
Se rabido victrix objecit prima furori
Mortis, et imperii sævas convellere leges
Orsa, satellitium mortis superavit, et ipsi
Terrorem incussit dominæ, quod corporis æqua

Temperies, vegetique artus, et vivida virtus   50
Lethiferis aditum præcluderet integra morbis.
Mors mirata suos contra hanc nil posse ministros,
Provectamque nihil solitis concedere telis,
Extremam imperio timet impendere ruinam.
Principiis igitur cupiens obsistere, totas   55
Intendit vires, atque omnia mente volutans,
Tartarei cogit proceres, monstra impia, regni.
Est vastum scabris sinuosum anfractibus antrum,
Solis inaccessum radiis, fundoque dehiscens,
Et ruptas reserans immani horrore cavernas.   60
Propatulo hic fluvius surgit Lethæus hiatu,
Ingentique ruens per concava saxa fragore,
Præcipitante rotat limosa volumina cursu,
Et dirum aggeribus spumans fremit unda repertis.
Hinc atque hinc atrata patent fuligine tecta,   65
Et loca senta situ, varios spirantia morbos,
Æternum spissæ squalent caligine mortis.
In medio solium, nulla spectabile pompa,
Informi obductum limo, sanieque perunctum,
Eminet, exesis diuturna ærugine fulcris.   70
   Hic annosa sedet canis mors horrida sætis,
Os macie, taboque genas confecta, cavisque
Immersos fossis oculos et livida circum
Dentes labra gerens turpique patentia rictu.
Hæc jubet : et raucis præco clamoribus auras   75
Personat, et medio manes compellat ab antro.
   Excita turba ruit cæcas furibunda per umbras,

Insolitos mirata sonos, atque ocius una
Conglomerata capit certas ex ordine sedes.
Fatales primum pariter sedere sorores,   80
Quæ levibus vitæ deducunt stamina fusis.[1]
Decrepita has sequitur baculoque innixa senectus,
Incultas diffusa comas, et membra caducis
Vix pedibus moribunda regens. Tum languida febris,
Et tussis, pituita, hydrops, et lurida pestis,   85
Phrenesis, cancer, porrigo, tormina, spasmus,
Et genus id, numerosa manus ; quibus undique septa
Mors spirans immane, oculis jaculantibus ignes,
Atque olidum truncis fumum de naribus efflans,
Terribiles ructat fremitus ; dein talia fatur.   90
       Atra cohors, nostris semper fidissima sceptris,
Olim quanta fuit Lethei gloria regni
Qua Phœbus, qua luna suos agit aurea currus,
Quas bello edidimus strages, quot funere reges
Mersimus, et totum quoties consumpsimus orbem   95
Non latet, et vestris cecidit pars maxima telis.
Vos etenim spissos animarum ad Tartara nimbos
Præcipites egisse subit, plenisque voracem
Exsatiasse hominum functorum messibus Orcum.
Numquid tanta ruet virtus ingloria, et uni   100
Noster cedet honos ? Sic formidabile numen
Imperiumque ruet, sic nostris hostia templis
Deficiet, tantique cadent fastigia regni ?
Est mulier, mulier nostris contraria fatis,

[1] In margin ' vel mensurant.' G.

Omni labe carens, nullæque obnoxia culpæ :   105
Illius hæc genetrix Christi est, qui immanibus ausis
Tartareos subiit fines, et victor opimis
Ditatus spoliis, superas evasit ad auras,
Et raptam æthereis prædam celer intulit astris.
Quem timeo, nostræ ne forte injurius aulæ   110
Antiquas violet leges, matremque (quod absit)
Viribus eripiat nostris, animosque ministret,
Ut prædas actura istis sine sole cavernis
Succedat, manesque suis exturbet ab antris.
Nec timor hic ratione caret, nam vidimus illum   115
Qui velut hæc sine labe fuit, victricibus armis
Tartareos superasse deos.   Pro dicite, cives,
Quid sit opis, quid consilii, qua hoc arte queamus
Propulsare malum. Vos ista pericula tangunt.
Cernitis ut nullos admittat corpore morbos,   120
Et vestras ludat vires?   Proh sola revellet
Jura per innumeros annorum fixa recursus
Femina?   Sic omnes cœpto desistere victos
Post tot sæcla decet? Scelus est... Hic plura volentem
Dicere, non patitur rabies, et marcida circum   125
Fauces spuma fluens, imis quam sæva medullis
Ira furorque ciet.   Veluti cum verbere tactus
Stat sonipes, pressisque furens detentus habenis,
Frena ferox pleno spumantia mergit in ore.
Mox varias edit confuso murmure voces   130
Circumposta cohors, strepitu reboante per auras ;
Qualis ad excussos sequitur de nubibus ignes.

Subjectis ardent irarum pectora tædis,
Atque odiis fervent animi, crudusque per artus
Livor et ossa ruit; cæcus rapit impetus omnes.   135
Arma fremunt, sævit belli scelerata cupido,
Certatimque feras sese exhortantur in iras,
Et patrias jurant tutari sanguine sedes.
Non secus ac subitis populus temerarius ausis,
Audito belli sonitu, furit undique præceps,   140
Atque omni sine lege ruit, nil mente retractans
Quid fieri expediat, sed quid novus ingerat ardor.

 Verum ita concussos animis grandæva senectus,
Longe aliud secum meditans, sic ore moratur:

 Siste gradum, generosa cohors, haud irrita forsan 145
Verba loquar, nostris aures advortite dictis.
Nobilis ut vidéo vobis vigor insidet, altum
Mens agitat bellum, claris crebrescere factis
Fert animus, juvat et superis indicere divis
Prœlia; nos etiam votis si cetera nostris   150
Congruerent, avidi tantos ambimus honores.
Sed frustra hoc temptamus opus. Quibus æthera telis
Pervia censetis? quæ non molimina vincet
Qui potis est totum delere et condere mundum?
Jampridem sensere immanes mole gigantes   155
In superos quid bella queant. Et Lucifer ille,
Orbe sub empireo rutilanti in sede refulgens,
Cum sibi divinos temere[1] poscebat honores,

  [1] 'Temerĕ' is an oversight, but we must leave it, as with
'nisi,' &c. G.

Haud potuit retinere suos, sed, pulsus in imas
Terrarum latebras, pœnas exsolvit acerbas. 160
His præstat didicisse malis, quam vana furentes
In cælum temptare nefas, et cedere victos.
Consilium rursus capitote, expendite causas,
In melius mutasse animos prudentia summa est.
Si mea canities, mea si sententia pondus 165
Momentumque habeat, bellorum insana cupido
Cesset, et in summi referamus verba Tonantis
Judicium, qui nec Stygiis injurius unquam
Sedibus esse potest, cujusque in numine lis est.

 Hæc ubi dicta dedit, torpent in prœlia vires, 170
Infractique cadunt animi, mentesque coacta
Pax tenet, et junctis rata fit sententia votis.

 Nuntius extemplo liquidas sublimis in auras
Tollitur, et facili tranans per inane volatu
Arduus insurgit, Lethæique acta Senatus 175
Exponens superis, avidus responsa requirit.

 Tunc Deus, ostentans æquato examine lances,
Esto, ait, æquus ero, causa exagitetur utrinque :
Cui ratio, cui jura favent, victoria cedat.

 Mox partes actura suas mors ferrea præsto est, 180
Et sævum frendens rabido sic intonat ore :
O rerum qui summa tenes, quid jura revellis,
Et male nil meritam dubiis terroribus angis ?
Quid merui, quid commisi, quæ crimina tandem
Sic multanda vides, nostris ut legibus istam 185
Eripias, et prisca ruat labefacta potestas ?

Mortalis nata est, et carnis credita moles
Communem redolet massam; caro terrea terræ
Reddatur, maneat[1] simili sub pulvere pulvis.
Adamo ex patre est, cujus cum cetera proles   190
Illius ob culpam parcis obnoxia sumat
Corpora, cur mortem hæc et ineluctabile fatum
Effugiat, cur funereas transire per umbras
Abnuat, et victrix reliquis magis una triumphet?

    Hæc ait, at Gabriel causam contrarius urget   195
Virginis, adversoque potens sermone tuetur.
Nosti, ait, alme Pater, quos mors tellure repostos
In sua jura rapit, primi contracta parentis
Aspergit maculosa lues; et cedere fatis
Culpæ pœna fuit.   Sed virgo hæc, criminis exors, 200
Cur luat immeritas omnino innoxia pœnas?
Id Christi genetricis erat sponsæque tonantis,
Ut pura infectos transiret sola per artus,
Communique carens culpa, mala debita culpæ
Haud ferret.   Nullis Deus est nisi sontibus ultor. 205

    His ita respondet solio Deus orsus ab alto:
Judicium hoc esto.   Venerandæ virginis almus
Spiritus astra petat, sanoque e corpore migret
Non mortis sed amoris ope, et violenta doloris
Vis nulla impediat, sit summa exire voluptas.   210
Tunc mors dira fremit, lapsumque in viscera torquet
Invidiæ furiale malum, disrumpitur ira

    [1] Above 'maneat' is written 'redeat;' but as 'maneat' is
not erased, we retain it. G.

Morborum infelix acies, et inutile frendens
Vipeream expirat rabiem. Demum acrius instat
Ut saltem extinctum liceat dissolvere corpus.   215
Ast superi contra insurgunt, et nescia labis
Cælo membra petunt, animæ decora alta beatæ.
   Annuit Omnipotens. Divum sonat aula triumphis.
Virgo poli regina sedet, mors victa fugatur.   219

FILII PRODIGI PORCOS PASCENTIS AD
PATREM EPISTOLA.

Sɪ tam longinquis rogites quis scripsit ab oris,
   Vel ferat unde rudes sordida charta notas,
Inspice, suffusis quamvis maculosa lituris
   Littera scriptoris nomen et omen habet.
Continet illa meos plenos formidine casus,[1]   5
   Illa dabit nati facta scelesta tui ;
Et licet ingrato sordent elementa colore,
   Sunt tamen hæc domino candidiora suo.
Quippe, quod emerui, lutulentis[2] versor in antris,
   Nilque nisi obscenum lumina nostra vident.   10
Non mihi divitiæ, non fulvi copia nummi,
   Præstitit ut quondam, nunc quoque præstat opem.

----

[1] In margin, as an apparent alternative line for this : ' Illa
meum referet ter lamentabile fatum.' G.
[2] Mis-written ' lutosis.' G.

Haud inopem fallax comitatur vulgus ut olim,
    Nec, qualis fuerat, jam famulatus adest.
Ornatæ desunt radianti murice vestes,   15
    Nec phaleris tecti subjiciuntur equi;
Omnia nimboso fluxere simillima vento,
    Nec facies rebus, quæ fuit ante, manet.
Hei volvit fortuna rotam, ventisque solutis
    Disrupit nostram perniciosa ratem.   20
Aurea deperiit, nunc ferrea prodiit ætas;
    Sunt læta in tristes tempora versa dies.
Quæque prius ventis pergebant vela secundis,
    Et pontum ut faciles edomuere lacus,
Acta ruunt inter Scyllas interque Charybdes   25
    Et fracta adversis dilacerantur aquis.
Heu parva infandum liquerunt gaudia luctum!
    Heu ruptum liquit vipera parta latus!
Jam placidæ periere dies, tristesque secutæ;
    Ultima lætitiæ prima doloris erat.   30
Sors ea dura quidem, sed nostris debita factis,
    Immo est errato lenior ira meo.
Cum miser ignotas veni peregrinus in oras,
    Pronus in interitum, pro dolor! ipse meum,
Totus in insanos effudi tempora luxus,   35
    Tempora vulneribus jam redimenda meis.
Seque mihi juveni juvenes junxere sodales,
    Et ruitura simul plurima turba fuit.
Raptus in exitium, sociis agitantibus, ivi;
    Aut comes aut princeps ad scelus omne fui,   40

Utque pudor faciem, pietas sic pectora liquit.
　　Calluit a multis mens hebetata malis,
Nec mihi cura Dei, propriæ nec cura salutis,
　　Sola videbatur cæca libido salus.
Sic ego tartareis merces certissima monstris,　　45
　　Tartareos retuli jam nova dira canes ;
Non furiis actus furiosa videbar Erinys,
　　Nec mihi sub stygiis par fuit ullus aquis.
Hæc mea vita fuit, si possit vita vocari
　　Quæ tulit ad mortis perniciosa fores.　　50
Hoc mea lustravit nimium vaga carbasus æquor,
　　Alta quoad plenam sustulit unda ratem :[1]
Sed modo saxosi portus anfractibus hærens,
　　Corruit ablatis naufraga puppis aquis.
Jamque luo pœnas, turpis fero præmia vitæ ;　　55
　　Obruor innumeris exul egensque malis.
Ah ! lacer ex humeris algenti pendet amictus,
　　Cetera marmoreo frigore membra rigent,
Et male contecti madefiunt imbribus artus ;
　　Quin lacerant nudam verbera sæpe cutim.　　60
Continuis lassæ callent grunnitibus aures,
　　Læta est in tales musica versa sonos :
Sunt etenim porci mensæ, lectique sodales,
　　Unus eis cibus est, unus et ille mihi.
Horridus inculto pendet de fronte capillus,　　65 .
　　Nec caput a ventis quod tueatur adest.

---

[1] There is little doubt SOUTHWELL meant 'quoad' and 'eis'
(line 64) for dissyllables. G.

Dum facies liquida pallens respondet ab unda,
    Quæ quondam a speculo reddita sæpe fuit,
Dissimiles surgunt antiqua ab imagine vultus,
    Nec species eadem, quæ fuit ante, manet ;   70
Quippe novas macies induxit in ora figuras.
    Vix cutis, exesis carnibus, ossa tegit ;
Squalida languentes febris depascitur artus,
    Imaquo pervasit tabidus ossa dolor,
Nec mihi curandis dantur medicamina morbis.   75
    Tu nisi succurras, non feret alter opem.
Hei ! tua sum, genitor, tua sum, licet impia proles,
    Ni mala quæ fuerit, desinat esse tua.
Te genitore fui proles, non impia proles,
    Impia, me misero, me genitore, fui.   80
Aspice tu prolem, proles dedit impia pœnas
    Atque tulit meritis præmia digna suis ;
Inque dies funesta magis tormenta supersunt,
    Et mala præteritis deteriora malis ;
Mille animum curæ, corpus mala mille fatigant,   85
    Intus nulla datur, nec foris[1] ulla quies.
O quam difficiles portendunt omnia casus,
    Tu nisi mature tristia fata leves.
Hei citus affer opem, dextramque extende cadenti,
    Quæ data vita mihi, morsque negata foret.   90

---

[1] ' Foris' is here an adverb = ' out of doors.' But in classical Latin the ' *is* ' is always and necessarily long; and so here again is a false quantity. G.

O pater, O nati spes summa et sola salutis,
 Sis pater et nati sit tibi cura tui.
En scelus agnoscit, lacrimis commissa fatetur,
 Parcere peccanti munus amoris erit :
Peccavi, fateor, sceleris mens conscia luget,   95
 Erroresque luunt singula membra suos ;
Scilicet et veniam sceleris mens conscia poscit,[1]
 Nec nisi peccanti parcere posset amor.
Parcat amor, vincat pietas, iræque facessant,
 Plus tua te virtus, quam mea facta regant.   100
Nec quia me cernis factum de prole rebellem,
 Tu fieri judex ex genitore velis.
Quamvis si fieres, nunquam te judice tantis
 Esset, credo equidem, subdita vita malis.
Cur tua deserui redamati limina tecti !   105
 Cur mea subtraxi lumina mæsta tuis !
Sic visum est superis, hæc me fortuna manebat,[2]
 Hæc mihi, dura licet, pœna ferenda fuit.
Ah, Deus, ecce tuli, sævos jam comprime fluctus,
 Et petat optatos lassa carina sinus.   110
Per mare, per scopulos, per mille agitata Charybdes,
 Mitius ah tandem, te duce, pergat iter.

---

[1] Line 97 is written in four ways in the MS., somewhat confusedly: 1. As above. 2. Scilicet et veniæ segetem mea facta ministrant. 3. Materiam veniæ mea sors miseranda ministrat. 4. Non quærit veniam qui nil commisit iniqui. G.

[2] This line is thus written on the margin : Scilicet hos superis placuit me volvere casus. G.

O mihi si patrios liceat revidere penates,
    O mihi si felix luceat ille dies,
Ante ruet cœlum tendetque ad sidera tellus   115
    Et mare siccatis fluctibus ignis erit,
Quam quæram ignotas iterum novus advena terras,
    Quamvis quærenti regia sceptra dares.
Patria ! dulce solum ! quod si mihi visere detur,
    Nec me divelli mortuus inde sinam ;   120
Condicio melior patriis in sedibus Iri est,
    Quam Crœsi magnas exulis inter opes.
Ergo cara tui pateant mihi limina tecti,
    Et videam notos post fera fata lares.
Sin minus, externis moriar peregrinus in oris,   125
    Nec tumuli ritum qui mihi præstet erit,
Sed sine funeribus nullo curante relinquar,
    Et miseranda feris præda cadaver erit.
O si forte brevi tales tibi littera casus
    Adferat, et nati talia fata tui,   130
Quæ sibi mens, quis sensus erit, cum, te orta parente,
    Audieris rabidas membra vorasse feras ?
Tunc fortasse gemens sobolis vel busta requires,
    Quam poteras vivam nunc habuisse domi.
Tunc, si me renuas, memorans renuisse dolebis,   135
    Atque tuo duplex imber ab ore fluet.
Obvia sæpe animo defuncti occurret imago,
    Junctaque cum lacrimis plurima verba dabis,
Ast aderit nullus nisi tristes fletibus umbræ
    Et rapiet gemitus ventus et aura tuos.   140

Tunc dolor invadet quem non invaserat olim,
    Quique sepultus erat, vulnere surget[1] amor.
Ille quidem surget, sed nostros serus in usus,
    Cum nulla optatæ spes opis esse potest.
Nunc igitur,[2] O nunc, dum spes manet ulla salutis, 145
    Succurre, et tantis obvius ito malis.
Quodque mihi, O genitor, solus concedere posses,
    Accipe supremum prolis ab ore vale.

---

[1] Above 'surget' is written 'vivet.' G.

[2] The 'ŭr' of 'igitŭr' is here made long. By transposing
the second 'nunc' and ' O,' and reading ' Nunc igitur, nunc O
dum,' &c. the false quantity would be avoided, whether the au-
thor's or not. G.

FRAGMENT OF A SERIES OF ELEGIES.

There appear to be a part of No. 7, the whole of No. 8, and a part of No. 9. These follow in the order of the MS. G.

*   *   *   *   *

Ex luctu populus, redditur ipse chalybs.
Conclamant Celtæ celsos periisse Monarchas,
    Nec conclamato funere liber Iber.
Ferales Nebrissa rotat mutata cupressos;
    Nulla premit laurum præfica, laurus abi.   5
Quin formidatos armat Carteia nepotes,
    Tam sævæ cupiens arma movere neci.
Cantaber et Vasco demptum sibi plorat honorem;
    Nunc onus est illis quilibet alter honos.
Hunc fati lusum flet Lusitanus et inquit,   10
    Quæ mors dicenda est, si jocus ille fuit ?
Bisseni,[1] clamant, ' bisseni' cedite menses :
    Omnis in hoc obitu scilicet annus obit.
Ecce jacet fusis gens Castellana maniplis,
    Hoc tumulo vires perdidit, atque viros.   15
Ex merito Latium nomen sortire latendi ;
    Hac terra, Latii condita terra, lates !

[1] Query, the Spaniards; so named from some province of Spain ? Biscay (?); and qy. read Biscani ? G.

Quid quod et Eoi pariter, gens altera mundi,
  Sensit de cælo lumina rapta suo !
Quid quod et Æthiopes membris nigrantibus horrent! 20
  A luctu credo provenit ille color.
Heu, dicunt, periisse Peru ! mens naufraga currit.
  Quo ferar? ah periit qui modo portus erat.
India tota gemit passis diffusa capillis :
  Ortus in occasum Margaris omnis abit.   25
Hei mihi ! cur lacrimas alio peto sole tepentes ?
  Ut doleam tellus nempe petenda nova est.
Quid faciam ? vidi lugentes fluminis undas ;
  Et vidi lacrimas, utraque terra, tuas.
Perge, anime, in fletum, tepuerunt marmora fletu,   30
  Ergone marmoribus tu mage durus eris ?
Ingemuit pontus, gemuit quoque terra dolore,
  Et ponto et terra tu mage sævus eris ?
Ah doleo ! testes superi ! mea Margaris, eheu !
  Margaris, heu ! luctus hæc quoque testis erit.   35
Non doleam? mea vita fugit, mea Margareta !
  Hoc solo steterat nomine vita mihi.
Non doleam ? sensus animæque evanuit ardor !
  Quis poterit vitæ jam superesse calor ?
Deficio, subsido : dolor ! dolor ! expirabo !   40
  Jam satis est, luctus tu tege, terra, meos.

ELEGIA VIII.

Dic ubi nunc quod amo est! ubinam quod semper
    amavi?
  Hei mihi! vel quod amo, vel quod amabo perit?
Non perit: illa præit; sed amans sectatur amantem;
    Haud sequor, haud igitur me præit; ergo perit.
Non perit, at patrium vivis bibit æthera labris :   5
    Me solum duplici morte perire jubet.
Sic quod amas animas? quod amas sinis ecce perire;
    Si sinis hoc, cinis est, nam calor inde fugit.
Si calor hinc remeat, mortis me frigus adurit :
    Dic ubi sit gemini pectoris unus amor?   10
Tu vel ego[1] duo sunt? non sunt : quid? fallimur ambo;
    Sint duo, non duo sunt, una vel unus eris.
Una vel unus ero : qui legem novit amoris,
    Unum non uno pectore pectus habet.
An bene dinumeras? Ego, tu; duo nomina fingis : 15
    Ast unum duplici nomine numen inest.
Numen inest; cor corde premit, mentemque maritat;
    Non duo tu vel ego, sint duo corda licet.
Sim tuus et mea sis, sint vincula bina duorum :
    Simus et hic ambo; non tamen ambo sumus.   20
Quid queror! haud moreris; duo sunt nam corpore in
    uno,
    Sic vivum nostro corpore corpus habes :

----

[1] See former note : egō. G.

Aut ego jam perii, duo sunt nam corpore in uno ;
    Sic mea sunt tumulo membra sepulta tuo.
Sed neque jam morior, neque tecum vivere possum : 25
    Hoc vivo, possum quod memor esse tui.
Hoc est, quod moriens, rerum pulcherrima, dixti :
    Nomen tu memori pectore semper habe !
Et licet hinc absim, sit præsens conjuge conjux :
    Defungor : functæ tu quoque vive mihi. 30
Dixi ego, ne dubita, memori vivemus amore,
    Quam tuus ipse tuus, tam mea semper eris.
Jam mea semper eris, licet hic mea diceris absens ;
    Pectoribus statuam dicta suprema meis.
Quamque mihi dictum, tam tu mihi semper adhæres, 35
    Et dicti et vitæ mors erit una meæ.
Non mihi votorum reddet lux ulla tuorum
    Tædia ; quis tantæ non meminisse potest ?
In præsente tamen præsentem quæro ; quid illud ?
    Fascinor ? absenti num mihi semper ades ? 40
At forsan nequeunt oculi te ferre sequentes ?
    Si nequeo visu te, modo mente feram.
Aut age ! quod menti deerit, supplebit ocellus :
    Sic mens, sic oculus testis amoris erit.
Sic animus lamenta dabit, lacrimabit ocellus ; 45
    Commodus ad partes fiet uterque meas.
Quodque animus celat, non hoc celabit ocellus ;
    Mens secum tacite, sed gemet ille palam.
Ite palam, lacrimæ, servati pignus amoris ;
    Ille mihi leto non nisi cedet amor : 50

E E

Ite palam, gemino dolor hic spectabitur orbe :
  Hic dolor est, hic est quem pius auget amor.
Lamentor, queror, usque queror, gemo, lugeo, plango,
  Langueo : languorem dicere vultis? amo.
Nunc molem sine mole feram, sine pondere pondus ; 55
  Nunc labor, minima nunc ego mole gravor.
Dicite quid sit amor? pondusne est, an mage penna?
  Penna mihi levis est, et grave pondus amor.
Excutio pondus, rapidis me intersero pennis,
  Queis vaga sublimis sidera carpit amor.   60
Ah amo ! sed quid nam? vel ubi? mea sidera novi :
  Hic quod amo superest, huc volo, terra, vale.

ELEGIA IX.

UMBRA REGINÆ NOBILES VIROS DOCET, QUID SIT DE
REBUS HISCE FLUXIS SENTIENDUM.

Quid conclamato jacis irrita vota sepulchro ?
  Quam petis, in vili non remoratur humo.
Nunc ingens cælorum heres, nunc hospita cæli,
  Affigo superis parta tropæa polis
Verte alio lacrimas, sanguis meus, inclytus ordo,   5
  Inde toga gravior, fortior inde sago.
Plange ; sed O quid nam ?   Stulti ludibria mundi !
  Pars magna est animi forsitan ille tui.
Quid pretii pretium ?   Quid habet decus omne decoris ?
  Non sunt hæc animo digna potente coli.   10

Cernis opes? Pictæ sunt fulva umbracula massæ,
 Est raptrix animi copia; cernis opes.
Divitiis vitiis inhias? reus aureus ipse es :
 Fies inter opes non nisi semper inops.
Vanus honor; tumidi sunt oblectamina sensus,   15
 Marcida gloriolæ pabula; vanus honor.
Res nulla est, bulla est, res futilis, utilis illis
 Queis inhonorus honor non honor est sed onus.
Vana Venus; cæcæ sunt irritamina culpæ,
 Dementis mentis toxica; vana Venus.   20
Fallacem faciem cerussat amaror amoris,
 Dum mala proponit mala venusta Venus.
Este procul tellus, et inania munera terræ;
 Munera non ullo respicienda die.
Pluma volat : pueri totis complexibus instant.   25
 Umbra fugit; pressus præterit illa tuos.
Ros est; si pelago rapitur, fit protinus unda.
Unda . . . .

The four following poems are written in a very small, careful hand, on a fold of paper (32mo) of eight pages: the poems occupy three pages only. G.

JESUS. MARYE.

AD DEUM IN AFF[LICTIONE] : ELEGIA.

Tu tacitas nosti lacrimas, tu saucia cernis
    Pectora, secreto quod cremer igne vides ;
Tu, quoties tristi ducam suspiria corde,
    Tu, quoties pro te mors mihi grata foret.
Vivo tamen, si vita potest quam duco vocari,   5
    Quippe cui[1] mors est vivere, vita mori.
Namque procul mea vita fugit qua vivere vellem,
    Et fera qua nollem vivere vita venit :
Hæc me dum fugio sequitur, fugit illa sequentem.
    Persequor et fugio, luctus utrinque mihi ;   10
Nec fugiens capior, nec euntem carpere possum.
    Hei mihi, qui versa vivere sorte dabit !

[1] SOUTHWELL makes 'cui,' according to very late usage, an iambus, cŭī, whereas in the silver age, Seneca, Martial, and Juvenal first began to use it as a dissyllable, but a pyrrhic dissyllable, cŭĭ. G.

AD SANCTAM CATHERINAM, VIRGINEM ET MARTYREM.

Tu Catherina, mei solatrix unica luctus,
  O soror et Christi sponsa decora, veni.
Dic mihi cur tacitis intus miser ignibus urar,
  Dic mihi cur mordax viscera luctus edat.
Nonne potes, si vis, nostros in gaudia fletus   5
  Vertere? quid prohibet? tu, Catherina, potes,
Quippe suæ nunquam sponsæ renegare maritus
  Vel minimum casto quod petit ore potest.
Huc igitur, dilecta Deo, tua lumina flecte,
  Aspice quam multis mens [labet] icta malis.[1]   10
Ferre cito O digneris opem, pulcherrima virgo,
  Atque extinguendis ignibus affer aquas.
Cui Deus injussus venit obvius, ipsa rogata,
  Quæso, veni nobis mitis, ut ipse tibi.
Quoque tuum pepulit[2] Christus medicamine morbum, 15
  Hoc nostro luctum pectore pelle, precor.
Cumque dolor similis, quæ te medicina juvaret[3]
  Cur potius nostris esset inepta malis?
Si mihi concedas, dubio procul angor abibit,
  Quæque tibi fuerat, nunc erit apta mihi.   20
Virgo sancta, vale, Christi sanctissima martyr,
  Terque quaterque vale, sisque benigna mihi.

[1] This line is defective: 'labet' filled in to complete it: 'ruat'
or 'cadat' will do equally well. G.

[2] In the ms. SOUTHWELL wrote 'pepulit,' and changed it him-
self to 'repulit:' but the former seems better. G.

[3] Or juvabat mis-written juvavit. The perfect is juvit. G.

IN RENOVATIONEM VOTORUM, FESTIS NATALIS DOMINI.

Vita venit, vitæ cnm votis obvius ito,
　　Et veniet votis obvia vita tuis.
Vita quod est tibi dat, tu vitæ reddę teipsum,
　　Et tibi per vitam vita perennis erit.
At quinam poteris melius te reddere vitæ,　　　　　5
　　Quam si, qui vita est, des tua vota Deo ?
Des igitur tua vota Deo, dabit ipse seipsum,
　　Et reddet votis præmia viva[1] tuis.

IN FESTUM PENTECOSTES, ANNO DOMINI 1580, 21 MAII.

Postquam, tartarei spoliis ditatus Averni,
Vi propria superas Christus rediisset ad auras,
Divino angelicas inter splendore phalanges
Conspicuus summas cæli se tollit in arces.
Tamque expectatum cælestis turba triumphum　　　5
Aspicit, atque hominum longi pars mortua luctus
Præmia degustat.   Solus miser incola terræ
Angustam patitur sortem, duroque laborum
Pondere depressus, querulo petit ore juvantem.
Respice sublimi clemens de sede gementes　　　　10
In terris populos.   Cur nos ardentibus ustos
Curarum flammis et saucia corda gerentes

　　　[1] The ms. reads vita, but wrongly: and we substitute ' viva.'

Deseris? hei miseris quis nos solabitur ultra?
Sufficit exilium, patriique absentia regni ;
Sufficiunt varii casus diuturnaque pœna 15
Quam caro, quam mundus, quam dæmonis impetus in-
    fert.
Si plura imponas, nimia sub mole gravati
Decidimus ; sed et hæc propria virtute nequimus
Ferre, nisi [et] nostras divina potentia mentes
Fulciat, et tenues confirmet numine vires. 20
Eja igitur, celer huc pietatis lumina flecte,
Ut, qui cælicolas dulci solaminis aura
Perfundis, Limbique patres sperata tenere
Præmia concedis, media regione locatos
Haud mæstos remanere sinas, sed qualia saltem 25
Mens humana potest, carnis complexa catenis,
Gaudia tam varios inter gustare dolores,
Non renuas ; ut, te triplicem solante catervam,
Te triplici laudet cælum, Styx, terra, camena.
    Has adeo mæstas pietas divina querelas 30
Suscipiens, miserum placido medicamine morbum
Atque infelices statuit curare ruinas.
Expansis igitur sacræ penetralibus aulæ,
Tertia de superis placido persona meatu
Sedibus egreditur, tenuesque elapsa per auras 35
Versus apostolicum properans se contulit agmen.

ADDITIONAL NOTES AND ILLUSTRATIONS.

1. As stated in Memorial-Introduction (p. lxxxvi.), I here give the remaining interlineations and studies for St. Peter's Complaint from the Stonyhurst autograph MSS., as follows:

VERSE II.

The bowes which [shott the fa . . .—erased] leveld at his dolful
    brest [*sic*]
The sharpest arows and most deadly flyghtes
Were theis of Chryste, when they on him did rest
These ey[erased] were bowes there lookes lyke arowes lyght
Which not content to hurt his heavy hart
glanced to the Soule
Even pea lanced the Sowle [erased] and wounded in such wise
      he was fayne till
That al his dayes while life did quyte departe
  so   still
He oynted it with liquour of his eies.
       [In margin—To oynt the wounde to bath the sores.]

VERSE III.

  This verse it is difficult to copy.
          once to a minion bold   face
Thre severall tymes [twyse—erased] by two handmades woyce
    Next to a man last to that revyl [or renyl] rout
[And last by meanes of that accursed crue—erased]
  bought [*sic*]   he was not of the fold
He sed and swore [that he new folower was, made his choise—
    erased].
      adherents   never
Of Chrysts whome he [denyed that he knew—erased]
[To folowe Chryst a man he never knew—erased]
But when
        The cocke had chased out this [stubborne—erased] brall
                as   thing
    [thrall?] and brought in day for witnes of the cryme

[When as—erased] the [whe—erased] wretch scarse markyng
stubborn
yet his fall
Did with his eies meete theies of Christ his King.

VERSE IV.

In what distresse pore peater did remayne
At this encountrynge ech with others eies
Let no man vant that he cann make it playne
No tunge can reache the truthe scarce mynde surmyse
It seemed that Chryst amids that juysh crew
Forlorne of frends these speaches did rehorse
Behold that which I sayed is now to viewe
O frende disloyall, disciple fierce.

VERSE V.

No youthful dame her beautuouse face in glasse
Of christall bryghtnes did so wel discrye easely prie
As thy old sely wret did in this passe
foul de-
In th' eies of Chryst his filthy falt espye
Nor egre eare though covetous to heare
preache
And without pause attent to teachers speache
Could learne so much in twyce two hundred yeares
in a turne
As with one looke he did in moment reach.

VERSE VI. ETC.

Lyke as sometyme (though it unworthy be
  To lyken sacred matters with profane)
  [In margin—Profaned things in holy talk to name]
By lookes a lover secret thoughtes can se
  And searche the hart thoughe it no wordes do frame
Let amorous knyghts traynd up in cupids schoole
Teache those which are unskilful in this art
How without usynge tong or wrytynge toole
By lookes the lovers know ech others hart
The eies may serve for to display the hart
Ech eie of Chryst a running tungue did seeme
ech lyk a listning
And peters eis so many eagre eared
  [In margin—Eche ey of peter like a listninge eare]

Prest to receyue the voyce and it esteame
According to that sense that it should beare
More fierce he seemed to say ar thy eis
Then the impious hands which shall naile me on the crosse
Nether feele I any blow which do so annoy me
Of so many which this gylty rable doth on me lay
As that blow which came out of thy mouth.
None faythful found I none courteous
Of so many that I have vouchsafned to be myne
But thow in whome my   was more kyndled [sic]
Art faythlesse and ungratefull above all other
All other with there (cowardly) flyght did onely offend me
                                    my
But thow hast denyed and now with the other [foes] ghilty
Standest feedynd thy eies with my damage [and sorowes]
As though part of this pleasur belonged unto the.

ANOTHER VERSE.

Who by one and one could count
The wordes of wrath and of love full
Which peter seemed to se imprinted
In the holy gyre [compasse] those two calme eyes, it would
          make him brast that could understand [conceive] them:
For if from mortall eie often cometh
Virtue, which hath force in us, He which proveth [this] let him
          gesse
What an eie divyne [or of God] is able to worke in man's senses.

As a fold [or feld?] of snow which frosen
The winter in close valew hiddyn laye
At the sprynge tyde of the son heated
Doth quyte melt and resolve into water
So the feare which enterred was in the frozen heart
Of peter then when the truth he conceled
When toward him his eies he turned
Did quyte thaw and unto teares was resolved.

He [sic] teres or weepyng were not as river or torrent
Which at the scorchyng hot season could ever dry upp
For though Chryst Kyng of heaven immayntenant
Did retorne him the grace which he had lost
Yet all the remnant of his lyfe

There was never nyght but therein he did wake
Herynge the cock tell him how unfayful he had ben
And gevinge new teares to his old falt
That face which litle before had ben
Attyned with the coloure of death
By reason of the blood which was retyred to the harte
Levyng th' other parts cold and pale
Of the beames of those holy eies warmed
    as red as fyre
Waxed flame and by the same dores
That feare entred it vanished away
And in his duo place shame appeared
Vewynge the wrech how diverse
From his former state he founde him self
His hart not suffysyng him to stand there presente
Before his offended lord that so had loved him
Without taryance for the fierce or mercyful
Sentence which the hard tribunal seat did give on him
From that odious house hated house that then he was in
Weepyng bitterly he went forth
And desyrous to encounter some that just penance [and payn]
Would geve him for his grevous error.

2. In the Stonyhurst MS. of a Discourse on Mary Magdalene,
these stanzas are written by themselves by SOUTHWELL—the
second incomplete:

> The Shippe that from the port doth sayle
> And lanceth in the tyde
> Must many a billow's boystrous brunt
> And stormy blast abyde.

> The tree that groweth on the hill
> And hye dothe shoot his bowes
> Besyde the danger of the axe,

3. 'Josephe's Amazement,' st. ii.-vi. (pp. 122-3). Joseph's
intention of flight is mentioned in Pseudo Matt. ch. x. xi.: and
with reference to this and SOUTHWELL'S use of such, it may here
be noted that the Protevangel or Apoc. Gospel was (then) new
to the Latin Church, being first published in Latin in 1552, and
so an object of curiosity to our Poet, who seems to have been
well-read. (See p. 132.)

4. SOUTHWELL uses 'sight' as = the instrument or organ of sight, *i.e.* the eye. Richardson and the Lexicographers give no example of such use, and it may therefore be well to confirm the sense and use. First, SHAKESPEARE (Venus and Adonis, lines 181-4):

> And now Adonis, with a lazy spright,
> And with a heavy, dark, disliking eye;
> His louring brows o'erwhelming his fair *sight*,
> Like misty vapours when they blot the sky.

Again (Coriol. ii. 1):

> All tongues speak of him, and the bleared *sights*
> Are spectacled to see him.

Once more, Midsummer Night's Dream (iii. 2):

> And laid the love-juice on some true-love's *sight*.

Similarly we use 'sight' as the eye opening or instrument of seeing, of optical instruments: and so Shakespeare:

> Their eyes of fire sparkling through *sights* of steel.
> *2 Henry IV.* iv. 1.   (See p. 155.)

5. 'Silly' (see p. 176: note on st. i. line 4 of 'I die without Desert'). The translator of The Rogue or Life of Don Guzman D'Alfarache, though a Spaniard, was as great a master of colloquial idiomatic English as Florio, and I think there is a clear example of silly=pavoreux, as late as 1629. Speaking of the innkeeper who is afraid that his mule veal will be discovered, Guzman says (b. i. c. v.): 'This poor Rogue (albeit a very villaine) pardned in roguery, and habituated in mischiefe, and being steeped, and lyen long in soke (as it were), in thefts, and all kinde of coozenages, was now out of heart, and grew silly and weake-spirited, and was ready to quake for feare. Besides, such kinde of men are commonly cowards, and have onely an outside of men, but no manhood at all.' The context quoted points to this meaning, and nothing in the rest of the context at all shows that he got foolish or silly in our present sense of the word.

6. In the 'Month' for January-February 1872 appeared an 'ELEGY ON EDMUND CAMPION' from a black-letter contemporary volume in the British Museum, where it forms one of several. Thereupon a correspondent in the 'Tablet' assigned reasons for ascribing it to SOUTHWELL, and received support from other well-known and accomplished critics. But a Letter from my admir-

able friend Rev. S. Sole, of St. Mary's College, Oscott, Birmingham, in 'Tablet' for Feb. 24th, shows that the external data are against such authorship, while the internal goes to prove that the Writer (probably Walpole, S. J.) must have been an eye-witness of the martyrdom, which Southwell could not have been. It must be admitted that there are Southwellian words and turns in the Elegy: but his non-authorship is equally certain. G.

THE END.

FLY-LEAVES

SUPPLEMENTARY TO GROSART'S EDITION OF FATHER
SOUTHWELL'S POEMS

(One Volume, 1872).

SHORTLY after the completion and issue of my edition
of the Complete Poems of Fr. Southwell, S.J., I had
the satisfaction of learning the discovery of an au-
thentic contemporary portrait, life-size, of the martyred
'sweet Singer,' in the House of the Society of Jesus,
at Fribourg (*not* in the Gesù at Rome, as originally
communicated to me inadvertently). Of this portrait
a very careful and daintily-finished crayon-copy was
taken by Charles Weld, Esq., of Chideock, in 1845, for
the portrait-gallery (a singularly rich one) of Stony-
hurst College, Lancashire; and it gives us the very face
—thin, worn, wistful, large-eyed, steep-browed, gentle
yet firm-lipped—that I ventured to imagine in my
Memoir with its quotation from the Hon. Mrs. Norton.
I owe the information of the discovery or recovery to
Father John Morris, editor (or author rather) of 'The
Condition of Catholics under James I.' (8vo, 1872),
and 'The Troubles of our Catholic Forefathers, related
by themselves' (8vo, 1872). I have had the head of
Fr. Southwell engraved in first style by Alais of Lon-

don, and issue of it twenty-five proofs before letters on India paper (folio), one hundred lettered (quarto) for insertion in our quarto edition of the Poems, fifty for the 8vo edition, and fifty for the 12mo edition.

Besides the Portrait, my good friend Fr. Morris has favoured me with an exceedingly interesting, touching, and in every way noticeable Letter from Fr. Henry Garnet, giving an account of the martyr-death of Southwell. By his kindness I am enabled to furnish both the original Latin letter itself and a translation of it. I wish again to express my deep sense of the liberality and courtesy of the authorities at Stonyhurst in facilitating my labours in all pleasant ways. It gratifies me also to announce that the folio impressions were all taken up within a few weeks of the issue of my proposals.

A. B. GROSART.

Park View, Blackburn, Lancashire.

DEATH OF F. ROBERT SOUTHWELL, S.J.

THERE is preserved at Stonyhurst College, in the hand-
writing of F. Christopher Grene, who died in 1697,
the copy of a letter written by Fr. Henry Garnet to
the General of the Society, Fr. Claud Aquaviva, in-
forming him of the death of Fr. Robert Southwell. It
was written on the day after that event. It must be re-
membered that it is a letter from the Superior of the
Jesuits in England to the General of his Order in Rome,
and that it was not written for publication. It may
serve to show what manner of men the proscribed Jesuits
of those days really were, and may fitly accompany the
Portrait of the Martyr.

'February 22 (March 4 N.s.), 1595
(in England 1594).

'The peace of Christ Jesus. At length I have a most
beautiful flower to offer to your paternity from your garden,
a most sweet fruit from your tree, an admirable treasure
from your treasury, "silver tried by the fire, purged from the
earth, refined seven times." It is Christ's unconquered sol-
dier, most faithful disciple, most valiant martyr, Robert
Southwell, formerly my dearest companion and brother,
now my lord, patron, and king, reigning with Christ.

'He had been kept for nearly three years in closer cus-
tody than any one ever was, so that no Catholic saw him
or spoke to him. He was often tortured, and that in a

more cruel manner than even this barbarity is accustomed
to inflict. He publicly declared that he had been tortured
ten times, and that with torments worse than the rack, or
than death itself. Thus deprived of all human aid, at
length they brought him forth, that it might be clear to all
how far the divine assistance exceeds all human help. For
all this long time he could neither say Mass, nor go to the
Sacrament of Penance, nor speak with any one, nor receive
consolation from any; yet he went to judgment and to exe-
cution with so calm and tranquil a mind, that you would
have said that he came from the midst of a monastery of
religious men, and that he was passing of his own free
accord from the breasts of his mother to the sweetest of
delights.

'He was taken from the Tower of London to Newgate,
the prison for thieves and murderers, and there he was kept
for three days in what they call *limbo*, with no comfort but
a candle. On the 20th of February he was brought into
court, where by a cunning device his adversaries took care
that very few people should be present; for the day before
they gave no notice of what they were going to do, either
to the gaoler or to any one else; and at the very time that
he was summoned a notable thief was led off to execution,
which was done that almost all the city might be drawn
to see him, and thus not notice what was done with the
Father.

'Yet not a few Catholics were present, who told us all
that passed. For the moment I have so little time, that
I omit these details just now; but I will write them next
week or the week after. At this time your paternity will
hear only those things that passed at his most happy tri-
umph on the following day, as I have been surely informed
by one of ours who was present.

'Having been drawn to the gallows, and lifted from
the hurdle on which he had been drawn to the cart, he
made the sign of the cross as well as he could, for his
hands were bound, and began his speech thus: "Whether

we live, we live unto the Lord; or whether we die, we die unto the Lord: whether, therefore, we live or whether we die, we are the Lord's." When he was beginning a sermon on these words, he was interrupted by the sheriff's deputy. He earnestly begged that he might be allowed to speak, promising that he would say nothing that could offend any one. He then began in this manner: "I have now come here to perform and accomplish the last act of this wretched life. I pray and beseech our Saviour, through whose precious death and passion I hope to be saved, mercifully to pardon me all the sins that I have committed since my birth into this world. I profess myself a priest of the Roman Catholic Church, and of the Society of Jesus; and for this I give God eternal thanks."

'A troublesome minister here said, "Master Southwell, explain yourself; for if you understand what you say, according to the Council of Trent it is damnable." The crowd of bystanders ordered the foolish minister to be silent, and the father replied: "Master minister, trouble me not, I pray you, at this time. I am a Catholic; and interpret it as you will, I trust to be saved by the merits and passion of our Saviour. As to the queen, I have never attempted or thought any evil against her. Indeed, I have always prayed to our Lord, and in this little space of time that I have yet to breathe I will not cease to pray, that of His great mercy, and for the sake of His precious blood and glorious wounds, He may vouchsafe to give her those gifts and graces which His divine wisdom sees to be fittest for the salvation of body and soul in this life and the next. I now commend to the hands of Almighty God my unhappy country, that of His mercy He may fill it with that knowledge and understanding of His truth which most may lead to the salvation of souls, and to His eternal glory."

'When he had said this, he caught sight of that one of ours who gives this account, and threw his handkerchief towards him, which, however, did not reach him. He then went on with his speech. "Lastly," he said, "I commend to the hands of Almighty God this my poor soul; this wretched body I leave to the queen's will; and I pray that this my death may be useful to myself and my country, and may be a consolation to others."

'And then, while waiting for the cart to be driven away, he made the sign of the cross; and lifting up his face to heaven, he said, "Into thy hands, O Lord, I commend my spirit." As there was still some time remaining, he uttered with the greatest devotion some sentences of the Psalms, as, "Blessed be the Lord God of Israel;" "The just wait for me until Thou reward me;" "Create a clean heart in me, O God;" "Holy Mary, Mother of God,. and all the Saints, intercede for me."

'As the cart was driven away, he signed himself, saying, "Into thy hands, O Lord." Whilst hanging from the gallows, he often made the sign of the cross, for the rope was badly placed on his neck, until the hangman pulled his legs (which is an unusual act of humanity with us) ; and then he closed his eyes, which till then were open. An officer often tried to cut the rope, but was prevented by Lord Mountjoy and by all the people, who three times cried out "Leave him, leave him!"

'The hangman took him down from the gallows with much reverence, and with his attendants carried him in his arms to the place of his disembowelling. Others they usually drag along the ground in a very inhuman way. One of the pursuivants declared that he had never seen a man die more piously; and some of the heretics wished that their souls might be with his.

'This is what I am able to write at present. Next week the rest shall be written, and perhaps the two letters will reach your paternity together. Meanwhile let this give you joy, and by your prayers prepare us, of all the most unworthy, for similar combats; for I cannot see how I can long escape the enemies' hands. This one thing I pray, that my sins may not keep me from the combat, or make me less valiant in the fight; and I do not doubt that

your paternity, by your holy sacrifices, will gain this for
me.

'Your reverence's unworthy son and servant in Christ,

'HENRY GARNET.

'London, February 22, 1594, O.S.; March 4, 1595, N.S.'

P. HENR. GARNETTUS AD P. GENERALEM

DE MARTYRIO P. ROB. SOUTHWELLI.

22 Feb. (4 Martii stilo nov.) 1595
(in Anglia 1594).

Pax X^i J. En offero jam tandem P. V^{ae} ex hortis suis
florem pulcherrimum, ex arbore sua fructum suavissimum,
ex gazophilacio suo thesaurum eximium, argentum igne
examinatum, probatum terrae, purgatum septuplum, invic-
tum X^i militem, fidelissimum discipulum, et fortissimum
martyrem, Rob. Southwellum, charissimum mihi olim so-
cium ac fratrem, nunc dominum, patronum ac regem una
cum X° imperantem. Hunc in arctiori carcere quam ullum
unquam tribus jam fere annis custoditum, ubi nullum Ca-
tholicum aut vidit aut allocutus est, saepius tortum et sup-
pliciis acerbioribus quam solet ista barbaries aliis infligere,
quippe qui decies se tormenta subiisse professus sit, quovis
equuleo et morte etiam ipsa crudeliora, omni denique hu-
mana ope destitutum, jam tandem protulerunt, ut constaret
omnibus quanto pluris valent divina subsidia omni humano
adjumento. Nam cum hoc toto tempore neque missas
celebrare neque poenitentiae sacramentum obire neque col-
loqui cum ullo aut a quopiam consolationem accipere
potuerit, adeo tamen tranquillo ac sedato animo et ad judi-
cium et ad supplicium venit, ut e medio religiosorum ho-
minum conventu, et quasi ab ubere sponte abductum ad
suavissimas delicias diceres. Translatus est a Turri Lon-

dinensi ad Novam-portam, qui latronum atque homicida-
rum carcer est, ibique in Limbo quem vocant triduo asser-
vatus, nullo alio solatio nisi candela. Vigesimo Februarii
die ad tribunal adductus est, ubi callido consilio adversarii
curarunt ut quam paucissimi interessent: nam neque cus-
todem neque ullum alium pridie admonuerunt quid essent
facturi, et eo ipso tempore quo illum accersebant insignis
latro ad supplicium ducebatur, ut ad ejus aspectum effusa
tota fere civitas, quid de patre fieret minime adverteret.
Aderant tamen Catholici non pauci, qui ea quae gesta
sunt nobis enarrarunt, quae tamen quoniam hoc tempore
quod mihi breve restat, scribere non vacat, omittam in
praesentia, proxima vel sequenti hebdomada eadem scrip-
turus: nunc ea solum P. V^a audiet quae in ipso felicissimo
ejus triumpho postridie contigerunt, prout ex quodam e
nostris qui interfuit pro certo cognovi. Cum ad patibulum
jam tractus esset, atque e crate qua trahebatur in currum
sublatus, facto crucis signo ut poterat, manibus videlicet
vinctis, dicere coepit: 'Sive vivimus, Domino vivimus, sive
morimur, Domino morimur; sive ergo vivimus, sive mori-
mur, Domini sumus.' Cumque in haec verba sermonem
institueret a vicecomitis deputato interpellatus est: rogavit
obnixe ut loqui permitteretur, nihil se dicturum asserens
quod quenquam offenderet: Itaque exorsus hunc in modum
est: 'Huc modo accessi ad ultimum hujus miserae [vitae]
actum praestandum atque complendum: Servatorem nos-
trum oro atque obtestor, cujus preciosa morte ac passione
me salvum fore confido, ut omnia mea peccata quae a pri-
mo meae nativitatis ortu commisi, benigne mihi condonet.
Profiteor me sacerdotem esse Catholicae Romanae Ecclesiae
et e Societate Jesu, Deoque propterea gratias ago immorta-
les.' Hic minister quidam importunus: 'Domine Southwelle,
inquit, explica te ipsum, nam si hoc intelligas, juxta Con-
cilium Tridentinum damnabile est.' Turba vero quae as-
tabat ministro ineptissimo silentium imperavit. Tum Pater:
'Domine minister, inquit, ne quaeso hoc tempore mihi mo-
lestus sis; ego Catholicus sum, et quomodocumque tu in-

terpreteris, ex meritis et passione Servatoris nostri salvum
me fore confido: quod ad reginam attinet, nunquam illi
malum aliquod aut attentavi aut cogitavi; quin etiam
Dominum semper oravi et tantillo hoc tempore quo spirabo
non desinam orare, ut pro sua immensa misericordia et ob
sanguinem suum preciosum et vulnera gloriosa dignetur ei
ea dona ac gratias donare quae sua divina sapientia saluti
animae ac corporis viderit esse in hac et futura vita maxime
consentanea: deinde in manus Omnipotentis Dei patriam
meam miseram commendo, ut Deus eam pro sua miseri-
cordia repleat illa cognitione et intelligentia suae veritatis
quae ad animarum salutem et suam aeternam gloriam
maxime conducat.' Dum haec diceret, quendam ex nostris
conspicatus, qui haec refert, strophiolum e manu projecit,
quod tamen ad socium non pervenit. Tum sermonem pro-
sequens: 'Denique, ait, in Omnipotentis Dei manus paupe-
rem hanc animam commendo, corpusculum autem istud
reginae voluntati submitto: petoque ut hanc mortem meam
mihi et patriae meae utilitati, aliis et solatio esse velit.'
Tumque expectans currus amotionem facto crucis signo et
facie in coelum sublata dixit, 'In manus tuas Domine' etc.
Cumque tempus adhuc superesset maxima devotione pro-
nunciavit sententias quasdam Psalmorum, ut 'Benedictus
Dominus etc. Me expectant justi. Cor mundum crea in
me Deus. Sancta Maria Mater Dei et omnes Sancti inter-
cedite pro me.' Dumque amoveretur currus signavit sese
dicens, 'In manus tuas Domine.' Dum e patibulo penderet
saepe se signavit, quod funis male applicatus collo esset,
donec carnifice tibias vellente (quae humanitas est apud
nos inusitata) oculos, ad id usque tempus apertos, ipsemet
clausit. Conatus est satelles aliquis saepe funem excin-
dere, sed prohibitus est a Domino Montjoy et ab universo
populo ter clamante, 'Mitte eum, Mitte eum.' Carnifex eum
e patibulo deposuit magna cum reverentia, et una cum suis
comitibus brachiis eum detulit ad locum eviscerationis,
cum alios soleat inhumane per terram trahere. Quidam ex
pursevantis asseruit nunquam se vidisse hominem qui

magis pie esset mortuus; quidam et hæretici optarunt ut animae suae cum illo essent.

Haec sunt quae hoc tempore scribere potui : reliqua sequenti hebdomada scribentur, quae forte una cum istis ad V. P. pervenient. Interim Vᵃ Pᵃ his fruatur, nosque omnium indignissimos suis precibus instruat ad hujusmodi certamina; neque enim video quomodo diu possum hostium manus evadere. Illud unum obsecro, ne mea me peccata impediant a certamine, aut minus fortem inter certandum faciant; quod Vᵃᵉ Pⁱˢ sanctissimis sacrificiis me impetraturum minime diffido. Londini, 22 Februarii 1595. Rᵃᵉ Vᵃᵉ indignus in Xᵒ filius ac servus,

HENR. GARNETTUS.

Near the beginning of the letter the following occurs in the margin, in Father Christopher Grene's handwriting :

De P. Southwello M. Garnetti epistola de ejus martyrio, 1595 Feb. 22. P. Southw. 3ᵒ Martii 1595 (21 Febr. stilo veteri) occisus feria sexta post Dom. 3ᵐ Quadragesᵃᵉ prima dies fuit 5 Martii, Pascha 20 Apr. stilo veteri.